Happiness Flows

Happiness Flows

Fakir M. Sahoo
Formerly Professor & Head
Centre of Advanced Study in Psychology
Utkal University, Bhubaneswar, India
(Now at, XIM University, Bhubaneswar)

Satyabrata Tripathy
Chief Manager (MM)
Coal India Ltd., India

Kalpana Sahoo
Assistant Professor (OB)
School of Human Resource Management
XIM University, Bhubaneswar

Black Eagle Books
2021

🦅 Black Eagle Books
USA address:
7464 Wisdom Lane
Dublin, OH 43016

India address:
E/312, Trident Galaxy, Kalinga Nagar,
Bhubaneswar-751003, Odisha, India

E-mail: info@blackeaglebooks.org
Website: www.blackeaglebooks.org

First International Edition Published by
Black Eagle Books, 2021

HAPPINESS FLOWS
by **Fakir Mohan Sahoo, Satyabrata Tripathy & Kalpana Sahoo**

Original Copyright © Fakir Mohan Sahoo, Satyabrata Tripathy & Kalpana Sahoo

All rights reserved. No part of this publication may be reproduced, stored in a retrieval system, or transmitted, in any form or by any means, electronic, mechanical, photocopying, recording or otherwise without the prior permission of the publisher.

Cover & Interior Design: Ezy's Publication

ISBN- 978-1-64560-221-7 (Paperback)
Library of Congress Control Number: 2021948776

Printed in United States of America

To the love and joy of my family: Reeta (Anju),
Voomika (Poly), Tapas, Tanisha (Tithi)
FMS

To my daughter Sarmistha.
There will never be another one like you for me ....
ST

To the happiness of my dear sons (Sonu & Monu)
KS

CONTENTS

Chapter 1 Windows into Happiness   13-30
    Paradox of Prosperity
        Wealth and Well-Being
        Mental Health Indicators
        Indian Scenarios
    Confluence of Constructs
        The Hedonic Perspective
        The Eudaimonic Perspective
        Self-Determination Theory
        Contours of Contents

Chapter 2 Measurement Issues   31-47
    Instruments
        Experience Sampling Method
        Life Orientation Scale
        Diversity of Measures
        Physiological Measures
        Measures of Psychological Well-being
        Appendix A : LOS
        Appendix B : Ryff's Scale

Chapter 3 Positivity Factors   48-108
    Self-efficacy
        Sources of Self-Efficacy
        Mediating Mechanism
        Well-being Benefits
    Optimism
        Nature of Optimism
        Antecedents of Optimism
        Training for Optimism
        Issues in Optimism
        Optimism and Well-being
    Hope
        Pathways and Agency Thinking

        Emotion and the Process
        Measurement of Hope
        Development of Hope
        Hope and Health
    Resilience
        The Lotus-in-the-Mud Phenomena
        Sources of Resilience
        Personality Factors
        Promoting Factors
        Resilience and Happiness
    Emotional Intelligence
        The Evolution of the Construct
        Framework of EI
        EI and Happiness

Chapter 4   Antecedents of Happiness   109-162
    Genetic Factors
    Personality
    Role of Gender
    Marital Status
    The Effect of Age
    Income, Social Class and Education

Chapter 5   Internal Amplifiers   163-221
    Religiosity and Spirituality
        Studies of Religion
        Components of Religion
        An Integration
    Meditation
        Varieties of Meditation
    Mindfulness and Happiness
        What is Mindfulness?
        Mindfulness Meditation
        Features of Mindfulness
        Meditation and Health
    Flow: Mechanism of Living in the present
        Benefits of Flow
        Increasing Flow Experience
    Savouring
        Strategies to Foster Savouring
    The Buffering Role of Humour

Theories of Humour
Humour Styles
Humour in Daily Lives
Attitude of Gratitude
    Practice of Gratitude
Fostering Creativity
    Training for Creativity
    The Creative Process
    Phases of Creative Process
Relevant Factors
    The Theoretical Position
    The Creative Person
    The Creative Environment

Chapter 6 Environmental Boosters   222-258

Physical Activity and Exercise
    Exercise
    Related Activities
Social Capital
    Parameters of Closeness
    Aversive Dimensions
    Friendship
    Building Flourishing Relationship
Cultural Factors
    Taxonomy of Cultures
    Culture and Happiness
    Functional Dynamics
    Structural Dynamics
    Issues of Comparability
    Resolution and Resources

Chapter 7 Social Ecology of Happiness   259-298

Family Happiness
    Adaptive Benefits of Family
    Features of Close Relationship
    Secret of Living Together
    Uniqueness of Lasting Marriage
Workplace Happiness
    Job Satisfaction and Happiness
    Contributing Factors
    Job Characteristic Model

　　　　　　　An Integrated Approach
　　　　　　Community Happiness
　　　　　　　　Person-Community Fit
　　　　　　　　Community Involvement
　　　　　　　　The Spirit of Giving

Chapter 8　Explanatory Frameworks　　　　　　　　　　　299-319
　　　　　　Telic Theories
　　　　　　　　Goal Contents and Happiness
　　　　　　Top-Down Versus Bottom-up Theory
　　　　　　Cognitive Theories
　　　　　　Associationistic Theories
　　　　　　Judgment Theories
　　　　　　Benefits of Downward Comparison
　　　　　　Neuroscience of Happiness

Chapter 9　Achieving Lasting Happiness　　　　　　　　320-347
　　　　　　Evolutionary Perspective
　　　　　　Mood Induction
　　　　　　Intentional Activities
　　　　　　Positive Life Events
　　　　　　Mind Over Matter
　　　　　　Rewiring the Brain
　　　　　　Therapeutic Application
　　　　　　Behavioural Interventions

Chapter 10　Looking Ahead　　　　　　　　　　　　　　348-372
　　　　　　Comparability and Equivalence
　　　　　　　　Measurement Equivalence
　　　　　　　　Etic and Emic Strategy
　　　　　　　　Alternative Strategies
　　　　　　Unresolved Issues
　　　　　　　　Intensity versus Frequency
　　　　　　　　Universality versus Specificity
　　　　　　Towards an Integration
　　　　　　　　Reconciliation Attempts
　　　　　　　　Hybrid Models
　　　　　　　　Future Directions

References　　　　　　　　　　　　　　　　　　　　　373-402

Books Authored by F.M. Sahoo

- Cognitive styles & amp; interpersonal behaviour
- Affective sensitivity & amp; cognitive styles
- Psychology in Indian context (Edited)
- Environment & amp; behaviour
- Child rearing & amp; educating assistance manual
- Dynamics of human helplessness
- Sex roles in transition
- Behavioural issues in ageing (Edited)
- Atlas of mind
- Mysteries of mind
- Wonders of mind
- Splendours of mind
- Mind management
- Tools of mind
- Landscape of mind
- Plasticity of mind
- Melody of Minds
- Happiness flows

Books in Odia

- Bichitra mana
- Manasika bikruti
- Jiban prabahare manasika bikruti
- Adhuni ka jibanare manasika chapa
- Manara manachitra
- Manastatvika bikasare saisaba parba
- Byaktitva & amp; netrutva
- Nari manastatva
- Manastatvika bikasara godhuli parba
- Sisu manara bigyan
- Sachitra mana
- Sabala mana, saphala jibana
- Manastatvika bikasara balya parba
- Manastatvika bikasara kaishore parba
- Manasika samasya O samadhan
- Manara rahasya
- Jibana O' manastatwa
- Tallinata
- Sahitya O' manastatwa
- Chapamukta jeeban
- Sakshyatakara
- Manastatwika bikashar jouban parba
- Sukhanubhutira marmakatha
- Mana Prikrama

Translation

- Divya sambasana (Part-v)
- Divya sambasana (Part-xv)
- Shiridi ru Puttaparti
- Siksha samparkare
- Bibeka sampritee
- Chetanadipta jiban
- Dhyanadipta jiban

Preface

River flows. Happiness also flows. It is the flowing quality of happiness that makes it an interesting area of exploration and exposition. Knowledge is never stagnant. Knowledge about happiness is not stagnant; it changes across time and space.

Despite the changing and flowing quality of knowledge about happiness, there are elements of stability and consistency. Without consistency it would not be possible to build a *cumulative* science of happiness. In this book, we have tried to discern the sustainable formulations (about well-being / happiness) that have stood the tests of time.

At the same time, attempts are directed to discover new age happiness. Since technology is changing and priorities are changing, researchers are keen to capture the "New Look" element in happiness theories. We are aware of this paradigm shift and we have attempted to keep a close look.

With respect to the elements of consistencies and specificities across cultures, we have adopted a resilient approach. We fully appreciate that both pancultural and culture-specific laws of human behaviours are recognized in science of mental health. The universals and specificities are precious. While generating conclusions and guidelines, our efforts are directed to strike a balance between universal knowledge base and indigenous conceptualizations.

Finally, we would humbly say that a book of this nature cannot be claimed as "one-size-fits-all" product. During application, a few things may change and things may change in course of time. Yet the book, we believe, would serve as a valuable guide for future study and research. How genuine is the effort can only be tested against crucible of time. Happiness in reading this book is just the beginning.

23 November 2020

F.M. Sahoo
S. Tripathy
K. Sahoo

Chapter 1

Windows into Happiness

The intention to open windows into happiness has two inner springs of motivation. First, it is a part of academic involvement. The first author of the book (F.M. Sahoo) has spent considerable amount of time in teaching and studying human happiness. In fact, some of the research scholars have carried out empirical studies on certain aspects of happiness under his supervision. The commitment to academic pursuit pulls the psychic levers in this direction.

The second inner prompting comes from everyday experiences. Everyday we meet people, greet with the expression. How are you? Although we are accustomed to hear "I am fine, thank you", words and gestures do not go together. Are people really happy? This is a great existential question enveloping all of us. While this is a question for all of us to think about, the community of social and behavioural scientists have to be responsive to act upon. This is a call the authors of this book have undertaken.

While opening the windows, a few chunks of information are to be presented. Prior to a detailed discussion of the how of happiness throughout the book, why and what of happiness would offer the keys. These two fundamental keys may openup the seminal discussion on "paradox of prosperity" and "confluence of constructs".

Paradox of Prosperity

We live in a time when affluence and adversity coexist. Our living conditions would echo Dickens' description in *A Tale of Two Cities*: We have the best of times, we have the worst of times, we have the spring of hope, we have the winter of despair. Prosperity-wise, we are in the best period of history. The technological revolution that has swept across human communities have brought affluence to our door-step. If we consider the United States as a prototype of affluence the signs of plenty and prosperity are visible on many facets of public life.

The economic indicators are dazzling. The mental health statistics are equally disturbing. In a recent review, Diener and Seligman (2004) present the paradox of progress. This review, in combination with Myers (2000a; 2000b) and Easterbrook's (2003) dispel the illusion linking wealth with well-being. The classic example is the United States where income has tripled during last 50 years. Yet life satisfaction has remained flat. More surprisingly the depression during these 50 years has increased ten-fold. (Diener & Seligman, 2004). A closer look at economic and well-being indicators provides hypotheses regarding wealth and health.

Wealth and Well-being: The obsession with economic development has galvanized human efforts for a long time. The industrial revolution triggered human motivation for industrial productivity. Adam Smith's book *Wealth of Nations* harnessed the money dynamics and people all over the world worked hard for mass production and mass consumption. No doubt, it solved some basic problems of food and shelter. Excepting countries afflicted by calamities, colonialization and political instability, people in many countries experienced a reasonable improvement in standard of living. Some countries aided by vast natural resources and planned economy became very rich. The features of material prosperity are conceivable if we survey some of the criteria in benchmarking nation the United States.

- Americans have tripled their purchase of cars, TVs, computers during last 50 years.
- Nearly one-fourth of households earn $75,000 per year.
- In 2001, Americans spent 25 billion dollars for recreational activities. This is more than gross domestic product of North Korea.
- The house area averages 2,250 square feet about double the size of the average house in 1950s.
- American eat out four times a week in a fast food restaurant and once a week in a sit-in restaurant.

The splendid economic record would create an impression of equally alluring expectation of well-being. Yet a large-scale national survey reveals that the American level of life satisfaction has remained "Virtually flat" (Diener & Seligman, 2004). For within-nation as well as cross-national comparisons, one-item life satisfaction scale is used where '1' indicates "very dissatisfied" and '10' indicates "very satisfied". The mean life satisfaction of Americans was 7.2 with little variation throughout the entire period from 1947 to 1988. The percentage of Americans reporting that they are very happy has remained relatively fixed at about 30% from 1950s through 1990s (Myers, 2000a). Most Americans are richer, but not happier than in the past. Americans' increased income over last 50 years has not led to a corresponding rise in their life satisfaction.

A broad source of comparisons of wealth-well-being linkage is produced by World Value Survey. A large group of international social scientists have conducted this survey for 25-year period. Robert Inglehart at the University of Michigan has coordinated the compilation of findings. Similarly, Veenhoven at the Erasmus University Rotterdam, Netherlands, has created the World Database of Happiness. Drawing on these international sources, certain common expectations are supported. Taking large number of countries into consideration substantial correlations (in the range of .50 to .70) are found between average per capita income and life satisfaction (Diener & Biswas-Diener, 2002).

Although people living in wealthy nations are happier than those living in less wealthy countries, the deviate cases are not smaller in number (Baumgardener & Crothers, 2009). The Irish have relatively high life satisfaction but only moderate income. The Japanese enjoy high income but only moderate life satisfaction. The U.S. is at the top of the income measure but 6th in self-reported life satisfaction. India and China both rank near the bottom in income but show significant ratings higher than Japan. Even countries fairly close in geographic proximity show large differences in life satisfaction. Denmark has consistently shown higher ratings on satisfaction than Germany, France and Italy. These surprises in the context of wealth–well-being relation implicate the role of noneconomic factors.

In contrast to the moderate correlations in cross-nation comparisons, within-nation correlations between income and happiness are quite small. Diener and Oishi (2000) report an average within-nation correlation of only 0.13 (with 40 different nations studied). In the United States, the correlation was .15. Specifically, income and well-being show moderate correlations within poor countries and very small or nonsignificant correlations in rich countries. In the Diener and Oishi study the highest correlation was found in South Africa (.38). Poor people living in Kolkata indicated the modest correlation (.45) between income and life satisfaction (Biswas-Diener & Diener, 2001). Studies showing relatively higher correlations between money and satisfaction in poor countries indicate the importance of money in situations where basic existential needs are not yet met. In contrast, lower correlations between income and life satisfaction in rich countries suggest increased income has no appreciable effect on happiness in rich countries. A Special Issue (Body & Mind Issue) of Time Magazine Survey reports that annual income beyond 50,000 dollars in the US has no incremental effect oh happiness (Jan 17, 2005, p.A33).

Mental health indicators. As developed nations have become more wealthier, they are also afflicted by a greater degree of mental disorder. Mental disorder is definitely a threat to well-being. In addition, recent developments in psychotherapies and medications have greatly improved the prevention and treatment of mental disorders. The practice goes beyond the alleviation of symptoms and add to the well-being of clients. Despite such positivity, the mental health scenarios in developed countries including the United States are surprising. These are some of the features of contemporary depressive scenarios.

- Mental disorders are growing in frequency. A structured psychiatric interview indicates that a national sample of adults in the U.S.A. presents disturbing incidence. About 50% of respondents show at least one disorder in their lifetime, and 30% report a disorder during past year. The rate of experiencing a disorder during past month is startling 18.2%.
- Similarly, 16% of young adults in a British national sample were found to have neurotic

disorder during the past week. About half of the disorders were anxiety and depression. In Ireland, 24% of the population is classified as clinically depressed during the past months, 6% during the past year, and 12.2% of the population had experienced a mental disorder of some kind during the past year.

- In sharp contrast to the improvement of economic indicators (income doubled or tripled), the incidence of depression has increased enormously during last 50 years casting apprehension of 10-fold risk across generations.
- A massive international study involving 40,000 adults in the United States, Germany, France, Italy, Lebanon, New Zealand and Taiwan show sharp decline in optimism and risk for depression in almost all national samples.
- A disturbing fact concerns young people. Fifty years ago, the average age for the first episode of depression was 29.5, and depression was almost unknown in adolescence. Now, teenagers are the vulnerable clients.

Viewed through the lens of development in affluent countries, the contradictions between economic prosperity and mental poverty are clearly visible. A similar picture of contrast is also seem when we survey conditions in developing societies such as India.

Indian scenarios. In recent decades, India's economic achievements have received wider acclaim. India's GDP more than trebled from Rs 32.53 lakh crore in 2005-06 to Rs 113.50 lakh crore (at constant prices) in 2015-16 even as per capita income more than trebled from Rs

25.696 to Rs 77.435 respectively during the period (Goyal, 2020).

However, the economic achievement is not consistent with India's position on happiness ladder. Every year United Nations Sustainable Development Solutions Network (UNSDSN) comes out with The World Happiness Report ranking of 156 countries. The report takes into account GDP per capita, life expectancy, social support and freedom to make life choices. In the 2016 report, the Scandinavian countries dominated the top positions with Denmark (1), Switzerland (2), Iceland (3), Norway (4), and Finland (5). India ranked 118th on the list. It slipped from 117th in 2015.

This is not inconsistent with poor records of mental health in India. A report by the World Health Organization (WHO) revealed that 7.5 per cent of the Indian population suffer from some type of mental disorder. Mental illness constitutes one-sixth of the health-related disorders and India accounts for nearly 15% of the global mental, neurological, and substance abuse disorder burden. The treatment gap which is defined as the prevalence of mental illness and the proportion of clients that receive treatment, is over 70 per cent. WHO also predicted that by 2020, roughly 20 per cent of India will suffer from mental illness. There are less than 4000 mental health professionals in India, WHO reports (The Economic Times, Sept 27, 2020).

Since modern practice of mental health science is not limited to ameliorating illness symptoms these have dynamic roles in boosting well-being. A complete model of well-being requires both the absence of mental illness and the presence of positive mental conditions. This assertion presupposes important roles of noneconomic factors in well-being.

Role of noneconomic factors: An extensive and analytical research on wealth-well-being linkage has discovered the role of many salient features in happiness.

First, a common assumption that money increases well-being is no longer tenable. A bulk of studies reveal that happy people gain more money subsequently. Moving beyond the simple correlations, researchers have challenged the direction of causality. They view that well-being is a greater cause of wealth than the case of wealth as a cause (Diener & Seligman, 2004).

Across nations, there are diminishing return for increasing wealth above 10,000 U.S. dollars annual income. Further, health, quality of government, and human rights all these correlate with wealth. When these variables are controlled the correlations between wealth and well-being are substantially reduced. Helliwell (2003), an economist, concluded that people with highest well-being are not those who live in the richest countries, but those who live where social and political institutions are effective, where mutual trust is high, and competition is low (p. 355).

One possibility for the observation that increasing income does not lead to increased well-being involves unrealistic escalation of material aspirations resulting in frustration. Well-being depends on some degree on the gap between income and material aspiration. When such gaps are filled it brings satisfaction. When aspirations grow more quickly than income, frustration becomes inevitable.

A number of investigators have carried out studies to explicate negative outcomes of wealth. Materialism is defined as placing a high importance on income and material possessions. Kasser and Kanner (2004) document detrimental effects of materialism. The authors evinced that materialistic individuals display lower self-esteem, greater narcissism, greater social comparison (comparing themselves with others), low empathy and lower intrinsic motivation. However, these effects are lower for those people who have very high income. Across nations, placing high importance to money is associated with less well-being. Materialism might lead to less well-being because materialistic people tend to downplay the importance of social relationships and tend to have larger gap between their achievements and aspirations (Diener & Seligman, 2004).

In the context of lottery winners, some studies have reported greater happiness in lottery winners in comparison with control groups, while other studies have indicated greater stress and anxiety amongst lottery winners. In an interesting study, participants received money from the welfare department to make up the gap between their low income and the basic minimum income (taxable threshold). It was expected that this receipt would significantly add to their well-being. Yet, no such positive impact was found (Thoits & Hannan, 1979).

The foregoing discussions highlight the salience of good life in terms of meaningful, engaging and fulfilling existence vis-à-vis economic affluence.

Towards a national well-being index: In view of the limitation of income criterion as an index of well-being, researchers have moved in the direction of evolving a national index of well-being. Well-being related research in European countries have persuaded scholars to use a common parameter of well-being termed **Eurobarometer** (Diener & Seligman, 2004).

The buzzword sounded in recent years is the King of Bhutan's (the Buddhist kingdom in the Himalayas) term of **Gross Domestic Happiness (GDH)**. The king asserts that the best way to foster good life and well-being is to focus on the GDH rather than on GDP. Bhutan's emphasis on happiness of its people above all else appears to produce world-wide support. The happiness and well-being of people is so vital that economic development is subordinated to this primary goal of flourishing. Beyond money, an understanding and enhancement of happiness requires a deeper analysis of noneconomic factors (Sahoo, 2007).

The scientific discussion on a construct requires definition and operationalization. The present conceptualization of happiness is product of an evolutionary process. The derivation of the current status is a confluence of **two major perspectives: the hedonic approach and eudaimonic approach.** The statement needs elaboration.

Confluence of Constructs

What do you want? The encounter with this question yields an infinite number of answers. Answers vary across persons, situations, contexts, cultures and historical periods. Answers also vary across age, gender, education, income and personality. Yet the single most important expression happens to be peace and happiness. These are the features of "good life" indicating optimal psychological functioning and experiences (Dalai Lama & Cutler, 1998).

In the publication sector we find a significant concern with quality of life around us. Diener and Seligman (2004) searched psychology journals, PsychLit. They found 94,650 publications on "depression" and 4,757 on "life satisfaction" in January 2004, but only 701 of these indicated. There were 2158 publications that discussed "positive affect", but only 91 of them mentioned "life satisfaction". Similarly, 3,520 publications discussed "negative affect" and 107 of them mentioned "life satisfaction". Thus, researchers in the past mostly gravitated towards the discussion on depression and related concepts, contemporary tilt is towards quality of life and life satisfaction. A Psychinfo search using the terms well-being and mental health brought forth 28,612 and 12,009 citations respectively, for the past 5 years (Ryan & Deci, 2001). When the search was broadened to include terms such as health, happiness, quality of life and other related concepts, the number increased further.

The proliferation of empirical facts regarding well-being happiness has been possible because of two significant developments. First, the construct of happiness has flourished under the aegis of two distinct theoretical perspective: hedonic and eudiamonic approaches. The hedonic view entails that happiness is basically pleasure. The eudiamonic perspective views happiness in terms of the actualization of one's own diamon or true nature. In other words, it denotes realization of human potential. Both the constructs have sound theoretical frameworks.

In addition to the evolution of theoretical frameworks, advanced analytical models have been helpful to further empirical research on well-being. The advent of multi-level modelling helped researchers to use hierarchical linear analysis. This was useful to go beyond the between – person (individual difference) analysis. Instead of confining oneself to answer why Person A is better than Person B with respect to well-being, one can probe into why wellness differs across different points of time. Further idiographic assessments of goals, values, aspiration, and other parameters are helpful for examining people's experience of happiness. Moreover, advanced statistical methods for examining cross-cultural data provided benefits of pancultural inferences (Little, 1997).

The principal perspectives, the hedonic and the

eudiamonic, have their early growth current expansion and future possibilities.

The hedonic perspective. The view that happiness is the hedonic enjoyment has its roots in Greek history. Aristippus, a Greek philosopher from the fourth century B.C., declared that the fundamental goal of life is to experience maximum pleasure. This gives totality to human life. Hobbes contended that happiness represents the successful pursuit of human appetite. Utilaterian philosophers including Bentham advocated human efforts to maximize pleasure and self-interest. They considered it as the foundation on which the society is built.

Psychologists who adopted hedonic view broadened its scope saying that hedonism entails the pleasures and preferences of both body and mind. The broader perspective of hedonism involving the enjoyment of pleasure and avoidance of pain implicates all judgments pertaining to good and bad aspects of life. Thus, happiness is not limited to physical hedonism, it is extended to the attainment of pleasures derived from valued outcomes in various domains of life (Diener, Sapyta, & Suh, 1998).

In a volume titled, *The Foundation of Hedonic Psychology*, Kahneman et al (1999) define hedonic psychology as the study of "What makes experiences and life pleasant and unpleasant" (p. ix). The authors view the terms well-being and hedonism are essentially equivalent. Although there are various ways to evaluate pain / pleasure continuum, hedonic psychology has used assessment of **subjective well-being (SWB)**. SWB consists of three components: life satisfaction, the pursuit of positive mood, and the absence of negative mood (Diener, 1984).

Although the measures of subjective well-being (SWB) have been extensively used in well-being research, all the questions relating to theory and practice have not yet been settled. We may expect a greater accumulation of facts before a robust theory and practice approach is built. In the meantime, there are *three* possibilities which may be proved or disproved in future. First, hedonism as a robust theory and SWB as its operationalization may go together. Second, SWB may be treated as operationalization of well-being and dynamics of well-being may be explained in terms of eudaimonic parameters (to be discussed later). Third, positions of hedonic and eudaimonic approaches may stand independently with possibility of proof or disproof of the either position.

The eudaimonic perspective. Seeking pleasure and its gratification has been denigrated as indicators of well-being. Aristotle viewed hedonic enjoyment as dehumanizing; he considered happiness as the expression of virtue. Drawing on Aristotle's view, many thinkers, philosophers, religious leaders and visionaries have regarded happiness as the realization of true human potential. This is the essence of eudaimonic view.

Humans have numerous needs. Some needs and desires are subjectively felt and their satisfaction brings momentary pleasure. In contrast, there are some objectively valid needs and their satisfaction foster human growth. The satisfaction of the objectively valued needs is the eudaimonic perspective, subjective happiness cannot be equated with well-being.

Waterman (1999) points out another feature of eudaimonic happiness. The eudaimonic conception of well-being calls upon people to live in accordance with their **daimon**, or **true self**. In other words, life activities must be congruent with deeply held values and holistically engaged.

Ryff and Singer (1998, 2000), while exploring parameters of well-being, concluded a model of human flourishing. Their articulation brings it very close to Aristotle's model. They describe well-being not merely as the attainment of pleasure, but as the striving for perfection representing the realization of one's own potential. Ryff and Keyes (1995) label it as **psychological well-being** (PWB) as distinct from SWB. It is presented as a multi-dimensional construct with six distinct components: autonomy, personal growth, self-acceptance, life purpose, environmental mastery and positive relatedness. These six dimensions define PWB theoretically and operationally. The model also specifies what promotes emotional and physical health (Ryff & Singer, 1998). Ryff argues that eudaimonic pattern of living improves immune system as well as better functioning in several psychological domains. Ryff further argues that hedonic view of well-being does not embrace all facets of well-being. However, Diener makes a rejoinder saying that SWB is people's well-being message to experts, whereas eudaimonia is expert's message to people. It is expected that a greater accumulation of empirical knowledge in future would offer solutions to this apparent contradiction.

Beyond these two fundamental perspectives (hedonic and eudaimonic), there are two other tributaries of thoughts that have enriched the confluence of perspectives. There are self-determination theory and positive psychology.

Self-determination theory. Ryan and Deci (2000) proposed a construct termed self-determination theory (SDT) that focuses self-realization. In a way it is akin to Ryff's eudaimonia. The SDT posits three basic psychological needs: competence, autonomy, and relatedness.

The SDT posits that humans are capable of being proactive and engaged at one end of the continuum and passive and alienated at the other end. The social-contextual conditions in which people live foster or forestall development along this continuum. As indicated earlier, three basic psychological needs – competence, autonomy and relatedness – determine the potential for movement along this path. When satisfied, people move in the direction of intrinsic motivation and well-being. When thwarted, the resultants are passivity and alienation.

Ryan and Deci's conceptualization highlights the underlying dynamics of eudaimonic living. At a pragmatic level, it suggests that these basic needs are to be activated in all relevant sectors of life (home, work, education, sport, health care, religion and psychotherapy) so as to bring out eudaimonic happiness emphasizing personal growth and meaningfulness.

Positive psychology. A shift of focus from pathology to positivity is basically an outcome of positive psychology movement (Seligman & Csikszentmihalyi, 2000). During the 1990s, Seligman and associates advocated a strong framework of positive psychology science. The centre of gravity was changed from disease-centric explanation of human behaviour to a strength-centric exploration. The new discipline brought many areas of virtue and vitality such as efficacy, optimism, hope and resilience. It respected the study of courage, forgiveness, gratitude, humility and honesty. The new discipline included topics such as religion and spirituality, knowledge and self-regulation.

With this broadened outlook and positivistic approach, the definition, scope and possibilities of well-being research were also changed. Mental health was no longer defined as the absence or presence of mental illness. Flourishing was defined as the absence of illness plus the presence of positive parameters such as competence and autonomy.

This complete state definition of mental health restructured the definition, prevention and practice of health care. It is important to recognize that both the approaches – hedonic as well as eudaimonic view of happiness have been greatly influenced by positive psychology framework.

Contours of Contents

The book is an attempt to trace the evolution of the construct of happiness. While the terms "happiness" and "well-being" are used interchangeably, other equivalent expressions (subjective well-being or SWB, flourishing, mental health, etc.) are defined and amplified at appropriate points.

Chapter 1 opens **Windows into Happiness** by defining the constructs of happiness / well-being. Two fundamental perspectives on happiness – the hedonic and the eudaimonic views – are explicated. Two other supplementary developments – Self-Determination theory and positive psychology movement – are also briefly indicated.

Chapter 2 deals with **Measurement Issues**. Major tests and instruments are indicated. More specifically, the measure of subjective well-being, the positive and negative affect schedule (PANAS) and Ryff's Eudaimonic measure are briefly described. A few methods of operationalization including experience sampling method (ESM) are mentioned. In addition, the Life Orientation Scale, developed and validated by the first author (F.M. Sahoo), is included.

Chapter 3 explicates **positivity factors**. The literature on happiness has been greatly enriched by positive psychological concepts. The constructs of self-efficacy, optimism, hope, resilience, and emotional intelligence are defined and operationalized. Their relationship with happiness / well-being are outlined.

Chapter 4 is devoted to the discussion on **antecedents of happiness**. The role of genetic factors and personality is explicated. The roles of sociodemographic factors such as gender, age, marital status, income, education, social class are also discussed.

Chapter 5 titled **Internal Amplifiers** highlight some intrinsic mechanism such as religiosity and spirituality. Contemporary research in these areas are pointed out. In addition, the process and technique of mediation is described. Further, topics of humour, creativity, flow and savouring are also included.

Chapter 6 presents a detailed discussion on **Environmental Boosters**. In this context, relevance of physical activity and exercise, social capital (relatedness) and cultural resources is elaborated.

Chapter 7 is focused on **Social Ecology of Happiness**. A number of context-specific well-being such as family happiness, workplace happiness, and community happiness are given detailed account.

Chapter 8 deals with **Theories of Happiness**. The why of happiness is addressed. In this context, the role of learning and memory, social comparison, judgment process, and other related constructs are examined. The recent neuroscientific evidence regarding happiness is also outlined.

Chapter 9 is addressed to **Achieving Lasting Happiness.** Several methods of lab-induced mood change methods are described. In addition, happiness enhancement strategies suggested by contemporary psychologists are highlighted. Modern discoveries in brain research are indicated with a new to helping individuals to rewire their brains for happiness.

Chapter 10 is titled **Looking Ahead**. This chapter briefly indicates achievement in the research area of happiness. It outlines the unresolved issues and suggests some directions for future research.

Chapter 2

Measurement Issues

The definition and conceptual issues with respect to happiness/well-being have changed across decades. Accordingly, measurement philosophy and techniques have also shown considerable alterations. Since the most nontechnical and least controversial definition of well-being consists of an individual evaluation of his or her life quality in cognitive and affective terms, single-item global measure surfaced as the earliest form. The question may take different forms: 'How happy are you now?'; 'How satisfied are you with your life?'; 'How do you feel about your life as a whole?' Generally, people are asked to answer this sentence on five -, or seven -, or ten -point scale.

Instruments
Professor Ed Diener aggregated data from 916 surveys of happiness involving over a million people in 45 nations around the world (Myers & Diener, 1996). He transformed all the data onto a scale that went from 0 to 10 where 10 indicated extremely happy, 5 was neutral and 0 was extremely unhappy. The average happiness rating was 6.75. It seems an average person is moderately happy. Fordyce (1988) developed a two-item happiness measure:

(1) "In general how happy or unhappy do you feel?" (With a 10-point indicating feeling of ecstasy and '0' indicating completely depressed); (2) "On average what percentage of time do you feel happy (or unhappy or neutral)?" Lyubomirsky and Lepper (1999) developed a 4-item measure of global subjective happiness. Participants are asked to rate their happiness on a seven-point scale.

More refined multi-item scales with good reliability were developed later. One such scale is the 29-item Oxford Happiness Scale (Argyle, 2001).

Exhibit 2.1

Items from revised Oxford Happiness Scale

Below are a group of sentences about personal happiness. Please read all four sentences in each group and pick out the one that best described the way you have been feeling in the past week, including today

a. I do not feel happy
b. I feel fairly happy
c. I am very happy
d. I am incredibly happy
a. I rarely laugh
b. I laugh fairly often
c. I laugh a lot
d. I am always laughing
Note: Sum scores where a = 0, b = 1, c = 2, d = 3

A comprehensive measure of well-being is provided by the World Health Organization Quality of Life Scale (WHOQOL Group, 1998). It contains 100 items; some of the sample items are presented in Exhibit 2. The measure includes a wider range of feeling facets.

Exhibit 2.2

- How much do you worry about money?   1. Not at all,   2. Slightly,   3. Moderate,   4. Very,   5. Extremely
- How much do you enjoy your free time?   1   2   3   4   5
- How dependent are you on your medications?   1   2   3   4   5

Factor analytic studies of happiness / well-being indicate two separate factors: cognitive and affective. Cognitive factors represent cognitive evaluations of satisfaction with various life domains. Affective components represent the emotional experience of joy, elation and other emotions. Cross-cultural data show that these two aspects of happiness are correlated at about $r = 0.5$ in individualist cultures and as low as $r = 0.2$ in collectivist cultures. Thus, joy and satisfaction, the affective and cognitive component of happiness, are relatively independent of each other. In order to get around this problem of complexity some measurement experts have blended both the components within an integrated framework. For example, Alfonso, Allinson, Rader and Gorman (1996) developed the *Extended Satisfaction with Life Scale* where five items are used. In each of eight domains (self, family, sex, relationship, social, physical, education and work).

A similar multi-dimensional scale for measuring quality of life is titled FACIT (Functional Assessment of Chronic Illness Therapy). Although the title of the scale imparts negative connotation, the measurement system developed and validated by Evanston North Western Healthcare system provides a convenient easy-to-use scale for overall assessment. It consists of five subscales.

The subscales are:
1. Physical Well-Being   7 items
2. Social / Family Well-being   7 items

3. Emotional Well-Being   6 items
4. Functional Well-Being   7 items

Exhibit 2.2
Below is a list of statements that other people with illness have said are important. By encircling one number per line, please indicate how true each statement has been for you during the past 7 days.

	Not at all	A little bit	Some what	Quite a bit	Very much
• I have a lack of energy (Physical well-being)	0	1	2	3	4
• I feel close to my friends (Social/Family well-being)	0	1	2	3	4
• I feel nervous (Emotional well-being)	0	1	2	3	4
• I am able to enjoy life (Functional well-being)	0	1	2	3	4

Later a more refined method of measuring subjective well-being evolved Kahneman (1999) argued that one-time measure of well-being may not be reliable since it is subject to moment-to-moment fluctuations. Data collected on a working day may not be same as data collected on weekend days. Similarly, data collected from home may not be same as data collected outside the home. It is not difficult to differentiate between a person's momentary feelings and thoughts about well-being and larger, more global evolutions. At the momentary level it is possible to record people's moods and feelings online through experience sampling method.

Experience sampling method (ESM). While single-item and multi-item scales measure global perceptions of persons' happiness, experience sampling method (ESM) provides moment-to-moment measure of happiness (Stone, Schiffman, & DeVries, 1999). With ESM people are randomly signaled by a pager which they carry throughout an extended time period such as a week or a month. When the signal occurs they record their mood at that time point. Kahneman et al (1999) argued that this is a valid measure of happiness/well-being. The basic form of ESM can be somewhat varied to suit external conditions. For example, participants may be provided with wrist watches programmed to emit random signals for a fixed number of times (say eight times) each day for 7 days (or 2 weeks or 3 weeks), between the hours of 7:30 am and 10:30 pm. In response to the signal, respondents answer a number of open-ended and scaled questions from an experience-sampling form (ESF).

Happiness is a positive emotional state that is subjectively defined by each person. The evolutionary function of negative affects such as fear and anger have demanded greater attention. Historically positive affects have received limited attention over the last century. However, the potentialities of positive affects have become more obvious in recent decades (Cohn & Fredrickson, 2009). The distinction between positive and negative affects has become clear. Caciopo, Gardner and Berntson (1999) reviewed evidence indicating that separate biological systems subserve pleasant and unpleasant affect. Similarly, a number of researchers believe that the relationships between negative and positive affects are weak and indicative of independence. Thus, it is desirable to measure them separately because different conclusions often emerge about the antecedents and consequences.

Drawing on this rationale, Watson, Clark and Tellegen (1988) developed and validated a measure of Positive and Negative Affect Schedule (PANAS). The scale presents 20 affects (10 positive and 10 negative) and respondent is asked to indicate the extent a respondent is feeling (see Exhibit 2.3)

Exhibit 2.3
THE POSITIVE AND NEGATIVE AFFECT SCHEDULE
Use the 1 – 5 rating scale to indicate how you feel now

1	2	3	4	5
Very slightly or not at all	a little	moderately	Quite a lot	Extremely

- interested (PA) -- irritable (NA)
- distressed (NA) -- alert (PA)
- excited (PA) -- ashamed (NA)
- upset (NA) -- inspired (PA)
- strong (PA) -- nervous (NA)
- guilty (NA) -- determined (PA)
- scared (NA) -- attentive (PA)
- hostile (NA) -- jittery (NA)
- enthusiastic (PA) -- active (PA)
- proud (PA) -- afraid (NA)

Scoring: To score your responses, add up separately ratings for the 10 positive affects (PA) and 10 negative items (NA). Your score would range from 10 to 50. Compute also the difference. It is important to note that your PA score should be higher than your NA score. Hence a greater degree of difference in the direction of PA score is indicative of your happiness.

In measuring happiness, it is common sense to combine the frequency and intensity of pleasant emotions. Generally, people view others as happy when they experience intense positive emotions more often. However, empirical findings suggest otherwise. In a classic article, Brickman and Campbell (1971) posited that all people move on "hedonic treadmill". As they experience greater accomplishments, they move upward on a happiness scale. Yet they habituate the new level and gradually get back to their original **set point**. For example, they may win a lottery and feel extremely happy for some time; but gradually they get back to their original level. Similarly, people may encounter a fatal accident and experience pain and agony. This causes extreme unhappiness. But gradually they get back to their set point. Hence intense emotion is not a reliable marker.

Thus, feeling pleasant emotions most of the time and infrequently experiencing unpleasant emotions, even if the pleasant emotions are only mild, is sufficient for high reports of happiness. In other words, *frequency, not the intensity of emotions, is a dependable marker*.

Life Orientation Scale (LOS). Drawing on the three-component model of well-being, Sahoo (2009) developed Life Orientation Scale (LOS) to measure well-being. It is a multi-part instrument to scale the components separately (see Appendix A).

Part 1 presents 10 life satisfaction statements borrowed from relevant cross-culturally used scale. The statements include items such as "I am pleased with the way I have fulfilled my duties" and "I feel good about my life". Respondents are asked to indicate their agreement / disagreement with each of the statements on a 7-point scale where '1' denotes "strongly disagree" and '7' indicates "strongly agree". The scoring is reversed for negatively keyed items. The overall score is computed by summing scores across items.

Part 2 measures domain-specific satisfaction. Several such domains are represented. These include education (for self and children), social relation, self, work, recreation, finance and family. Under each domain, a number of sub-domains (such as coaching, examination performance, teacher, school/college environment) are included.

Respondents are required to indicate their level of satisfaction on a 7-point scale with respect to each subdomain. The scale ranges from '1' to '7' where '1' indicates "terrible" and '7' denotes "delightful".

Part 3 measures the frequency of positive feelings. Twenty-four affect denoting (12 positive and 12 negative) adjectives are presented. The positive items include cheerful; and joyful whereas negative items include sad and lonely. Participants are asked to indicate the frequency with which they have been experiencing each of these during last two weeks. The rating scale ranges from 1 to 5 where '1' denotes "never" and '5' denotes "almost always". Positive affect score is computed by summing scores across 12 positive items; similarly, negative affect score is computed by summing scores across 12 negative items. In addition, the balance score is computed by finding the difference between positive affect score and negative affect score.

It is important to note that Sahoo's Life Orientation Scale (LOS) provides a composite assessment based on three-component model. However, Part 2 of the scale measuring domain-specific satisfaction can be suitably adapted to deal with particular contexts. For example, application of the scale to samples of students may incorporate necessary changes in terms of replacing *work* by *study*.

Diversity of measures. In addition to some of the modal measures, a number of researchers have advocated alternative methods. For example, Sandvik, Diener and Seidlitz (1993) developed and validated a measure of well-being based on memory inclination. Respondents are asked to generate as many positive and as many negative events from their lives as they can during a short time period. With this method, it is possible to determine the relative accessibility of memories for good and bad events. Thus, we can determine the structure of how respondents view their lives. Additional measures are likely to provide complementary information. one potent source of additional information involves the objective category of physiological measures.

Objective (physiological) measure. In addition to psychological measures, it is useful to include psychological assessment. The cardiovascular indices (heart health and blood pressure) are helpful. Biochemical indicators such as uric acid, blood sugar, steroid hormones (cortisol), serum cholesterol, chatecolamines (adrenalin / noradrenalin / epinephrine) offer complementary information.

Since stress triggers the production of some of the most powerful chemicals influencing our health, a brief explanatory note is needed. Adrenalin from our adrenal glands (sitting just above our kidneys) is often correlated with increased 'sympathetic" activity in the autonomic nervous system commonly recognized as the "fight, fright and flight" or short-term stress response. Cortisol (from another part of our adrenal glands but stimulated by the hypothalamic – pituitary axis in the brain) is associated with long-term or chronic stress responses.

The steroid hormone cortisol is a key part of our stress hormone. It mobilizes our energy, affect the immune system and essentially enables the brain to cope better with the stimuli that have created the stress. We know that a level of challenge can be beneficial, heightening our ability to respond to stressors. However, chronical; sustained, unavoidable stress, which stimulates an excess of cortisol is very harmful, and can lead to death in the brain, and even, in extreme situation, to death. Indeed, chronic stress has symptoms very similar to aging in the brain and excessive cortisol causes significant damage to the hippocampus, crucial to the retention of memory.

Although there is evidence that mild stress (good stress) plays a role in adaptive changes in the immune system, chronic and long-term stress causes damaging changes in the immune system.

A major change in the study of stress and health came with the accumulation of reports that stress might reduce a person's resistance to infection. The theoretical and health implication led to the emergence of a new field called psychoneuroimmunology (PNI) the study of interaction among psychological factors, the nervous system, and the immune system.

Microorganisms of every description revel in the warm, damp, nutritive climate of our body. Our immune system keeps our body being overwhelmed by these invaders. Before it can take my action against an invading microorganism, the immune system must have some way of distinguishing foreign cells from body cells. That's why **antigen** – protein molecule that identifies it as native or foreign – plays a major role in specific immune reaction.

Immune system barriers to infection are often considered to be indicators of health. There are specific barriers that act against invaders. **Lymphocytes** are specialized white blood cells that are produced in bone marrow and stored in the lymphatic system. **Cell-mediated immunity** is directed by **B-cells (B – Lymphocytes)**.

In sum, T cells (T Lymphocytes) and B cells (B lymphocytes) count is an indicator of efficacious immune function. In other words, these could be regarded as an objective of measure of well-being.

Measure of Psychological Well-Being

As discussed earlier, two streams of research characterize the study of well-being. The first, termed subjective well-being (SWB), started in 1950s as part of hedonic tradition. The measures seeking to quantify life quality in terms of overall life satisfaction, domain-specific satisfaction and positive affect experience have been described earlier.

The other tradition, termed psychological well-being (PWB), has its roots in Aristotle's notion of *eudaemonia* – the realization of one's true potential. This conceptualization obviously emphasizes goals, values and realization in promoting positive functioning. Although a tremendous amount of work was undertaken employing Diener's three-component model of well-being, the major limitation was its atheoretical climate. Well-being research was found to be rather data driven rather than based on a clear conceptual framework.

An objective approach to psychological and social well-being was proposed by Ryff (1989) and Keyes (1998). On the basis of extensive empirical research and factor analysis, they explicate *six-component* well-being model and found that this multi-dimensional model is a superior fit over a single-factor model of well-being.

Ryff (1989) posits that this six-component model of well-being provides a holistic, integrated model of psychological well-being. Self-acceptance, personal growth, purpose in life, environmental mastery; autonomy, and positive relations with others are the six components of psychological well-being **(see Appendix B)**. The model has been examined in various studies and the predictions have been supported. The findings also reveal that the six components are independent, though correlated (Ryff & Singer, 1998).

Carol Ryff's Scales of Psychological Well-Being is a holistic measure based on eudaimonic tradition. It contains six 14-item scales to measure dimensions of autonomy environmental mastery, personal growth, positive relations with others, purpose in life, and self-acceptance. Although the 14-item scales have been used in many empirical studies, the author has also derived the 9-item scales for use. In recent years, the extensive use of this six-component model has generated a bulk of research and application.

Appendix A
The Life Orientation Scale (LOS)
F M Sahoo
Part – 1

Instruction

Below are ten statements that you may agree or disagree. Using the 1-7 scale, please indicate the amount of your agreement or disagreement with each item by placing the appropriate number on the line beside that item. Please be open and honest in your response.

1. Strongly disagree
2. Disagree
3. Slightly disagree
4. **Neither agree nor disagree**
5. Slightly agree
6. Agree
7. Strongly agree

- The life I live is close to my ideal.
- I enjoy the respect I am given.
- My family members would describe me as satisfied.
- I wish I had more respect given to me.
- I am pleased with the way I have fulfilled my duties.
- I wish I were more at peace.
- If I could live my life once again, I would want it to be almost exactly the same.
- I feel good about my life.
- My family members approve of my life.
- I feel at peace.

Part -2

Instruction

As an individual, you have several areas of your activity. Listed are such domains. Examine your feeling in each of these domains. Consider your feeling and experiences and indicate the degree of satisfaction with each of these domains. Put a number from 1 to 7 where "1" represents "terrible" feeling '7' represents "delightful" feeling.

- **Education (of self or children)**
- Coaching
- Exam Performance
- Teachers
- School environment
- College environment
- **Social Relation**
- Neighbours
- Friends
- Colleagues
- Visitors
- **Self in general**
- Physical health

- Achievement
- Morality (ethical)
- **Recreation**
- Games and Sports
- Social get-together
- Hobbies
- TV/Movies
- **Work**
- Pay
- Boss
- Physical surrounding
- **Finance**
- Income
- Expenditure
- Investment
- Debt
- **Family**
- Spouse
- Children
- Relatives
- Daily Living

Part-3

Instruction

Reflect on your experience for last two months and indicate the degree you have been experiencing each of these mental states. Using the 1-5 scale, indicate the number to express the intensity of your experience.

1. Never
2. Rarely
3. Sometimes
4. Often
5. Almost always

Cheerful   Depressed

Irritable	Lively
Happy	Gloomy
Joyful	Spirited
Nervous	Energetic
Scared	Lonely
Sad	Disgusted
Delighted	Optimistic
Shaky	Relaxed
Tired	Withdrawn
Excited	Enthusiastic
Alert	Dissatisfied

Part-4

Instruction

Please indicate these personal information.

Name (optional):   Sex:
Age: Residence:
Occupation: Income (Monthly):
Education

                Thank you for your cooperation

Scoring Notes

The scoring is self-explanatory. Part 1 item score keyed in positive directions excepting 4th and 6th items which are to be reverse-scored. Sum of scores across ten items is indicative of total life satisfaction. For Part 2, domain-specific satisfaction can be determined in terms of general satisfaction and specific satisfaction. For example, the rating for education is the general satisfaction with education. The ratings given for coaching, exam, etc. can be added across these sub-items. The average of these summed rating denotes specific satisfaction with education. For Part 3, positive affect score can be computed by adding ratings across 12 positive items. Similarly, negative affect score can be determined. The difference of these two scores is indicative of PANAS score. This is indicative of happiness / unhappiness.

Appendix B

Ryff's Scales of Psychological Well-Being

Dimension	Indicators	Sample Items
Autonomy	• Self-determining and independent • Resists social pressure • Evaluates self by personal standard	• I tend to worry about what other people think of me • I have confidence in my opinions, even if they are contrary to the general consensus.
Environments Mastery	• Has a sense of competence in mastering environment • Makes effective use of opportunities	• The demands of everyday life often get me down • In general, I am in charge of the situation in which I live.
Personal Growth	• Feels continued development • Has a sense of realizing potential	• I am the kind of person who likes to give new things a try. • I do not enjoy being in new situations.
Positive Relations with Others	• Has warm, satisfying relationship • Capable of strong empathy	• My friends and I sympathize with each other problems. • I find it difficult to really open up when I talk with others

Purpose in Life	<ul><li>Has goals and sense of directedness</li><li>Feels there is meaning in present and past life.</li></ul>	<ul><li>I have a sense of direction and purpose</li><li>My daily activities often seem trivial and unimportant to me.</li></ul>
Self-Acceptance	<ul><li>Has positive attitude towards the self</li><li>Accepts multiple aspects of self-including good and bad qualities</li></ul>	<ul><li>In many ways, I feel disappointed about my achievement in life.</li><li>For the most part, I am proud of who I am and the life I lead.</li></ul>

Chapter 3

Positivity Factors

The construct of happiness / psychological well-being as it stands today is the product of many transitions and transformations. Its evolutionary history is fairly complex. Although it has now been recognized as a distinct subfield within the broader framework of psychology, its journey towards its present status with distinctive definition, objectives, and methods was not without impediments. The heroic march from the status of science of mental illness to science of mental health is an event of humanistic aspiration and scientific achievement.

It is but natural that the deepest concerns of human beings were rooted in their survival and security modes. As with other domains, mental functioning concerns were also centered on issues of illness. Commencing from the prehistoric age to medieval ages, attempts were directed to prevent and treat mental illness. During the juncture of the nineteenth and the twentieth centuries, systematic investigations yielded certain positive outcomes. Sigmund Freud pioneered talk therapy to deal with mental illness. Other Freudians, post-Freudians and neo-Freudians expanded the contours of healing. While the issue of individual development and community empowerment was tangentially addressed, the main focus was on the healing process.

The second wave of mental health movement inspired several organized efforts across many nation states. During war periods, the mental-health movement basically involved three goals: (a) curing mental illness, (b) making individual lives productive and fulfilling, and (c) identifying and nurturing high talents. Despite these goals, the first one was actively pursued while other two goals were neglected. In a developed country like the U.S.A., the Veterans Administration was founded in 1946. It provided great employment opportunity for psychologists in the healing sector. Similarly, the National Institute of Mental Health (NIMH) was set up in 1947. It greatly promoted the research in the area of mental illness; it also yielded significant benefits in providing curing services for the mentally ill. Yet, it underutilized the idea of fulfilled individual and thriving community. Critic wondered whether NIMH is an institute of *mental health* or *mental illness*?

During the third wave of mental health movement, there were two significant developments. First, there was a paradigm shift in terms of redefining the concept of mental health. The World Health Organization stated: Health is not the absence of diseases or infirmities, it is an integrated system of physical, psychological and social well-being. This implies that only the absence of mental illness would not denote mental health; mental health would require the presence of a number of positive parameters such as job involvement.

In consonance with this proposition, empirical research in psychology provided supportive evidence. Specifically, measure of psychological well-being correlates on average - .51 with the Lung depression inventory and - .55 with the Center for Epidemiological Studies depression scale. Measures of life satisfaction and happiness also tend to correlate - .40 to - .50 with scales of depression (Keyes & Lopez, 2005). Based on these findings, Keyes posits that health is a complete state (WHO, 1948). Mental health is not merely the absence of mental illness, nor is it merely the presence of high well-being. Rather mental health is defined as a complete state consisting of (a) the absence of mental illness and (b) the presence of high level well-being. The model of complete mental health is depicted in the Figure below;

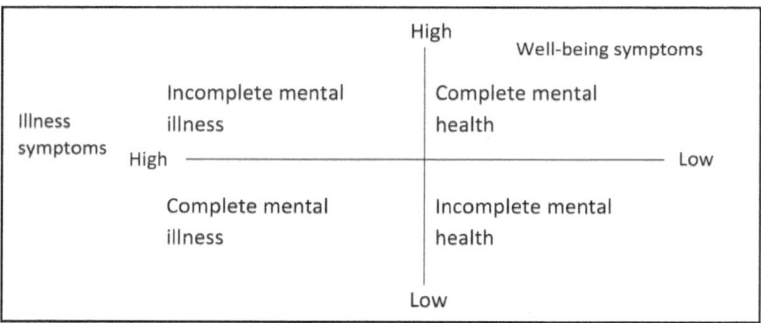

The model of complete mental health (as depicted in Figure) combines the illness and well-being dimensions, thereby yielding two states of mental illness and two states of mental health. In this model, mental health consists of a complete and an incomplete state; mental illness also consists of an incomplete and a complete state.

Complete mental health is the syndrome that combines high levels of symptoms of emotional well-being, psychological well-being and social well-being, as well as the absence of recent mental illness.

In other words, mentally healthy individuals are free of pathologies. However, some individuals without mental illness will also have low levels of well-being, which is a condition, described as **languishing** by Keyes. In contrast, adults who are free of mental illness but who have high levels of well-being are designated as **flourishing**. This state is aptly described by the Surgeon General of the US Department of Health and Human Sciences (1999) as is given below:

> Mental health is a state of successful performance of functions resulting in productive activities fulfilling relationships with people and the ability to adapt to change and to cope with adversity. (p.4)

The essential gap created by the paradigm crisis in the disease model was filled by the paradigm shift to the construct of complete health (Keyes& Lopez, 2005). Since the construct of complete health is synonymous with the concept of flourishing, it becomes an academic imperative to delineate the nomological network of flourishing. This process of delineation is greatly facilitated by developments in **positive psychology**.

Mainly under the leadership of well-known psychologist Martin Seligman, the positive psychology movement emerged from a reaction to an exclusive preoccupation with disease model in psychology. Seligman and a few others became concerned about the neglect of human strengths and virtues. They started positive psychology to shift atleast some of the emphasis away from the worst things in life to the best things in life. The aim of positive psychology is to use scientific methodology to discover and promote the factors that allow individuals, groups, organizations, and communities to prosper. The center of gravity was shifted from pathological functioning to individual and community empowerment.

With such a focus, the study of well-being included positive parameters of human behaviours. Included in the list of major factors are self-efficacy, optimism, hope and resilience. The capacity for love and vocation, courage, interpersonal skills, aesthetic sensibility, perseverance, forgiveness, originality, future mindedness, spirituality, talent and wisdom were also considered.

Self-Efficacy

The self-efficacy construct rests upon a long line of historical thinking related to the sense of *personal control*. Famous thinkers such as William James focused on willfulness and volition in human thinking. McClelland and Atkinson spoke of achievement motivation. White stressed effectance motivation. Rotter emphasized locus of control. It was this classic line of control-related research, the Stanford University psychologist Albert Bandura (1977, 1997) posited the construct of self-efficacy.

Bandura (1977) defined self-efficacy as "people's beliefs in their capabilities to produce desired effects by their own actions". Similarly, Maddux (2005) has described self-efficacy as "what I believe I can do with my skills under certain conditions".

In the context of self-efficacy, it is important to make a distinction between *skill acquisition* and skill *execution*. We acquire skills by going through schools/colleges, by undergoing training programmes, and by observing various performance. However, skill execution requires a supportive belief system. It requires the belief that the person can do the work competently. In other words, self-efficacy denotes the extent of belief that the person can execute a function competently.

The belief could be very general in its tone. The

person could have a generalized belief regarding his or her capabilities. This is *generalized self-efficacy* – a trait-like concept. Now let us examine a paradox. A person may possess a very high level of generalized self-efficacy. Yet would he/she save a drowning child? The answer is: NO. Even if the person has a very high level of self-efficacy, the person would not venture out saving the child as he/she does not know how to swim. Hence what is more important is the context-specific efficacy such as swimming efficacy, driving efficacy, teaching efficacy and child-management efficacy. These *domain-specific efficacies* are *state-like concepts* (subject to learning and training).

Generalized self-efficacy is measurable. So also is the domain-specific efficacy. For example, driving efficacy can be measured by presenting a number of questions which can be answered in the form of 'yes' or 'no'. A sample of representative questions may include:

- Can you drive well when the road condition is not good?
- Can you drive well when you are feeling feverish?
- Can you drive well when it is raining?
- Can you drive well when traffic signals are not clear?
- Can you drive well when your friends are distracting you?

Obviously driving efficacy would be considered very high if a respondent offers a large number of 'yes' responses. On the other hand, a small number of affirmative responses would be treated as low driving efficacy.

Apart from the notion of generalized self-efficacy and context-specific efficacy (e.g., driving efficacy), there is a third form of efficacy: *collective efficacy*. It is otherwise known as *team efficacy*. It is the collective belief of a group of people regarding their team capability. For example, the faculty members of an educational institution may collectively believe in the successful implementation of a new programme of studies. The self-efficacy of isolated members may not matter much. What would ultimately matter is the collective belief regarding successful implementation of the programme.

Sources of Self-Efficacy

The strong theoretical foundation and considerable research have demonstrated mechanisms for its development. These include the opportunities to experience mastery/success, vicarious learning/modeling, social persuasion and positive feedback, and psychological and physiological arousal and well-being.

Mastery experiences: While practice makes perfect, success builds confidence. It is advisable to start from the tasks of moderate difficulty level. Such an exposure increases the possibility of greater success and builds confidence. Once the confidence is strengthened, difficult tasks can be undertaken in future.

There are many approaches that can help to build mastery experiences. For example, a trainer can break down a complex task into sub-components and teach the trainee each of the simple subskills, one at a time. This allows the trainee to experience "small success" more frequently. These simple tasks and skills can then be gradually integrated into their broad, more complex whole, with opportunities for practice and mastery at each step of the way.

Another way to provide trainees with mastery experiences is to intentionally place them in situation where the probability of success is relatively high, where they have a good chance to experience success. This is why selection, orientation, placement, and career planning are so important. People need to be set up for success as much as possible rather than put into uncertain environments that turn out not to be a good fit for them.

Vicarious learning / modeling: It is documented that observational experiences allow individuals to process and learn them from success and mistakes of others and to selectively *imitate* their successful actions. This learning enhances the observer's own chances for future mastery experiences and success. However, in order for modeling experiences to be effective, there must be both model and situations similarity, and time should be allowed by the learner for some degree of reflection.

The trainer may bring a far-fetched model (say a very successful leader in the USA) to the notice of the trainee. In this case, the trainee may admire and worship the model, but the trainee would not imitate. The dissimilarity between the trainee and the model would create a gap. On the other hand, the more similar the role model is to the trainee (target), the more likely the observer's (trainee's) efficacy would be influenced by the role model's success. This implies that peer-mentors, models from the vicinity are preferable. The similarity between the model and trainee would prompt imitation. Once role models are accepted on the basis of similarity, the model would be a source of information and inspiration for the target.

Social persuasion: Simply hearing others urge you on (i.e., have confidence in you) and provide positive feedback on your progress can transform your self-doubting beliefs into efficacy expectancies. As you listen to others' encouraging "you can do it" and "you are doing so well in accomplishing the first step of _ _ _ _ _ _ _ ", your thoughts and beliefs begin to shift to a confident "I can do it" perspective.

The impact of these nonfinancial positive reinforcers such as attention, recognition, and positive feedbacks has been recognized in efficacy literature.

Psychological and physiological arousal: Feeling good and being in good physical condition can have positive impact on one's cognitive and emotional states, including efficacy beliefs and expectancies. On the other hand, being ill, fatigued and out of shape can have a negative impact.

Importantly the mental and physical arousal and wellness do not have as big an impact as the other more focused sources of efficacy. Yet, if negative, they can be a major blow to one's level of efficacy. Hence, the level of people's emotional states (or, arousal) must not be lost sight of.

Mediating Mechanisms

People with self-efficacy manage their thoughts, motivation and emotion in specific ways. In contrast, inefficacious individuals adopt different methods.

At the cognitive front, thoughts of efficacious individuals are regulated by fore-thoughts and self-appraisal. The higher the goal challenge, firmer is their commitment. They visualize success scenarios that provide positive guides and support for performance. They also remain task-oriented throughout.

In the context of motivation, they set goals themselves and plan course of action. They mobilize resource and value outcomes. They make consistently self-monitoring and are open to periodic feedbacks. Three types of self-influences do operate. These include self-satisfying, and self-dissatisfying reaction to one's performance, self-efficacy for goal attainment, and readjustment of personal goals based on one's progress. They appropriately utilize proximal, tangible and achievable goals.

With respect to affective process, it is observed that efficacious individuals adopt effective coping strategies. Inefficacious people magnify the severity of possible threats and worry about things that rarely happen. In contrast, efficacious persons believe that they can exercise control over possible threats. In coping with adaptation to new social domains, efficacious people treat it as a challenge, whereas inefficacious people view it as a threat (Bandura, 1991).

Well-being Benefits

Self-efficacy has produced a large body of research documenting adaptive benefits. Self-efficacy has been implicated in successful coping with a variety of psychological problems. In addition, it has been linked with several forms of satisfaction (e.g., work, family, social relation). Self-efficacy influences health in *three* possible ways.

Efficacy and adaptation: General beliefs of efficacy serves as a personal resource factor in the process of adaptation. People with a high sense of perceived efficacy trust their own capabilities to master different types of environmental demands. Even if the constraints are heavy, they interpret the events as challenging. Cognitively they leverage their confidence and sense of control, feel motivated by physiological arousal and effectively deal with negative emotions. They firmly believe that positive events are caused by their own efforts and negative events are caused by external circumstances. In contrast, inefficacious individuals perceive environmental demands as threats. They are prone to self-doubts, anxieties and coping deficiencies.

There have been several studies that have examined

the role of self-efficacy in stressful life transitions. Jerusalem and Mittag (1995) investigated the adaptation process of young East German migrants and refugees during a stressful life transition following the collapse of the Eastern system. Perceived self-efficacy emerged as a powerful personal resource regarding the impact of migration stress on cognitive appraisals as well as psychological and physical well-being. Highly self-efficacious youths' experiences lower anxiety, better health and fewer health complaints than low self-efficacious migrants.

Elimination of health-impairing behaviour: The promotion of well-being requires both the adoption of health–promoting behaviour and elimination of health–impairing behaviour. Numerous studies have shown that health cognitions are greatly influenced by the level of perceived self-efficacy (Schwarzer & Fuchs, 1995). Self-efficacy is not only a major contributor influencing decision-making process but also the initiation and maintenance process.

We live in a world where a variety of health-risk behaviour, such as smoking, alcohol consumption, poor nutrition, lack of physical exercise, risky sexual practices, and ignoring preventive health screening abound. Many people try to cope with environmental stress by regulating their emotions through risky behaviours such as smoking and addiction. Although the public health agencies in every country try to reduce risky behaviour (smoking, addiction, so on) through prevention and remediation, the attempts are not always successful. Hence a fundamental question concerns the identification of personal and social variable that could be utilized for the adoption of health behaviours.

Studies have been conducted to compare the role of perceived self-efficacy with that of risk perceptions and past behaviours. The intention to use safe sexual practices was best predicted by past behaviour. However, the intention to stop smoking, to eat healthy foods, and to exercise were mainly determined by self-efficacy. The intention to undergo cancer screening was also influenced by self-efficacy, but the effect was moderated by sex, age and interactions with outcome expectancies. These findings have implications for the promotion of health behaviour.

Behavioural control over health-quality: As people's belief in their self-regulatory efficacy influences three basic phases of personal change, efficacy operates to foster lifestyle changes that enhance health and to alter those that impair it.

Abuse of addictive substances is a highly prevalent problem Marlatt, Baer, and Quigley (1995) have evinced the unique role played by perceived self-regulatory efficacy in every phase of addictive behaviour. After people give up an addictive substance, relapses often occur even though withdrawal symptoms are no longer present to drive one to resume use of alcohol, drugs, or cigarette smoking. The challenging problem involves the elimination of psychological reliance on addictive substances for their positive effects or as an escapist mode of coping with difficult realities. In sum, the role of personal efficacy in weakening (or eliminating) faulty lifestyle and strengthening healthy lifestyle is a key factor in health promotion.

Optimism

The term optimism is a relatively recent arrival on the historical scene. Optimum and pessimism are not strictly polar opposites. Optimism is cognitive in its emphasis, reflecting a reasoned judgment that good would predominate over evil. In contrast, pessimism has an affective (emotional) tone. Pessimistic individual is one for whom suffering would outweigh happiness.

When asked to distinguish people generally use the metaphors "glass half-filled" versus "glass half-empty" to demote optimism and pessimism respectively. More recently an author has written a book titled *"Zebra Questions"*. A person asks zebra: "Zebra! Are you white with black stripes or black with white stripes?" The zebra puts some counter questions: "Are you happy with occasional unhappiness or unhappy with occasional happiness? Are you elated with occasional depression or depressed with occasional elations? Are you fresh with occasional fatigue or fatigued with occasional freshness? Are you frank with occasional restraints or restrained with occasional frankness?"

The message inherent in these questions is obvious. This is a stylistic dimension; it conceptualizes as to how one categorizes one's environment.

Nature of Optimism

A useful definition of optimism was offered by anthropologist Lionel Tiger (1979): "a mood or attitude associated with an expectation about the social or material future – one which the evaluator regards as socially desirable, to his (or her) advantage, or for his (or her) pleasure" (p.18). Contemporary thinkers usually treat optimism as a cognitive characteristic – a goal, an expectation, or a causal attribution. Optimism is not simply cold cognition, it is both motivated and motivating. Optimism and pessimism have both defensive as well as ego-enhancing aspects.

Inherent human nature: Optimism has been posited as an inherent aspect of human nature. However, early approaches to optimism as human nature were basically negative. Classical authors such as Sophocles, Neitzsche and Freud argued that optimism was illusory, and it handicaps humans in handling the crosses of life. According to Freud, the accurate perception of reality is an indicator of good psychological functioning. Similar opinions were expressed by a large number of celebrated psychologists such as Allport, Erikson, Fromm, Maslow, and Rogers (from the 1930s through 1960s). "Reality testing" became the defining feature of the healthy individual and psychologists attempted to train people to appraise reality.

Approaches began to change in the 1960s and 1970s in light of research evidence that most people are not strictly realistic, and their thoughts are biased in the optimistic direction. A large number of studies indicate that language, memory, and thoughts are selectively positive. People use more positive words than negative words in their writings and speaking. In free recall, people produce positive memories sooner than negative ones. Most people evaluate themselves more positively than they evaluate others. In many testing situations such as examinations, examinees self-rate themselves above the median although only 50 percent of the participants are theoretically placed above the median. This is clearly a self-serving bias.

In the context of therapeutic interventions there is widespread belief that psychologically healthy people show the positivity bias. Richard Lazarus (1983) described what he called *positive denial* and showed that it can be associated with well-being while dealing with adversity. Aaron Beck (1967) developed influential cognitive approach to depression and asserted that depression is characterized by pessimism and helplessness. By implication depressives are illogical and nondepressive are logical. However, Beck (1991) more recently gave a changed version saying that nondepressives bring a positive bias towards their ongoing experiences and expectations about the future.

Greenwald's (1980) opinion linking human nature to a totalitarian regime was another supporting clue for positive bias. According to Greenwald, the self organizes its history and identity as a totalitarian state. Everyone engages in an ongoing process of structuring and revising his or her own personal history. The story each of us talks about ourselves is necessarily ego-centric. Each of us is the central figure in our own narration. Each of us takes credit for good deeds and passes the buck for failure. In sum, the ego maintains and furthers its own interest.

A major break through came in the form of Shelley Taylor and Jonathan Brown's (1988) work on *positive illusions*. They reviewed a large number of studies indicating that psychologically healthy people show bias towards the positive; these are *creative illusions* even if these are illusions. Taylor (1989) persuasively argued in her book *Positive Illusions* that people's tendency to present themselves in the best possible light is a sign of well-being. For Taylor, optimism as an illusion is responsive, whereas delusions are health-impairing.

Tiger's (1979) assertion that optimism is an inherent aspect of human nature is explicated in his book, *Optimism: The Biology of Hope*. Tiger argued that optimism has adaptive characteristics and it has played dynamic role in human evolution.

Individual difference construct: While optimism as an inherent aspect of human nature is amply recognized, psychologists interested in the predictive role of optimism looked at it as an individual difference construct. There were numerous research traditions that stimulated the interest in the study of the extent of belief or expectation (e.g., Kelly, Rotter).

A significant change was the waning of traditional stimulus–response (S-R) approach to learning and its replacement with cognitive perspective emphasizing expectancy. According to S-R framework, learning denotes the acquisition of particular motor response in particular situation. Skinner's S-R view essentially entails the association strengthened by way of *contiguity* between stimulus and response. The cognitive view, on the contrary, emphasizes the element of *contingency* the degree to which stimuli provide new information about responses. The behaviouristic orientation (S-R) stresses on temporal contiguity between the response and the reinforcer, viewing the individual as tapped by the momentary co-occurrences of events. In contrast, the contingency view of learning proposes that individuals are able to detect cause-and-effect relationships, separating momentary noncausal relationship from more enduring ones. So, learning at its essence entails the discovery of "what leads to what".

Since learning of this sort extends over time, it is logical to view in central (cognitive) terms. Most proponents of this view consider the representation of contingency as an *expectation* to explain how learning is generalized across situations and projected across time. Most approaches to optimism as an individual difference construct adopt this approach, in which optimism is regarded as a generalized expectation that influences any and all psychological processes.

Within the framework of optimism as an individual difference construct, there are quite a few approaches. Despite the distinctiveness across approaches the findings with respect to the benefits of optimism are uniform.

Optimism is related to desirable outcomes: health, happiness, success and academic attainments.

Although most of the studies of optimism are geared to explore consequences and correlates of optimism employing psychometric measures, a brief survey of the two major approaches is likely to provide inputs for investigation of other issues.

Optimism as a self-regulatory process: Many researchers study optimism extensively as a self-regulatory process. They identify it as **dispositional optimism**: the global expectation that good things would be plentiful in the future and bad-things scare.

The authors (Scheier and Colleagues) argue that optimistic people in the face of difficulties, continue to pursue their valued goals and regulate themselves and their personal states using effective coping strategies so that they are likely to achieve their goals. Dispositional optimism is associated with good health and a positive response to medical intervention. The impact of dispositional optimism on recovery from medical procedure is mediated by effective coping strategies such as redefinitions and reframing. Pessimists, in contrast, use avoidant coping strategies or disengage from coping with problems.

Scheier and Carver (1985) measured optimism (vs. pessimism) with a brief self-report questionnaire called the Life Orientation Test (LOT). Representative items from this test include the following:

1. I am always optimistic about my future
2. I rarely count on good things happening to me.

Respondents indicate their agreement/disagreement on a five-point scale. Positive expectations are combined with (reversed scored) negative expectations; the resulting measure is investigated with respect to various outcome factors (health, happiness, achievement and coping).

Optimism as explanatory style: Professor Martin Seligman and his colleagues have conceptualized optimism as an explanatory style, rather than a broad personality trait. Optimistic people, according to this perspective, explain negative events or experiences by attributing the cause of these to external, temporary and specific factors. In contrast, pessimists explain negative events or experiences by attributing the causes to internal, stable and global factors. For example, an individual encounters a street accident. How does an optimistic explanatory style compare itself with a pessimistic explanatory style? An optimistic individual is likely to explain that the accident is caused by erratic behaviours of the other motorist (an *external* factor); the effects of injury would stay for a while and then would disappear (a *transient* or *temporary* factor), the bad effects of the accident would be confined to his or her hand injury (a *specific* factor) and the person can do other works. In contrast, a pessimist tends to explain the negative event differently. The pessimist thinks that the accident is caused by his or her faulty driving (an *internal* factor); the effects of injury would stay for a long period of time (a *stable* or *permanent* factor); the effects would generalize to a number of domains of his or her life (*global* factor); he or she would be deprived of using his or her hands, legs and other limbs for a long period of time.

How do optimistic individuals explain good (positive) events? Compared with the task of explaining negative events, optimists need to do the reverse. They attribute the positive events to internal (personal) factors, they view the effects of positive events relatively lasting (permanent) and they also spill the effects of positive events over multiple domains (global or pervasive) of life. In short, they employ personal, permanent and pervasive attributions. For instance, if their project succeeds, they tend to explain the cause of this success in terms of their own efforts or strategy (internal factor). Similarly, they view that the good effects of their success would be prolonged (stable) and it would positively influence a number of domains (global factor) of their lives; the good effects would spill over to family life, professional life and other domains. In contrast, the pessimist would view the cause of success in terms of external factor like outside support. The pessimist would also perceive the good effects of positive events as temporary (unstable) influencing only limited aspects (specific) of his or her life.

In sum, any encounter with good events or bad events trigger *three* questions in mind: who is responsible for the event? How long would the effect stay? How pervasive would be its impact? As indicated, optimists explain positive events in terms of internal (personal), stable (permanent) and global (pervasive) terms; they explain negative events in terms of external, unstable and specific factors. In contract pessimists explain positive events using external, unstable and specific factors; they explain negative events employing internal, stable and global factors. Research shows that optimistic explanatory style induces a number of positive outcomes whereas pessimistic explanatory style generates helplessness and depression.

Explanatory style is typically measured with the help of a self-report questionnaire called Attributional Style Questionnaire (ASQ). It presents hypothetical events (both positive and negative) followed by two alternative explanations. Respondents are asked to select one that fits with their perception. The measure generates scores of internality, stability and globality for positive events and scores of externality, instability and specificity for negative events. These are indicative of optimism. In addition, there is another robust measure of explanatory style called Content Analysis of Verbal Explanations (CAVE). Trained experts can rate the writings and speeches on the dimension of internality, stability and globality (also on externality, instability, specificity). CAVE is used for diaries, interview transcripts, newspaper, quotations, and other documents.

In addition to the ASQ and the CAVE, a children's version of the ASQ has also been developed: Children's Attributional Style Questionnaire (CASQ). A Relationship Attribution Measure (RAM) has been developed to evaluate optimism within marriage (Finchman & Bradbury, 1992).

Antecedents of Optimism

Seligman and his colleagues carefully describe the developmental roots of the optimistic explanatory styles. To begin with, there appears to be some genetic components of explanatory style, with optimism scores more highly correlated for monozygotic (identical) and dizygotic (fraternal) twins.

Optimism appears to have roots in the environment. For example, parents who provide safe, coherent environment are likely to promote optimistic style in their offspring. Likewise, the parents of optimists are portrayed as modeling optimism in their children by making explanations for negative events that enable the offspring to continue to feel good about themselves (i.e., external, variable/unstable, and specific attributions for negative experiences), along with explanations for positive events that help the offspring feel extra-good about themselves (i.e., internal, stable and global attributions). Moreover, children who grow up with optimism are characterized by having parents who understood their failures and generally attributed those failures to external rather than internal factors. On the other hand, pessimistic people had parents who were pessimistic.

Television watching is yet another potential source of pessimism. Some studies document that pessimism-related behaviours stem from television watching.

Training for Optimism

As indicated earlier, optimistic explanatory styles offer a number of benefits. Optimism is significantly related to academic success, career success, professional success, effective coping and well-being. In view of these positive consequences, emphasis has been placed on attributional retraining. Seligman (1998) has developed programmes to help children and adults to change their explanatory style from pessimism to optimism. Drawing on the cognitive therapy models of Aaron T. Beck and Albert Ellis, Seligman train participants to analyze mood-altering situations and then modify their pessimistic beliefs to optimistic beliefs. In situations of adversity, participants conduct an ABC Analysis of their adversity. Here is an example of an ABC analysis of a particular situation.

Adversity: My project did not succeed

Belief: I am inefficient

Consequence: I changed my feeling ok to feeling depressed.

Following ABC analysis of adversity, three sets of skills are practiced. These include distraction, distancing and disputation.

Distraction entails doing something to shift attention from pessimistic thought to optimistic thought. This may involve saying "STOP" loudly or carrying a flash card with 'STOP' written on it in large letters. The person may also wear an elastic band on the wrist or do similar things to divert the attention.

Distancing involves reminding ourselves that pessimistic explanation of adversity is only one possible explanation of the situation. Distancing is a strategy to reduce the impact on mood by asserting that beliefs are not facts.

Disputation is the strategy of conducting an internal dialogue. Its aim is to convince oneself that there is equally strong or stronger optimistic explanation for the adversity. When disputing pessimistic explanations, we may ask these questions:

1. What is evidence for the explanation or belief? Is there any evidence that it is not true?
2. Are there alternative optimistic explanations for the adversity? (optimistic explanations for adversity: external, specific and temporary factors)
3. If I cannot justify an optimistic explanation foe the adversity, are the implications of pessimistic explanation catastrophic or just a bit of a temporary inconvenience?
4. I cannot decide whether there is evidence for an optimistic or pessimistic explanation, which explanation or belief is most useful for my positive mood?

With the help of ABC analysis skills and distraction, distancing and disputation strategies, the next step is to put them together in ABCDE (Adversity, Belief, Consequence mood change, Disputation and Energization) practice.

The disputation skill would remove the thought of negative consequence and the resulting positive mood change would stimulate energization. The Penn Optimism Programme was designed to help school-age children develop optimistic explanatory style. The 12-week programme contains elements of ABCDE model.

Issues in Optimism

While a wealthful of information concerning optimism has been collected in recent years, there are issues that remain unresolved. A couple of issues may briefly be noted.

Little optimism versus big optimism: It is important to make a distinction between *little optimism versus big optimism*. Little optimism denotes specific expectations about positive outcomes. Two representative thoughts can be indicated: "I would find out a suitable restaurant for eating out this evening"; "I would complete my today's assignment in time". Big optimism refers to largest and less specific expectation on: The best in my life is yet to come". The other example reads: "My ambition in life would be definitely fulfilled". The big versus little optimism reminds us that optimism can be described at different levels of abstraction. Furthermore, it may function differently depending on the level.

What exactly is the relationship between little and big optimism? Are they positively correlated or are they independent dimensions? In case of independence of dimensions, it would be possible to imagine someone who is a little optimist but a big pessimist, or vice versa. Researchers need to probe into this distinction more carefully.

The reality basis. Optimism can have costs if it is too unrealistic. People's perception of personal risk for illness and mishaps may be considered. People need not be too optimistic so as to avoid regular health examinations.

Similarly, optimism in the form of wishful thinking can distract people from making concrete plans about how to attain goals. In other words, the **functional or realistic or dynamic optimism** is the call of the day. However, what constitutes reality is not an easy problem to solve. Schneider (2001) has attempted to delineate some criteria of *realistic optimism*.

Optimism and Well-being

The growing interest in optimism springs from its demonstrated relationship with happiness. A bulk of studies clearly evinces the positive association between optimism and health. The positive association could be surveyed from three different perspectives.

Empirical studies. Several studies reveal that optimism is linked with health promotive behaviour and pessimism makes people vulnerable to stress and illness. Harvard graduates who were most pessimistic when interviewed in 1946 were least healthy when retested in 1980. Similarly, Virginia Tech students who reacted to bad events pessimistically suffered more colds, sore throats and flu a year later. Optimist people are less bothered by various illnesses and recover better from coronary bypass surgery and cancer. Blood tests provide a reason linking optimism with stronger immune defenses (Myers, 1990).

Relationships between optimism and well-being have been examined in diverse groups of people facing adversity. An early study of the effect of optimism examined the development of depressed feelings after child birth. Women completed the Life Orientation Test (LOT: A measure of optimism) and a depression scale in the last third of their pregnancy. They then completed the depression measure again 3 weeks after their babies were born. Optimism was related to lowering of depression. Optimism also predicted lower levels of depression postpartum, even when controlling for the initial levels. Thus, optimism seems to buffer depression after having a baby.

In another study, Scheier and associates (1989) examined men undergoing and recovering from coronary artery bypass surgery. Patients were tested a day before surgery, a week after surgery, and 6 months after surgery. Before surgery optimists reported less hostility and depression than pessimists. A week afterward, optimists reported more happiness and relief, more satisfaction with their medical care and more satisfaction with emotional support from friends. Six months after surgery, optimists continued to report greater subjective well-being. In a follow-up 5 years after surgery, optimists continued to experience greater well-being compared with pessimists.

Later research on the positive relationship between optimism and bypass surgery provides clues with respect to mediating mechanism. Optimism appears to operate on feelings of life satisfaction through a more focused sense of confidence about the surgery. The general sense of optimism about life apparently is funneled into a specific optimism regarding the surgery, and from there to satisfaction with life (Carver & Scheier, 2005).

Optimism also has been studied in the context of other kinds of health crises. One study examined adjustment to treatment for early stage breast cancer. Patients were interviewed at the time of diagnosis, the day before surgery, 7 to 10 days after surgery, and 3, 6, and 12 months after surgery. Optimism inversely predicted distress over time. Optimism predicted not only initial distress but also resilience against distress during the year following surgery.

Similar results have been obtained with respect to adjustment to procedure called *in vitro fertilization* and adjustment to abortion. Optimism not only has a positive effect on the psychological well-being of people with medical problems but also influencing well-being among care-givers. The range of population diversity studies is quite large. Included are the experiences of students entering colleges, employees of organizations, survivors of missile attacks, Alzheimer's patients, and medical professionals. There is converging evidence that optimism is significantly related to adjustment and well-being.

The positive role of optimism is not confined to the phenomenon of preventing and dealing with the bad, it also promotes the good. Seligman found that new Metropolitan Life Insurance representatives who put an optimistic spin sold more policies and were half as likely to quit during their first year. Apart from success in market behaviours, optimists display greater success in domains of academic, sports, and other achievements.

The relationship networks. The attempts to tap nomological network concerning optimism generates many testable predictions. A very salient feature relating to optimism and pessimism is that these two constructs, though inversely correlated are not polar opposites (Peterson & Chang, 2003). Obviously, the strength of prediction varies depending on the target of prediction. Generally, it is found that pessimism is a stronger predictor of outcomes compared with optimism (Peterson & Chang, 2003).

Optimism appears to be a part of subjective well-being. In a study, it was found that among a sample of lawyers, optimism was the best predictor of general well-being, better than hardiness. In another study, the researcher for law students found that those high in optimism in time 1 had more active immune systems in time 2. This was partly due to their having more positive moods, perceiving less stress and not having avoidance methods of coping.

Individuals with optimism recall more good things in the past and have a positive view of others, and produce pleasanter items in free association tests Scheier and Carver (1985) found their Life Orientation Test (LOT) score is found to correlate with happiness (a correlation of .75)

Several investigations have found that while both optimism and pessimism both correlate with other aspects of well-being, the pessimism factor do so more strongly (negatively). Pessimism is a stable predictor of psychological and physical health.

Intervention inputs: The procedure of combating pessimism and promoting optimism has been discussed in terms of reattribution training. However, an effective intervention procedure requires the identification of culture-specific contents in the remediation methods.

Optimism and pessimism are not simple opposites. Findings with respect to the one construct cannot be flipped into conclusions about the other. Furthermore, the constructs of optimism and pessimism are likely to have multiple features. It is important to recognize that different features are relevant to differing segments of population. Although all the features of optimism/pessimism have not yet been identified and these are still in the process of research, future attempts need to take care of the both identification and population-specification.

More specifically cultural context is an important consideration. Considering the view that some form of optimism and the absence of some form of pessimism is linked to the good life, a one-size-fits-all approach may not work well. Research has indicated that easterners including Asians and Westerners including Americans do not show similar sensitivities to optimism and pessimism. Accordingly, a culture-specific intervention consistent with Beck's cognitive framework might focus distinctly on increasing optimistic thoughts in distressed Asians rather than decreasing their pessimism. By decreasing pessimism in Asians, one could take away a major portion of motivation, and adaptive coping. On the contrary, it may be more valuable to use intervention that focuses on increasing decreasing pessimism of Americans.

Hope

Viktor Frankl is a revolution in the domain of human thought. He was the illustrious neurologist, psychiatrist and psychologist. He was the founder of the Third Viennese School of Psychotherapy (after Freud's psychoanalysis and Adler's individual psychology) – the school of Logotherapy. Yet, his life was a life of suffering. During World War II, he spent three years in Auschwitz, Dachau, and other concentration camps. As a longtime prisoner in bestial concentration camps he found himself stripped to naked existence. His parents, bother and his wife died in camps or were sent to the gas ovens. He witnessed the horrific scenes of thousands of people being sent to gas chambers. How did he manage to live? How did he survive to find meaning in the suffering, was it not the hopeful view of man's capacity to transcend his predicament and discover an adequate guiding truth? The poet Alexandar Pope echoes: Hope springs eternal in human breast.

Hope, a construct closely related to optimism, has been articulated by Rick Snyder (2000) as the perceived capability to plan pathways to desired goals. Goals could be short-term or long-term. Goals could be tangible (i.e., to increase per capita income from Rs X to Rs Y) or intangible (i.e., reducing poverty). Goals could also be attainable or uncertain.

Pathways and Agency Thinking

In order to reach goal, people must view themselves as being capable of generating workable routes to these goals. This process is called *pathway thinking*. It reflects one's capabilities of finding out alternatives for the attainment of goal. They are found to be using self-talks ("I would find out ways to get it done"). In a way the plurality of pathways is beneficial because it offers the advantage of evaluating desirability and feasibility of pathways.

The motivational component of hopeful thinking is called *agency*. It denotes the perceived capacity to use pathways to reach the goal. High hope people use a greater degree of agentic thinking. They are found to be using substantial amount of internal dialogues ("I can definitely do it"; "No obstruction can stop me"). Agentic thinking not only reflects the strength with which a performance can be executed, it also denotes the strength of belief regarding the removal of blockades.

Emotion and the Process

While some researchers have indicated hope as an emotion, the current focus is on its cognitive component. It is posited that positive emotions should flow from perception of successful goal pursuit. Perception of successful goal pursuits may result from unimpeded movement towards desired goal. It may also reflect instances in which the individual has effectively overcome any problems. Negative emotions, on the other hand, are product of unsuccessful goal pursuits. Thus, *goal–pursuit cognitions cause emotion*.

High hopes have positive emotional sets and a sense of zest that stems from their histories of success in goal pursuits. In contrast, low hopers have negative emotional sets and a set of emotional flatness that stems from their histories of having failed in goal pursuits. High or low hope people bring these overriding emotional sets with them as they undertake specific goal-related activities.

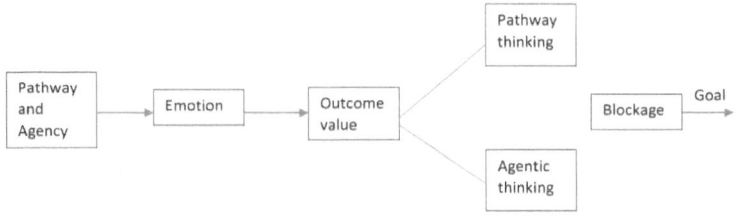

Figure: The Process

As shown in the Figure, the interactive relationship of pathway and agency thoughts is depicted in the left. This leads to the emotional sets that are taken to specific goal pursuit activities. Next in the Figure are values associated with specific goal pursuits. Sufficient values must be attached to goal pursuits before the individual continues the hoping process. At this point, the pathway and agency thoughts are applied to the desired goal. The person may encounter blockages along the route. However, successful pursuit of the desired goal circumvents the impediment. It results in positive emotion and pursuit efforts.

Measurement of Hope

Snyder and his associates have developed and validated several forms of measurements.

The Trait Hope Scale is a 12-item rating scale where four items are indicative of pathway thinking while four

items are indicative of agency thinking. All these eight items are keyed in the positive direction. The other four items are distractor and not scorable. All items are randomized. Respondents are asked to rate items on a 8-point scale where '1' indicates 'definitely false' and '8' indicates 'definitely true'. The sum of ratings across pathway items represents pathway score; similarly sum of ratings across agency items denotes agency score. The sum of scores across all 8 items represents hope. The Hope Scale is also known as Future Scale. Two sample items (one from agency and one from pathway thinking) can be cited below:
1. I energetically pursue my goals.
2. There are lots of ways around my problem.

The State Hope Scale is similar in format. It contains 6 items and respondents are asked to indicate their response on a 8-point scale. Respondents are asked to take a few moments to focus on themselves and to attend to what is going on in their lives at that moment. Once they have "here and now" set, they should indicate their response. Half of the items represent pathways thinking while other three items denote agency thinking. As with Trait Hope Scale, pathway thinking, agency thinking, and total score can be computed. Two sample items are given below:
1. Right now, I see myself as being pretty successful. (Agency)
2. I can think of many ways to reach my current goals. (pathway)

The Children's Hope Scale is specifically meant for children. It contains six items that describe how children do things in general. For each sentence, children are asked to think about the situation depicted and indicate the option they would choose in that situation. Depending on the option chosen score is assigned on a six-point scale. Half of the items are indicative of pathway thinking whereas other three items denote agency thinking. Pathway, agency and total score can easily be generated. A representative item is given below:

1. I think I am doing pretty well (*Agency*)
- None of the time
- A little of the time
- A lot of the time
- Most of the time
- All of the time

2. I can think of many ways to get the thing in life that are most important to me.
- None of the time
- A little of the time
- A lot of the time
- Most of the time
- All of the time

The Children's Hope Scale is applicable to school-age children.

In addition to these scales, Snyder and his associates have also the Young Children's Hope Scale to be used for pre-school children. The scales discussed do have also observational rating formats to be used by researchers, parents and teachers. Furthermore, an **Adult Domain-Specific Hope Scale** has been developed which assesses hope in specific domains such as social, academic, family, romantic relationships, occupation, and leisure activities.

Development of Hope

Snyder (2000) posits that hope develops in a predictable pattern across developmental phases such as infancy, childhood, adolescence, adulthood and later in life. Goals do change and goal-related thoughts also change. Hence hopeful thoughts evolve accordingly.

The infant, by the end of the first year, develops some faint ideas of cause and effect. The infant kicks a ball and it rolls. The infant babbles and the care-giver reciprocates. The baby cries and it is picked up by responsive mother. All these events create an impression in the infant that the infant can create events. The idea of self as an agent evolves during this period. In the second year, infants learn that they can instigate goal-directed activities to follow pathways to desired goals.

During early childhood, child further learns goal-directed activities. A strong bond develops between the child and the primary care-giver. This *secured attachment* helps a lot. The child can effectively deal with barriers and anxiety. The security of the child's attachment to caregivers and the resulting child's ability to deal with adversity is very important. In other words, children who are securely attached to their parents or caregivers and are provided with sufficient warmth and social support develop hope and resilience.

During the pre-school period (age 3 to 6 years), the rapid development of language, pre-operational intuitive thinking, interest in story-telling, and predictable routines stimulate further growth of hopeful thinking. Physical development helps in putting the plan into action. Another important clue in this period is the development of perspectivism. Child's own observation and his playful activities gives an impression that the same child or adult can play several roles. The same person can be father to someone while uncle to someone else. Hence solution of problems become contextualized and the child "sees" the value of context.

In middle childhood and pre-adolescence, there is rapid growth in logical thinking, abstract reasoning, memory skills, reading skills, and social perspective taking skills. These promote hopeful planning and pursuing pathways towards valued goals. The assistance and guidance of parents, teachers and mentors become increasingly useful.

In adolescence, youngsters develop autonomy, intimacy with friends and abstract reasoning skills. Career plans also emerge. These resources provide inputs for young people to think beyond conventional settings. Increasing autonomy from family pressures provide new opportunities to deal with barriers.

By the time individuals get into adulthood, it is likely that they might have encountered setbacks and barriers. Yet it is also likely that they might have come across *role models*. Typically, parents, teachers or similar personalities could be role models. The contact of role model is very critical. It becomes a source of information and inspiration. It provides both cognitions and positive emotions. Hopeful role models and coaches play very dynamic role in nurturing and strengthening hope. However, role models identified in the vicinity are more effective than far-fetched models. The distant models may be great and attractive, but people may not imitate them even if they admire the distant role models. This is primarily because of the fact they see the dissimilarity and psychological distance between themselves and the role models. In contract, it is plausible to see similarity between themselves and role models when role models are adopted from the vicinity. This perception of similarity prompts them to imitate role models. Thus, mentors and trainers need to use role models from the immediate surroundings while making interventions to induce hope.

Hopeful adults have distinctive profiles (Snyder, 2000). They might have encountered setbacks and adversity. Yet they have the tendency of defining adversity as challenging, an ongoing positive internal dialogue ("I can do it; I won't give up"). This kind of cognitive style helps them to build hope.

In contrast, individuals who have encountered very difficult circumstance (broken homes pathogenic parents, etc.) are likely to miss the opportunity of healthy development. A small proportion of this battered population deal with traumatic events because of protective factors and other support systems and grow in a resilient manner.

Hope and Health

In general, hope is positively related to academic, sports, physical health, adjustment and psychotherapy (Snyder, 2002). For example, higher Hope Scale scores taken at the beginning of college have predicted better cumulative grade point averages. Similarly, Higher Hope Scale scores taken at the beginning of college predicted the superior performance of male athletes and have done so beyond the coach's rating of natural athletic abilities (Snyder, Lopez & Pedrotti, 2011).

The positive role of hope in terms of primary and secondary prevention has been evinced. *Primary prevention* involves thoughts or actions that are intended to reduce or eliminate the chances of health problems (both physical and psychological). *Secondary prevention* involves thoughts or actions that are geared at eliminating, reducing, or containing a problem once it has occurred.

At the individual level hope and the primary prevention

of physical illness are shown to be correlated. People with higher levels of hope are seen to use information about physical illness to their advantages. High-hope persons use information about the etiology of illness. Within the framework of hope theory, knowledge is used as a pathway for prevention.

In addition, higher hope women report greater intentions to engage in cancer preventive activities than their lower hope counterparts. Moreover, people with high hope report engaging in more preventive behaviours (physical exercise) than those with low hope. It is shown that hopeful thinking is related to activities that help to prevent physical illness.

Apart from the individual level of primary prevention, hope theory can be applied at the societal level. Societal primary prevention involves thinking that reduces risks and prepares the entire society against illness. Societal primary prevention includes increasing desired behaviours and decreasing targeted undesirable behaviours through the use of advertisements, laws and social communications while the positive role of hopeful thinking as has been evinced in a number of cases in the past (Snyder, 2002), its application to test and predict human behaviours during COVID19 of present crisis is an interesting issue.

Once a physical illness develops the role of hope in secondary prevention becomes crucial. Consistent with the prediction, hope has been related to better adjustments in conditions involving chronic illness, severe injury, and handicaps. In addition to individual level of secondary prevention, societal secondary prevention is also evinced. For example, successful television advertisements may also persuade people to make wise decisions relating to health behaviour.

There are many ways in which hope plays positive role in promoting psychological adjustment. One way in which psychological adjustment is influenced by hope is through the belief in one's self. Snyder et al (2005) have found that hope bears a strong relationship with affectivity. It is related positively with positive affect and negatively with negative affect (correlations in .55 range). Furthermore, manipulations to increase levels of hope have resulted in increases in positive affects and decreases in negative affects.

Based on Snyder's hope theory, Snyder (2000) has evolved *hope therapy*. It is cognitive behaviour, solution-focused therapy. It is also narrative. Hope therapy aims to help clients formulate clear goals, produce numerous pathways to these, motivate themselves to pursue their goals and reframe obstacles as challenges to be overcome.

In the context of hope theory, the stressors represent that which is interfering with one's normal ongoing goal of being happy. When confronting a stressor, one must find alternative paths to attain the desired goal. Since higher hope people produce more pathways (strategies), they are likely to be mobilized to path of attaining happiness. The hope therapist essentially creates such favourable condition.

Another significant parameter that adds value to hope therapy involves Viktor Frankl's concept of *"meaning in life"*. According to Frankl (2004), basic human problem springs from existential vacuum – the perception that there is no meaning or purpose in universe. The perception of this existential vacuum can be remedied to the extent that persons actualize values. Frankl attempted to remedy through his logotherapy. Hope therapy seeks to achieve this target through induction of pathway and agency thinking.

More recently Wilde (2001) has advanced the construct of *expectationism* – the preventive strategy for reducing undesirable behaviour by enhancing people's perceived value of the future. Once people value the future, they may engage themselves in certain advocated behaviours. Thus, a blend of certain value systems increases the vitality of hope therapy and it enhances positive association between hope and happiness.

Resilience

Exceptional events trigger exceptional insights. It is a common observation that great discoveries and inventions are not limited to laboratories. Sometimes extra-ordinary events taking place in societies, unique happenings in human lives and unusual circumstances occurring in the globe engage our attention. Many people are elated or frightened; yet a few of us pursue certain interesting aspect of the event and come across a wonderful law of universal significance. The concept of psychological resilience is one such unique law.

In 1945, following World War II an orphanage in the village of Lingfield in Surrey, England, arranged to take twenty-four young child survivors of the Holocaust. Most of the children, between the ages of three and eight years old, were either arriving from concentration camps like Auschwitz and Terezin or had been living in hiding. They were already victims of traumatic stress. Children from the Terezin group had been present at mass hanging and many of them had been forced to pass boxes of human ashes back and forth. The Auschwitz children had been surrounded by the stench of dead bodies, waking to the sight of the crematoria smoke each day.

The four youngest children were only months old

when they arrived in the Terezin concentration camp. Subsequently they were placed in the Lingfield orphanage. In 1979, when all four of them were thirty-seven, an American psychologist named Sarah Moscovitz found these child survivors (originally described by Anna Freud, Sigmund Freud's daughter). She conducted a series of interviews with them both in 1979 and 1984, to document their progress over time.

Berl and Leah, the smallest and the weakest of the youngest four, suffered the most. They struggled socially and academically. They survived but they struggled, riddled with anxiety, shame and sadness about the past. More surprising were the interviews with Jack and Bella, the other two members. When Moscovitz met him, Jack was happily married with a supportive wife and had two children. He owned his taxi in London and he described his pleasure of meeting new people. He admitted that he had occasional depressive thoughts relating to his mother, but, by all accounts, he was managing life well. When Moscovitz met Bella she was sunny, vital and confident. Despite her husband's recent heart surgery Bella believed that they could come through anything together. She had started a business dealing in art and she was doing well. She also worked as magistrate on cases involving children. Here was a puzzle for Moscovitz. *How could four children brought up in the exact same traumatic circumstances land in such vastly different places in life? Why do the Berls and Leahs of the world languish while the Jacks and Bellas cope and even flourish?*

These questions began getting serious attention for the first time in the 1970s when a number of psychologists working at the intersection of child psychiatry and developmental psychology began to investigate the early childhood factors that impeded healthy growth and development. Much of credit goes to Norman Garmezy (University of Minnesota). While studying children with schizophrenic mothers, Garmezy came across a curious finding. Even in the face of very difficult circumstance, some children could blossom into very decent individuals. Garmezy termed the process as resilience or invulnerability and children as *resilient* or *invulnerable* or *stress-resistant*. It seems that the expression *"resilient"* has become oft-used. The situation can be schematically presented

	Poverty	Prosperity
Competence	Resilient	Advantaged
Incompetence	Vulnerable	Spoiled

The Lotus-in-the-Mud Phenomenon

The foregoing discussion need not create an impression that cases of resilience are limited to successful survivors from the concentration camps. There are other instances in the world context.

In 1989, people of Romania overthrew brutal dictatorship of Nicolae Ceasescu. During his regime, 150000 children were living under appalling conditions in the name of so-called Centre for Family Development. Ceasescu took power in 1965 and his regime required women to have five children by the time they were 45 years of age. They had no access to birth control programmes. Children were malnourished. They slept in dirty cribs. Four children were provided with a single cot. Blankets were soaked in urine and infected with lice. Nearly every ingredient for healthy physical and psychological development was missing.

After the fall of dictatorship, many generous individuals in the developed countries came forward to adopt some of those children. Researchers tracked the development of these adopted children. A leading researcher compared the development of 46 children who spent between 8 months to 4 ½ years in Romania and were adopted by Canadian parents. They were compared with a group of 46 non-adopted Canadian children. Many adopted children showed significant problems in four specific area:

- IQ was below 85
- Behaviour problems
- Insecure attachment to adopting parents
- Persistence of stereotyped behaviour

However, 2 years after adoption there was significant improvement in physical and psychological conditions. Children who were adopted prior to their 6-month-age were indistinguishable from non-adopted Canadian children. The ability of many children to recover from truly horrific conditions were amazing. Ann Masten (2001), a leading researcher in the area, calls it an *ordinary magic*. According to her, healthy functioning is similar to a rubber band that is stretched but does not break.

There is another incident which is more recent and frightening. On September 11, 2001, the World Trade Center in New York faced terrorist attack and a large number of people were victims of posttraumatic stress disorder (PTSD). The University of California (San Francisco) professor George Bonanno wanted to investigate people's psychological response to such unusual shock.

Bonanno used extensive interviews and was able to break responses down into five main patterns: (1) chronic depression, (2) chronic grief, (3) depressed improved, (4) recovery from grief, and (5) resilient. As indicated by the pattern names, the chronic depression group suffered from pathology both before and after the loss. The chronic grief group functioned well preloss but were paralyzed by grief both immediately after the loss and several years later. The depressed improved group experienced depression before the loss and during the loss, but gradually improved after the loss. The recovery from grief group experienced feelings of grief like yearning, shock, and anxiety that eventually subsided. The resilient group experienced no significant trauma.

The fact that these five patterns emerged did not surprise Bonanna. The real surprise was their relative distribution. over and over again-in natural disasters, after the SARS epidemic following the loss of a child or spouse – Bonanno's longitudinal studies on loss and trauma revealed the same pattern. No matter how bad the trauma, rates of PTSD never exceeded one-third and rates of resilience were always found in at least one-third and never more than two-thirds of the population. It bears repeating that Bonanno was not defining resilience as a lack of feeling or absence of sadness. He used the term "resilient" *to identify people capable of functioning with a sense of core purpose, meaning, and forward momentum in the face of trauma.*

In Indian context, there are also case of resilient personalities. The resilience phenomenon could otherwise be described as *lotus-in-the-mud phenomenon* (Sahoo 2010). The most fundamental question pertaining resilience concerns the source of resilience.

Source of Resilience

It is fairly difficult to list all possible sources of human resilience. However, a close scrutiny of possible sources may help us to categorize resources into *three* rubrics:
1. **I have (Protective Factors)**
2. **I am (Personality Factors)**
3. **I can (Promotion Factors)**

Protective Factors

The role of protective factors is very important in the development of resilience. The child / youth must have feelings that *I have someone* to count on. Despite poverty / adversity, there is an oasis in the desert of life. The protective factors provide psychological insulation. The person functioning as a protective factor may be one parental figure, or a friend, or a relative, or a teacher, or a neighbor, and so on. It is interestingly found that the child has an empathetic relationship with this protecting individual. If there is disharmony in the family, the child does not report his or her pain / pleasure to parents. If the child receives praise or prize in the school, he/she reports it not to his/her parents, but to the empathetic figure. Similarly, personal agonies are first reported to the protector.

The support of an adult role model buffers the effect of adversity and appears to predict positive outcomes. Such role model is not necessarily a single individual, it could be a small collectivity. High functioning social networks – friends, family, religious and community organizations – may provide protection and support. Werner and Smith (2001) followed nearly seven hundred children growing up in Hawaii with risk factors like poverty, parental discord, and parental stress. Werner and Smith concluded that social factors like supportive relationship function as protective factors.

Two major implications are derived. First, what is important in resilience is the role of a sympathetic adult or institutional agency. Second, such mentoring relationship develops within the framework of everyday experience.

Personality Factors

Theories abound about what produces resilience, but

certain fundamental characteristics seem to set resilient people apart from others. The first characteristic is the capacity to accept and face down reality. In looking hard at reality, we prepare ourselves to act in ways that allow us to endure and survive hardship. A common belief about resilience is that it stems from an optimistic nature. That's true but only as long as such optimism does not distort our sense of reality. In extremely adverse circumstances, rose-coloured thinking can actually spell disaster. In other words, *a blend of realism and optimism or dynamic optimism or functional optimism is desirable.*

The ability to see reality is closely linked to the second building block of resilience, the prosperity *to make meaning of terrible times*. Generally, people under stress throw up their hands and cry, "How can this be happening to me?" But resilient people devise constructs about their suffering to create some sort of meaning for themselves and others.

The concept is beautifully articulated by Viktor Frankl, Austrian psychiatrist and Auschwitz concentration camp survivor. In the midst of staggering suffering, Frankl invented *meaning therapy*, a humanistic technique that helps individuals make the kinds of decisions that will create significance in their lives. In his book *Man's Search for Meaning*, Frankl describes the pivotal moment in the camp when he developed meaning therapy. Although he was not sure that he would survive, Frankl imagined himself giving a lecture after the war on psychology and concentration camp, help outsiders understand what he had been through. He created some concrete goals for himself. In doing so, he succeeded in rising above suffering of the moment. As he put in his book, "We must never forget that we may also find meaning in life even when confronted with a hopeless situation when facing a fate that cannot be changed". Since finding meaning in one's environment is such an important aspect of resilience, it should come as no surprise that the most successful people possess strong value system. Strong value system infuses an individual with meaning because they offer ways to interpret and shape events.

The other building block of resilience is the ability to do with whatever at hand. Psychologists follow the lead of French anthropologist Levi Strauss in calling this skill *bricolage*. The root of that word is closely tied to the concept of resilience. It literally means "bouncing back". Levi Strauss wrote: "In its old sense, the verb "bricoler" was used with reference to some extraneous movement: a ball rebounding, a dog straying, or a horse swerving from its direct course to avoid an obstacle".

Bricolage in the modern sense can be defined as a kind of inventiveness, an ability to improve solution to a problem without proper or obvious tools or materials. In the concentration camp, for example, resilient inmates knew to pocket pieces of string or wire whenever they found them. The string or wire might later become useful to fix a pair of shoes, which in freezing conditions might make the difference between life and death.

Apart from these main observations, a few other predictors of personal resilience have been identified. In the foregoing discussion, the case of Jack and Bella has been cited. According to Moskovitz's study, Jack and Bella were able to charm the adults and function with self-agency at the Lingfield orphanage, creating a positive feedback loop with the staff and their families that resulted in better and better care. This *ego-resilience* – defined as the capacity to overcome, steer through – was first noted by developmental psychologists. Jack and Jeanne Block in 1968, in a highly regarded longitudinal study documenting the lives of one hundred young adults over more than thirty years. In addition to ego-resilience, the Block study measured a characteristic they called *ego-control*, or the degree to which an individual has the ability to delay gratification in service of future goals. Individuals exhibiting the combination of ego-resilience and ego-control were better able to adapt flexibly the different circumstances and succeed in the midst of challenges.

Such personality traits are rooted in belief systems that allow one to cognitively reappraise situations and regulate emotions. Social psychologists refer to this as *hardiness* a system thought, based, broadly on three main tenets: (1) the belief that one can find a meaningful purpose in life, (2) the belief that one can influence one's surroundings and the outcome of events, and (3) the belief that positive and negative experience will lead to learning and growth. Considering this it should come as no surprise that people of faith also report greater degree of resilience.

The role of *religious belief* is a complex issue in the context of resilience. Psychologist Kenneth Pargament has spent the lion share of his academic career investing the links between religion and resilience. Pargament attributes the power of religion to its invocation of the sacred. This connection between religious faith (or, more broadly, a personal spiritual cosmology) and resilience presents an intriguing rejoinder to atheist critic of religious beliefs. While such beliefs may or may not be *true*, they may nonetheless be *adaptive*. That is, religious belief persists and thrives, in part, not because it necessarily guarantees persistence of one's soul to the next life, but precisely psychological resilience upon its possessors.

All of these factors are rooted in our beliefs and our experiences. Whether cultivated through wise mentors, vigorous exercise, access to green space, or a particularly rich relationship with faith, the habits of personal resilience are habits of mind – making them habits we can cultivate and change when armed with the right resources.

This brings us to another less appreciated aspect of personal resilience: the influence of genetics. While the sequencing of human genome in the last decade has provided some useful information regarding genetic triggers, the current research has focused the effectiveness of tools that complement other forms of intervention for promoting resilience.

Promoting Factors

There are quite a few mechanisms that can be used as intervention to promise resilience. Yet one tool is portable, teachable, free and it has been on the market for more than two thousand years. It is meditation.

Researchers who study mindfulness and attention often conceive our emotions differently. In their view, emotions are not things that happen to us. Rather they exist – metaphorically, of course – as a kind of psychic currency, held in reserve. When we waste the reserve – giving over our attention to every single distraction from the outside environment – it dwindles down into an empty account, and we are left feeling fatigued or worse, in a downward spiral of negative affects like anger and greed. With practice, on the other hand, we can train ourselves to spend judiciously, keeping us from draining our emotional coffers.

Mindfulness meditation training is the tool that lets us do so. It allows us to take more intentional control over our emotions. Some of the training is drawn from Buddhism. These tools of mediation, mindfulness, and increasing awareness have been proven to aid in resilience training. Richard Davidson, the leading light in the area of neuroscience, opines that the eastern tradition in meditation is even effective in neuroplasticity – the process of rewiring (changing) the brain (Davidson & Begley, 2012).

There are many systems of meditation. Meditation experts often refer to two different styles: focused-attention and open monitoring. Focused-attention meditation maintains attention on a specific object of concentration. When thoughts and sensation arise, the mind allows them to pass without clinging to them and then brings itself back to focus on the chosen object.

In open monitoring, on the other hand, the object of focus recedes, and a sustained awareness of all sensory experience is cultivated. Open monitoring is characterized by an open, present, and nonjudgmental awareness of stimuli in the environment.

There is a third type of mediation that plays pivotal role in personal resilience. It is often called "loving kindness" or a practice of compassionate meditation. This is the technique of cultivating greater empathy through mediation. Such practices produce significant activity in the insula – a region near the frontal portion of the brain that plays a key role in bodily representations of emotion. In this practice, the mediator first focuses on loved ones and then expands the focus of compassion to towards all beings. Neuroscientist Davidson appreciates its role in altering our brain chemistry.

Finally, it is important to recognize that positivity of psychological resilience is not limited to the triumph over adversity. The gains are not confined to getting around the problem of post-traumatic stress disorder (PTSD). Rather the resilience may bring the benefits of *post-traumatic growth*. It has been shown that a number of people experience growth following traumatic events. They may change their lifestyles in the positive direction. They may give up smoking, renew family harmony and do many other prosocial activities. In view of these positive expectations, researchers are now gravitating from the study of PTSD to the exploration of *PTG (Post-traumatic growth)*.

Resilience and Happiness

The notion that stress and success are inevitably interwined has become so ingrained in contemporary cultures and work habits that we take pride in our stress levels. We brag about the length of our to-do lists. Success is popularly equated with aggressiveness. Yet science shows that the drive-and-stress theory of success has limited value; it backfires in the long run. Stress in small doses may help us to achieve short-term goal. In fact, there is good stress and bad stress. Without a small dose of stress, we may be knocked down by a speeding car. In a sense of landmark studies, Dhabhar, a professor of psychiatry at Stanford University, has shown that stress of lower intensity can provide physiological and psychological benefit including enhance immunity. Despite this benefit, intense and chronic stress is very harmful.

Furthermore, we value high intensity emotions like excitement (as opposed to low intensity emotions like calm). However, emotions like excitement – despite being positive-activate our body's stress response due to their intensity. In contrast, low-intensity emotions such as calmness and contentment generate enduring happiness. These Low-intensity emotions induce such mental states that we don't have to struggle to acquire self-restraint; with calmness in mind self-restraint prevails naturally and spontaneously.

Tapping into Natural Resilience

Resilience – our ability to quickly recover from stressful situations or setbacks – is not only needed to combat traumatic life events, it is also required to deal with micro-stressors. It is a common experience that an incessant flow of emails, an angry face of our boss, unnecessary delay at the railway stations bombard large number of micro-stressors on us. Without our ability to maintain and further natural resilience, our happiness would be at stake.

We have all learned about the fight-or-flight response, where our bodies prepare to either fight off a potentially deadly attack or run away. However, when the threat has passed, and our bodies return to their normal state – the rest-and-digest responses. The whole mechanism of these two conditions (fight-or-flight and rest-and-digest) is managed by the autonomic nervous system. The signal from the sympathetic division of the autonomic nervous system activates the stress response, heightens blood pressure, increases heart rate, and organism receives extra energy. After the threat is passed off, parasympathetic division of the nervous system signals to regain the normal state. The time for the return to optimal state is a key factor.

It is an interesting observation that animals do experience quick transition period. On seeing a lion, a deer runs for its life and sympathetic division is very active. But once the lion is out of sight, the deer gets back to rest-and-digest state very quickly. Even pets and young children display quick transition. The pets and infants show all symptoms of restlessness in the presence of doctors. But once the doctor's intervention is over, they get back to normal state. That does not happen with human adults. Even if the danger is passed off, the thought persists leading to the continual activity of the autonomic nervous system. This causes misery for humans.

Hence the key to our resilience is our ability
- to quickly return to the restorative rest-and-digest state,
- to remain in that state until an extreme life-threatening situation arises
- to overcome the next challenge at full strength

How can we tap into natural resilience? Breathing is life. We are typically not taught about the importance of breath and its impact on the mind and body. There are different patterns that relate to different emotions. Just as our mind influences the breath, we can influence the state of our mind through the breath as well (Seppala, 2016).

A revealing study by Belgian psychologist Philippot shows that our emotion change our breathing. In Philippot's study, people's breathing patterns were measured when the participants felt the emotions like sadness, fear, anger and happiness. They found that each emotion is associated with a distinct way of breathing. When we experience anxiety, we are likely to take rapid, shallow breaths. When we feel calm, we take deep, slow breaths.

Philippot's team conducted a follow-up study. They invited a different group of people to breathe in the patterns that corresponded to various emotions from the first study. Then they asked the participants how they felt. The participants indicated the emotions that corresponded to the breathing patterns. In other words, when they took deep, slow breaths the participants felt calm. When they took shallow, rapid breath, they felt anxious, or angry.

Breathing training is a surer way to build noted resilience. While voluntarily changing our breath can help us calm down in a particular situation, the long-term effects of a daily breathing practice are profound. Empirical studies have found that regularly practicing breathing exercises normalizes our level of cortisol – the stress hormone. As a regular practice, breathing can recondition our body to a state of greater calm, helping it bounce back from stress more easily and quickly perhaps reducing reactivity in the face of challenge.

There are various tradition of breathing training. Indian spiritual leader Sri Sri Ravi Shankar has spent much of his life teaching yoga-based breathing practices across the world through his organization the Art of Living Foundation. Many researchers have found benefits of Sri Sri Ravi Shankar's breathing technique (the *Sudarshan Kriya*). Many other researchers have experiments with *alternate nostril breathing* and abdominal breaking. In India, Swami Ramdev has popularized pranayama and various forms of breathing exercises. In sum, tapping into natural resilience through various yogic and breathing practices reduces stress, help us to return to the restorative rest-and-digest state and induces in us the low-intensity emotions like calmness contentment and happiness.

Emotional Intelligence

In every field of human activity, there are *paradigm crises* leading to *paradigm shift*. Once upon a time people believed that the earth was flat. Based on this conception they were carrying out navigation. But when they computed to arrive in a particular place but actually arrived in a different place, that created a tension. This was paradigm crisis. They concluded that something was wrong with their conception. When men of science worked hard to solve this crisis, there was paradigm shift. They discovered that earth's shape is not flat but oval. Similarly, our concept of objects and their motion have changed with the development of quantum physics. While Newtonian laws were fine to explain movement of objects, it could not explain motion of subatomic particles. Thus, quantum physics provided the new explanation, the paradigm shift took place in the physical world.

Similar is the case with emotional intelligence (EI). It developed as a reaction to the inadequacy in rational intelligence.

The Evolution of the Construct

Intelligence is a universal term which refers to all forms of man's complex mental activities. Intelligence, more specifically *rational intelligence,* evolved as a formal necessity to meet classroom requirements in French schools. In 1904, French Education Ministry personnel met psychology professors in Paris and requested them to solve a problem. The Ministry people told psychologists that children in the school do have varying intelligence and hence fail to derive benefit out of classroom instruction. In general, the teacher teaches for the average. The under-achiever dozes in the class because he or she cannot make out what the teacher is teaching. Similarly achieving students lose interest in the class because the teaching contents appear trivial.

The Ministry people requested the experts to evolve a mechanism of dividing students into three categories: the underachievers, the averages, and the achieving students. If such a classification is possible, then teachers could teach three distinct groups (averages, underachievers, achievers) using three different styles.

The psychologist Alfred Binet agreed to find out a method. Binet with the help of his doctoral scholar Simon, developed an interesting project and formulated the concept of *"mental age"*. They observed children in Paris and listed their abilities age-wise. For example, what one-week age children can do, what two-week-old children can do, and so on were listed. With the listings of all age-appropriate abilities, Binet determined mental age of a particular child.

An illustration would clarify the procedure. Suppose a child is ten-year-old, hence his/her chronological age is 10. Now the child can be given ability tests meant for nine-year-old. If the child is fully successful, he/she may be given materials meant for ten-year-old. If totally successful, the examiner can move forward. In this way the child may falter when test materials meant for 12-year-old is given. Let us presume that the child answers 50 per cent of test materials meant for 12-year-old, 25 per cent of materials meant for 13-year-old and '0' (zero) per cent of materials meant for 14-year-old. Full credit ca be given for 11-year-old material (the uppermost level at which the performance was cent per cent), fractional credit can be given to cases where success was within the range of 1 to 99 percentage. Mental age of the child can thus be fixed as is given below:

Mental age = $11 + \frac{1}{2} + \frac{1}{4} = 11 \frac{3}{4}$

Binet's contribution is unique in the sense it represents an objective level of mental functioning. If a child's chronological age is 10 years and mental age 11 ¾ years, the implications are clear and unambiguous. Even if the child's chronological age is 10 years it shows the capability of 11 ¾ year old of that society. To make it a convenient label psychologist used the expression, Intelligence Quotient (IQ).

$$\text{Intelligence Quotient, IQ} = \frac{\text{Mental Age}}{\text{Chronological age}} \times 100$$

In the illustrative case cited above, the 10-year-old child has the IQ of 115. The interpretation of IQ is simple and connotative. If somebody has an IQ of 100, it means that the person shows ability of his or her age-mates; a nine-year-old shows the ability of nine-year-old, a 32-year-old shows the ability of 32-year-old and so on. If someone has IQ of 50, it means that a 14-year-old shows the ability of 7-year-old and a 30-year-old shows ability of 15-year-old. Similarly, IQ of 150 implies that a 8-year-old displays the ability of 12-year-old and 16-year-old reveals ability of 24-year-old. Since IQ of 100 is indicative of the average, anyone having IQ 70 or less (2 standard deviation units below the mean) is considered to have the status of mentally challenged and any one having IQ 130 or more (2 standard deviation units above the mean) is considered to be gifted.

The construct of rational intelligence dominated the intellectual climate of the twentieth century. A number of standardized measures became very popular in Europe and America. Some of the oft-used measures include WAIS (Weschler's Adult Intelligence Scale) and WISC (Weschler's Intelligence Scale for Children). The scales have verbal and nonverbal components. Scores are generated with respect to memory skills, inductive reasoning, deductive reasoning, spatial-visual ability and various forms of linguistic skills. In order to get around the problems of language barriers, a British Psychologist developed a nonverbal intelligence test "Raven's Progressive Matrices" (RPM) where nonverbal reasoning is measured with the help of geometrical forms and figures. Raven claims it to be culture-fair test. Infact this is one of the oft-used test across the globe.

The basic strength of rational intelligence tests involves its high predictive power. It has strong positive correlation with academic achievement (approximately correlation coefficient being .7). This high correlation implies that almost 50 per cent of variance (square of .7) in academic attainment can be accounted for with the help of intelligence scores. Intelligence is also a stable and strong predictor of job and other forms of achievement. Because of this strong and stable predictive power, rational intelligence became an all-explanatory concept in the twentieth century. But the *paradigm crisis* was encountered during last part of the twentieth century.

Limitation of rational intelligence. The IQ movement received a setback in the cross-cultural domain. Many cross-cultural psychologists advocated cultural relativism and criticized measures of intelligence. For example, African Americans in the USA voiced: "It is not fair to assess how well *we* can do *your* tricks. You should measure how well *we* can do *our* tricks". While some psychologists evolved alternative nonverbal tests to do away with linguistic loadings, the solutions were not fully acceptable. For example, the use of geometrical forms and figures does not fully control the exposure factors, since some cultural groups live in carpentered world (like Europeans and Americans exposed to geometrical forms and figures in their environments) whereas other cultural groups live in open vastas (Eskimoes in Tundra, Bushmen in Kalahari desert, farmers in Prairies). The differential exposure introduced elements of bias in testing.

Another blow came from Gardner who spoke in the language of *multiple intelligence*. According to Gardner (1993), we prefer to learn and process information in different ways. People learn best when they can apply their strong intelligence to the task. He proposed eight types of intelligence: *verbal, mathematical, spatial bodily kinesthetic, musical, intrapersonal, interpersonal,* and *naturalist* intelligence. Gardner argues that the singularity of intelligence puts constraints on the recognition and utilization of human talents. In contrast, the appreciation of multiple intelligence paves the way for flourishing and development.

Another shortcoming of rational intelligence entails its low relationship with *creativity*. Research has shown low positive correlation between creativity and rational intelligence (approximately .4). This implies that only 16 per cent of creativity is accounted for by rational intelligence. Since creativity constitutes a very fundamental resource both at the individual and collective level, an overemphasis on rational intelligence at the cost of creativity appears to be a human error.

The most powerful blow against rational intelligence came from the scientific research of the neuroscientists. Neuroscience achieved a major break-through in 1980s when Roger Sperry's research on split-brain conclusively proved that brain structurally may be one, but it is two functionally. The more surprising element in brain research was that the feeling brain is older than the thinking brain.

Neuroscientists have posited that brain is a product of evolution. When species were evolving and they were at reptile stage, certain ring-like structures began to form near the brain-stem (where the spinal cord ends and brain structure begins). Since *limbus* is the Greek word for ring, scientists called it *limbic system*. more importantly, the limbic system took care of emotions. Subsequently the main brain (cortex) developed and different cortical centres were formed to deal with different sensory experience. The first such centre was the "nose brain" – the cortical centre to deal with smell. Smell is more vital from evolutionary standpoint, because animals would die if they consume decomposed food. Later other cortical centres were formed.

Later Roger Sperry (1981) received Noble Prize for his split-brain research. He showed that brain may be structurally one, but functionally it is two: Feeling brain and Thinking brain. A thick fibre of neurons divides the brain into two halves: left hemisphere and right hemisphere. They have distinctive functions. Left hemisphere is associated with logical thinking and language whereas right hemisphere is linked with emotion and pattern recognition. Interestingly enough the left hemisphere is neurally connected with right side limbs of the body and right hemisphere is connected with left side limbs of the body. Its implications are easily conceivable. If you want to listen music, the left side ear is more adaptive as auditory patterned signals would go through the; left ear and it would be processed by the right hemisphere. Similarly, counting pebbles with the use of right hand is more appropriate because stimulation going through the right hand would be processed by the logical and analytical left hemisphere of the brain. Sperry proved elaborate scientific lateralization. Other neuroscientists supported and furthered these findings.

In essence, the neuroscience clearly demonstrated *two* basic formulations: (1) *Although brain is structurally one, it is functionally two: feeling brain and thinking brain.* (2) *The feeling brain is older than the thinking brain.*

The early development of limbic system to deal with emotion and subsequent specification of right hemisphere as the specialized hemisphere to process emotion gave credence to the role of emotion in our lives. Perhaps Nature gave us first what was needed first. The primacy of emotion in lives signaled the significance of emotional intelligence (EI).

Framework of EI

In 1960, Mowrer addressed the prevailing thoughts about emotion undermining intelligence by proposing that emotional intelligence is "a high order of intelligence" (p.380) Peter Salovey of Yale University and John Mayor of the University of New Hampshire shared Mower's viewpoints. In their original 1990 paper, Salovey and Mayer posited a theoretical framework for emotional intelligence. Although there are several standardized measures of EI, Bar-On's (2000) test represents a model format. The EQ (Emotional Quotient)- I (Bar-On) primarily measures personality and mood-related variables such as self-regard, empathy, tolerance and happiness.

Daniel Goleman popularized the concept of emotional intelligence in his 1995 book, *Emotional Intelligence.* Goleman argued that rational intelligence explains only 10 per cent of our success whereas emotional intelligence accounts for a very large proportion of our achievement and happiness. Goleman has several books such as *Destructive Emotion*, and *Focus*; all these publications have contributed significantly towards the expanding popularity of EQ over IQ.

Exhibit
Factors Represented in Bar-On's Model

Intrapersonal: Self-awareness, Assertiveness, Self-Regard, Autonomy, Self-Actualization
Interpersonal: Empathy, Social responsibility, Interpersonal relationship
Adaptability: Flexibility, Problem solving, Reality testing
Stress Management: Impulse control, Tolerance
Mood: Happiness, Optimism

A simpler way to dimensionalize EI would involve the self and the other. On each of these two fronts, there could be theory or knowledge and application or skill. This could be schematically represented in the Exhibit given below:

Exhibit
Factors of EI

Domain	EQ Skills
Self-Awareness:	Self-confidence Self-Assessment Emotional self-awareness
Self-Management	Self control Trust Conscientiousness Adaptability Self initiative
Social Awareness	Empathy Service oriental Organizational awareness
Social Skills	Leadership Communication Influence Conflict management Team work Building bonds

EI and Happiness

A close examination of factors involved in EI clearly shows the strong linkage with happiness. Since positive emotions have happiness – promoting roles and negative emotions are detrimental to well-being, the postulated relationship is easily conceivable. People with high EQ use more of positive emotions, especially low intensity emotions. At the same time, they also have a great deal of control over negative emotion. Their ability to control anger is a positive asset.

There have been several empirical studies that show positive association between EQ and happiness (Myers, 1990). Fredrickson's classical study on emotion has demonstrated the role of positive emotion. Her theory "build-and-broaden-theory" of emotion posits how positive emotions generate internal resources. This study, in combination with other investigations, provides evidence regarding the positive linkage between EI and happiness.

Chapter 4

Antecedents of Happiness

The scientific investigation of a phenomenon requires cause-and-effect analysis. Because an experimental manipulation is relatively difficult in social and behavioural sciences, researchers find it convenient to examine the network of relationships amongst variables. Once the relationship pattern is identified, the prediction of the desired outcome becomes a possibility. This is the case with happiness as a valued outcome.

A large number of empirical studies have been conducted to examine the role of various antecedent factors. Some of these factors are socio-demographic variables such as gender and age while others are of psychological nature such as self-esteem and religious affiliation. Once the relationship nature (the magnitude and direction) is identified it may provide cues relating to the cause of the linkage. For example, the positive association between marriage and happiness may suggest several hypotheses relating to the supportive roles of the feeling of security, or feeling of being cared, or the satisfaction of physical needs. Subsequent studies may probe into which of these alternative hypotheses is valid.

Prior to delineating the role of specific antecedent factors, it is useful to begin with a general framework suggested by Lyubomirsky (2007). She presents a pie chart (as given below) which is largely shared by other

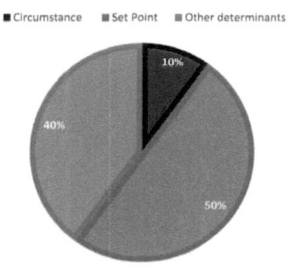

psychologists. As shown by the Pie Chart, a large number of events in our lives determine only 10 percent of our happiness. Genetics and predisposional factors account for 50 per cent of our happy experiences. The picture is not pessimistic though. There is a large area of 40 per cent which is free and controllable. Lyubomirsky (2007) argues strongly in favour of *intentional activities* in this area to boost happiness. The discussion on the contributions of specific factors would provide a broad canvass of determinants of happiness.

Genetic Factors

The strongest evidence for the predominant role of genetic factors comes from a series of fascinating studies involving identical and fraternal twins. Lykken, Tellegen and associates at the University of Minnesota took data from the Minnesota Twin Registry. They followed a large number of Caucasian twins born in Minnesota. The findings of one of the most famous twin studies, the *Happiness Twin Study*, was revealing. The data showed that there were moderately high correlations (.44 to .53) between the well-being scores of monozygotic twins and negligible correlations (.08 to .13) between scores of dizygotic twins. These findings support the conclusion that well-being is approximately 50 per cent heritable.

This has an interesting implication. The prediction of average happiness in an identical twin on the basis of the counterpart is much more powerful than the prediction based on the facts and events of target's life.

We may be curious to know the predictability in the context of fraternal twins. Compared with identical twins, fraternal twins are one-half genetically similar to each other. However, researchers found that fraternal twins were no more alike than any two siblings. This fact that identical twins, but not fraternal twins, share similar happiness levels posits that happiness is largely genetically determined.

However, the conclusion may have one problem. While comparing identical twins with fraternal twins, it is assumed that the family environment is same for both twins of identical variety, it is also same for both twins of fraternal variety. But is it really true? In the case of fraternal twins, there would be some differences in physical appearances and other features. Consequently, parents may behave with them differently; they may also have differing expectations from parents. Hence the environment and upbringing of fraternal twins are not as similar as those of identical twins.

Fortunately, this problem can be handled by a different kind of arrangement. It is possible to compare twins reared together with twins separated in infancy and reared apart. The findings were striking. The identical twins were extremely similar in their happiness regardless of whether they were reared together or reared apart. In contrast, happiness scores of fraternal twins were uncorrelated in both the contexts of similar rearing environment and differing environments.

Set-point. The empirical data from the Happiness Twin study leads to the conclusion that the genetic twins for happiness is very strong. It seems that each of us is born with a happiness set point, a characteristic potential for happiness throughout our lives. The set-point is stable point around which people's mood varies over periods such as a decade. It is about 98 per cent genetically determined (Carr, 2004).

The essential point is that even if we encounter major life events such as getting a job, having business success, meeting a car accident, or demotion in job, the event may push our happiness level up or down. Yet we tend to revert to this genetically determined set point. Evidence for this principle comes from studies that follow people over time as they face positive and negative events.

Heady and Wearing (1989) tracked Australian citizens every two years from 1981 to 1987. They found that several events (new friends, marriage, problems with children, and unemployment) happened; the events generated feelings of happiness and unhappiness as expected. But after the events had passed, their feelings returned to the original baseline. In another study, Suh, Diener and Fujita (1996) observed American undergraduate students and noted their feelings over time. They found that big and small events boosted or deflated their well-being for a while, but they returned back to their set points.

An important implication of the set point concept involves the principle of **adaptation**. It is a common experience that we feel uneasy when we leave a dark room and go out in the sun. but gradually our eyes adapt to changing conditions, and we feel fine. Similarly, we feel uncomfortable when we leave bright and lighted area and enter a dark room. Yet eyes gradually adapt to dark area. These are the cases of *sensory adaptation*. In general, our senses respond more to changing stimulation than to constant stimulation.

The idea of *hedonic adaptation* is similar to sensory adaptation. It means adaptation to stimuli that arouse emotion. The adaptation level theory was developed by Helson (1964). In a classic article on adaptation, Bruckmon and Campbell (1971) posited that people are placed on a **hedonic treadmill** that results in stable and fixed level (set point) of happiness. Like a treadmill, people walk and walk but don't get anywhere; similarly, people's emotional experiences may fluctuate but their overall level of long-term happiness remains unchanged. For example, people may win lotteries and become euphoric, but they return back to their original level in course of time. Similarly, people may suffer from paralytic attacks and become utterly miserable, but they resume their normalcy in course of time. The new buildings, the bigger job offer, and the new car make people happy for a while, but the good feelings fade. This occurs because people quickly adapt to both positive and negative events and they return back to their predetermined levels.

Researchers have attempted to explain adaptation by employing the concepts of contrast and habituation. The contrast principle suggests that a major positive event like winning the lottery may cause everyday pleasures (watching TV and playing cards) to pale by comparison. The pleasure-giving contributions of these mundane events are greatly reduced. As a result, the happiness gained by the thrill of winning lottery is offset by a decline in everyday pleasure. Habituation means getting accustomed to new events so that their emotional impact is reduced.

The hypotheses relating to contrast and habituation have been tested. Empirical support has been generated.

While the empirical demonstration of adaptation has provided support in favour of set point and hedonic treadmill, newer studies provide some of the strongest evidence against the hedonic-treadmill theory. Lacener and his associates note that even if people have genetically predetermined levels of happiness, these levels are pretty high. Most people (75% or more) report being very happy or more happy most of the time. In the context of big events people may return to a positive level of happiness – not to neutrality as suggested by adaptation process in the hedonic treadmill theory. Diener and colleagues also indicate that people have multiple set-point rather than one overall set-point. Happiness has distinct components (positive and negative effects, and life satisfaction) related to different domains (work, family, social relations). Each of these components may vary independently, similarly domain-specific happiness may also can increase or decrease independently. Happiness at work may be coupled with unhappiness at home. Thus, the idea of a single base-line or set-point does not appear appropriate; it is likely that people have multiple set-points. In addition, several large-scale longitudinal studies have shown significant changes in people's baseline levels of happiness. Fujita and Diener (2005) found in a 17-year longitudinal study that 24% of their participants changed their set-points in their last 5 years compared with first 5 years. It seems unlikely that our long-term happiness is determined by the great genetic lottery that occurs at conception. As an anecdotal report by Lyubomirsky (2007), she notes there is also exception to the phenomenon of adaptation. A mother may cuddle her baby and feel wonderful. Even one thousand times repetition of cuddling would feel wonderful 95 per cent.

In the context of hedonic treadmill and predetermined set-point, it would be appropriate to discuss briefly the concept of "depressive gene" – A finding obtained from genome research and modified by recent biopsychologists.

Depressive gene: At one point of time some researchers were interested to find out why stressful experience trigger depression in some people but not in others. The scientific exploration led to the identification of a particular gene called the 5-HTTLPR, which comes in two forms, the long and the short. The short allele is the bad gene and it is linked with depressive symptoms. Caspi and associates (2003) tracked the presence of this bad gene in a sample of 847 infants born in New Zealand. At the time of study, those infants were now twenty-six years old and researchers traced stressful events during last five years. The researchers also measured their depression. A quarter of the sample (26 per cent) reported having experienced three or more adverse life events and 17 percent had major depressive symptoms.

The critical finding was the stressful experiences led to depression only among those who carried "bad" short form of the 5-HTTLPR gene. Interestingly, same result was found for stress experienced during childhood.

So, our genes play an important role in depression as well as in happiness, but they need to be "expressed" – turned on or off. The findings of the New Zealand study are striking. It posits that the short allele variety of 5-HTTLPR gene is activated by an environmental trigger – the stress. Similarly, the long "good" allele appears to protect us from responding to stressful experience by making us resilient.

A major implication of these findings signals an optimistic note. Many of us may carry the gene for a particular vulnerability (e.g., pku, coronary problem, happiness). Yet, the genetic predisposition may not be expressed. It depends on the environmental trigger.

The issue of depressive gene brings to the fore another concern relating to affective positivity. Since the experience of positive emotions is at the core of happiness feelings, it is crucial to consider the extent positive affectivity is genetically determined.

Positive affectivity: Positive affectivity denotes stable individual disposition to experience positive emotions. People high on this trait are cheerful, energetic and enthusiastic. In contrast, those who are low on this disposition display reduced happiness, low levels of energy and confidence. There is cross-situational and temporal stability of this trait.

In 1975, Paul Meehl introduced the concept of **hedonic capacity** in a landmarking publication. Meehl argued that individual difference in hedonic capacity were present at birth and partly heritable. His frequent use of the expressions *"born with three drinks behind"* and *"born with three drinks ahead"* were indicative of predetermined genetic influence. He also implied that some people are born with more **cerebral joy-juice** than others.

It is conceivable that the research on positive affectivity was somewhat limited owing to the perceived importance of negative emotions. Throughout the most of the 20th century evolutionary perspectives underlined the adaptive value of negative emotions (e.g. aggression). The seminal influence of Freud made "anxiety" a pivotal concept of psychopathology. The emotion researcher Cannon and stress researcher Selye also emphasized the role of negative emotion (fear, anxiety, disgust) in our adaptation process.

Gradually two independent dimensions of emotionality were recognized. The Negative Affectivity dimension represents the extent to which an individual experiences negative emotional states such as fear, anger, and sadness. Positive affectivity reflects the extent to which an individual experiences positive emotion such as interest, confidence and joy. These two affect dimensions further represent two general biobehavioural systems: approach (Behavioural Facilitation System, or BFS) and withdrawal (Behavioural Inhibition System or BIS). While the adaptive benefits of BIS were already recognized the value of BFS was now highlighted. The BFS is adaptive in the sense that it ensures the acquisition of resources (food, water, warmth, shelter, competition, sexual partners).

During the last decade of the 20th century, a larger number of empirical studies were carried out to demonstrate the benefit of positive emotion. Barbara Fredrickson's (2001) experimental study led to the theory of *broaden-and-build theory of emotion*. Thus, trait of positive affectivity was placed on a solid footing.

The robustness of the construct was expanded in the form of temporal and cross-situational consistency. Watson (2005) presents a review of relevant studies supporting the consistency of the trait. It was shown than an individual standing on the trait was relatively stable over time, such that people maintain a consistency across measurements. Similarly, people were found to be consistent with respect to their positive affectivity across various situations such as home, work, social contexts.

The analysis with respect to causes and correlates of positive affectivity clearly shows that the trait is strongly heritable. The contributions of sociodemographic factors such as gender, marital status, age, job, education and income is very negligible. Males have as much positive affectivity as do females.

However, there are two variables that have consistently emerged as significant predictors of positive affectivity. First, a large number of studies have revealed that positive affectivity – not negative affectivity – is moderately related to various forms of *social behaviours*. These behaviours include number of friends, frequency of contact, making new friends, quality of social interaction and overall social activity. The second most important variable is *spiritual* or *religious* bent of mind. It is plausible that spiritual/religious attitude answers the basic existential questions of life (e.g., why am I here? What is the meaning of my life?).

Since positive affectivity is somewhat synonymous with happiness (Watson, 2005), a fundamental question concerns the *enhancement mechanism*. Watson (2005) suggests *three* principles that seem to work in this direction.

First, a lot of studies show that positive affectivity is related to action rather to thought. It is desirable to enhance positive affectivity by strengthening active engagement with the environment. Two specific forms of activity are very important. The first is the socialization and social interaction. The second is the exercise and physical activity. The positive effects of these activities are likely to be reflected in positive mood.

Second, the *goal striving is more important than goal attainment*. We have to respect the maxim that the process is more important than the product. Happiness does not spring from the passive experience of positive events; it stems from the active involvement in desirable circumstances. The construct of flow is a fine example.

Finally, we have to be sensitive to the internal rhythms. Whatever activity we do, we need to impute a sense of importance. The work may or may not be important. Yet we have to carry the internal message that the work/activity is important. This kind of mind-set would offer us self-efficacy, a cognitive strength, as well as an affective strength of positivity.

Personality

Is it possible to identify happy people? It is a common observation that people become happy when they encounter very happy situations. But it is not very unusual to come across persons who report positive affects across a wide variety of situations. Theoretically it is possible to divide up the sources of emotional sources between persons and situations. In one of these studies Diener and Larson (1984) found that positive and negative affect in situations are more due to persons (52%) than to situations (23%). Individuals are more consistent for negative emotions than for positive emotions.

There is also interaction between the effects of person and situation. For example, extraverts react more strongly to positive stimuli than do introverts. Hence the combination of extraversion and pleasant situation produces positive affect. These is another kind of interaction between persons and situations. People may choose some kind of situations in congruence with their temperament. They may also avoid and evade certain other kinds of situations which are not in harmony with their temperament. For example, outgoing persons seek more and more social contact whereas anxious individuals choose to avoid social situations.

In view of the predictive role of personality in the context of happiness, it is appropriate to delineate specific personality dimensions that are systematically related to happiness, life satisfaction and affect experience. British and European personality research has most often used the Eysenck's Personality Questionnaire (EPQ) with three dimensions of *extraversion, neuroticism* and *psychoticism*. American personality research has used the 'Big Five' scales of *extraversion, agreeableness, neuroticism, openness,* and *conscientiousness*. In recent years, Big Five Factors Personality or Neo-Personality Inventory (McCrae, Costa & Martin, 2005) has been extensively used across cultures, though some modification has been incorporated. For example, in China, a sixth Big Factor (Factor of Tolerance) has been identified and included as the sixth Big Factor. A basic strength of this measure involves the inclusion of *six* facets (sub-factors) to each of the big factors. Thus, the use generates scores on five big factors plus thirty facets.

A compelling reason for examining the relationship between personality variables and happiness involves the stability of measures concerned. Subjective well-being is stable across the life span despite the events, stages and turning points in lives. Many researchers have shown that people's emotional lives are heavily influenced by genetic factors (Lykken & Tellegen, 1996). The **"Nun Study"** provides a classic demonstration of the stability of positive emotion across lifespans (Danner, Snowdon, & Friesen, 2001). These researchers from the University of Kentucky collected from the data archive 2 to 3-page autobiographical sketch as part of religious vows. The sketches were submitted by nuns when they first entered the Church. The investigators coded each submitted sketch and counted the number of positive, negative and neutral emotion words. Scores obtained from the coding system were analyzed in relation to nuns' mortality and survival. Researchers found a strong relationship between longevity and the expression of positive emotions early in life. The most cheerful nuns lived a full decade longer than the least cheerful.

A biological basis for people's characteristic emotional orientation is expressed in genetic terms. Research by Tellegen and his associates suggest that genetic factors account for 40% of the difference in long-term levels of positive affect, and 55% of the difference in negative affect. Incidentally the temperament difference emerges early in life.

Temperament refers to a genetically-determined physiological disposition to respond in a stable and typical way. Even in the very first few weeks of life, infants show temperament differences in activity level, mood and responsiveness. Some infants are cranky whereas others are calm.

Jerome Kagan and his associates made very systematic observations of infant behaviours and classified major types called "**reactive**" and "**non-reactive**" (Kagan & Snidman, 2004). An interesting pattern of this observation leads to a very stable and dependable prediction. Reactive and non-reactive infants retain their adult personalities in a remarkable way.

The Big Five. The application of "Big Five" scales of extraversion, neuroticism, agreeableness, openness and conscientiousness has generated a bulk of findings linking personality with happiness. In a meta-analytic study of 197 samples containing over 40,000 adults, DeNeve and Cooper (1998) found that hedonically subjective well-being was consistently related to extraversion, emotional stability (the high functioning pole of neuroticism) and agreeableness. The overall correlations are presented below:

Exhibit: The Big Five and Happiness

Big Factors	Overall r	Number of studies
Extraversion	.17	82
Neuroticism	-.22	74
Agreeableness	.17	59
Openness to Experience	.11	41
Conscientiousness	.21	115

Source: DeNeve and Cooper (1998)

These correlations are small than those for the Eysenck's Personality Questionnaire (EPQ), both for extraversion and neuroticism. This may be due to the fact that Big Five taps personality traits in a generic manner. The third dimension relevant to happiness is the factor of conscientiousness. Furnham and Cheng (1997) used the Oxford Happiness Inventory (OHI) and the Big Five and found that neuroticism had the highest correlation with happiness (-.44), extraversion .39 and conscientiousness .31. It is plausible that the Big Five does not contain some of the cognitive dimensions which are relevant to the construct of happiness. Factor-wise brief description may offer useful information regarding the causes of the linkage.

Extraversion: Extraversion is strongly related to well-being in general and positive emotion in particular. The relation is so robust that extraversion could predict happiness 17 years later (Costa, McRay & Norris, 1981). When extraversion is split into sociability and impulsivity components, sociability correlates more strongly. Since Eysenck's Personality Questionnaire is remarkably loaded on sociability factor, it yields higher correlation (.50) with happiness. Further analysis of the relationship in terms of facets of extraversion in Big Five scale shows that the facet with strongest correlation is assertiveness (for males) and warmth and gregariousness (for females).

Gray (1972) offers a more subtle reason for the positive link between extraversion and happiness Gray posited that because of difference in brain structure extraverts are more responsive to *rewards*, and hence are happier. Neurotics are more responsive to punishment and hence are unhappier. Happiness of extraverts partly stem from their social interaction and social skills. Argyle and Lu (1990) asked participants to indicate the frequency of their participation in 37 leisure activities. The result was factor-analyzed. It was shown that extraverts generally make use of greater participation in socially-inclined activities (teams, clubs, dances, etc.).

However, there is still a substantial minority of happy introverts. It is conjectured that these introverts have a more intense inner life of fewer and deeper social relation. A possibility exists that happy introverts score higher on some of the facets and personality variables. Future research may probe into the matter.

Neuroticism: This has strong negative correlation with happiness. DeNeve and Cooper (1998) report a meta-analysis of 74 studies using various measures of neuroticism. Neuroticism was found to have an overall correlation of -.22, the strongest of the Big Five groupings in this analysis. The relation between neuroticism and negative emotion was so strong that the two variables can be regarded as equivalent. Neurotics have high levels of anxiety and depression. In contrast, happiness is characterized by the absence of anxiety and depression. This explains the predicted pattern of negative association between neuroticism and happiness.

Openness: Openness to experiences denotes the

difference between people who are imaginative and creative and those who are more conventional and closed-minded. Openness includes fantasy, preference for variety and novelty. In contrast, non-openness denotes practical-mindedness, preference for routine and conformity. Research indicates a moderate positive relation between openness and happiness.

Conscientiousness: Conscientiousness refers to people's level of control and discipline. People with high scores on this factor show a greater degree of competence, patience, dutifulness and striving for achievement. In contrast, people with low scores display the lack of confidence. They also exhibit impulsivity, negligence, carelessness and incompetence. Research shows a positive association between conscientiousness and happiness.

Agreeableness: Agreeableness refers to the mindset of getting along and cooperating with others. Specific traits include being trusting, helpful, modest, compliant and determined. Conversely people on the other end of the dimension are characterized by suspicion, selfishness and distrust of others. Agreeableness shows low positive correlation with happiness.

As discussed, the positive association between extraversion and happiness and the negative relation between neuroticism and happiness are highly significant while a number of possible reasons for this relationship has been indicated in the foregoing section, the overlap of extraversion and neuroticism with affectivity suggests a strong link of these traits with happiness. As a consequence, it is not possible to delineate cause-and-effect relationship between personality traits and personality; it would be somewhat *tautological*.

Other traits among the Big Five show more modest

associations with well-being (DeNeve & Cooper, 1998). Openness to experience is only weakly related to happiness. Agreeableness shows a small positive correlation with positive affect. Conscientiousness shows a modest positive relation with well-being.

Personality and eudaimonic happiness: The foregoing discussion mainly illustrates the relationship between Big Five factors of personality and well-being (SWB) as defined in hedonic tradition. However, psychologists working from eudaimonic perspective have also examined personality-health linkage. It may be indicated that Ryff's conception of psychological well-being (PWB) involves *six* components: *self-acceptance, environmental mastery, positive relations, purpose in life, personal growth,* and *autonomy*. Schmutte and Ryff (1997) studied 215 adults. The participants were administered five big factors and Ryff''s measure of PWB. As with previously stated hedonic measures of SWB, neuroticism was inversely related with each of PWB measures, while extraversion, agreeableness, and conscientiousness showed positive association with PWB. Openness to experience showed weak positive correlation with PWB. The comparison can schematically be presented in an Exhibit.

Exhibit: Personality – Well-being Links

Dimension	SWB Tradition	PWB Tradition
Neuroticism	Negative relation	Negative relation
Extraversion	Positive relation	Positive relation
Openness	Positive relation	Positive relation
Conscientiousness	Positive relation	Positive relation
Agreeableness	Weak positive	Weak positive

Despite similarity across perspectives, there are important differences. Schmutte and Ryff's findings suggest that personality influences well-being in multiple ways.

Within SWB model, neuroticism and extraversion are related to well-being in terms of affective linkages. Hence traits not directly related to affects (conscientiousness, openness and agreeableness) show smaller correlations with happiness. On the other hand, within the eudiamonic (PWB) tradition, conscientiousness shows stronger association with self-acceptance, environmental mastery, and purpose in life. It appears that components of conscientiousness contribute to healthy functioning even though they do not increase happiness. Similarly, openness is related to personal growth, even if it has a weaker relation with happiness.

The major implication of Schmutte and Ryff's study highlights the distinction between hedonic and eudiamonic approach. The relation of personality to well-being depends on how well-being is defined. Personality is clearly related to both happiness and health. However, certain personality dimensions enhance health more than happiness and vice versa. For example, conscientiousness is a strong predictor of good physical health practices and longevity. Conscientious people take good care of their health because of their self-discipline and restraint. Whether they are happier or not, their healthy living and long life are considered valuable in society. While attempting enhancement programmes, the manipulation of predictors would depend on the targeted outcome.

Explanatory models. Diener and Lucas (1999) have proposed five conceptual explanations for personality-well-being linkage. *Temperament model* posits that personality traits and happiness set-points are both predominantly genetically determined. Hence the correlation between the two is well-predicted. In *cognitive model*, it is maintained that genetically determined temperament influences the way we perceive and process information. This is likely to influence our happiness. In *socialization model*, it is posited that the process of learning influences both the formation of attitudes and personality; learning also influences our well-being. The common source of learning provides the linkage. The *congruence model* considers both the person and the environment. It is assumed that there may be a good fit between the two in the process of person's growth and the changing environment. When such compatibility occurs, these two processes mutually reciprocate each other. As a result, a relationship is built into the two. Finally, *goal models* stress the selection, strivings and attainment of specific goals. The pursuit of specific goals molds personality as well as behavioural routes. The attainment of goals bring personality and happiness to similar semantic space.

Cognitive aspects. The analysis of personality–happiness linkage offered conceptual clarity about the role of sociability (extraversion) and positive affect. Yet the cases of "happy introverts" remained problematic. What are the contributing factors for happiness in some introverts. Hills and Argyle (2001) computed partial correlations with the Oxford Happiness Inventory before and after controlling for extraversion. The correlations with some cognitive factors were striking. The correlation of happiness with respect to self-esteem, control belief and purpose in life were significant (Hills & Argyle, 2001). It is important to recognize that Ryff's eudaimonic perspective on happiness stresses self-acceptance, autonomy and purpose in life. It is quite plausible that happiness is mediated through some of these cognitive aspects of personality. The role of self-esteem, control and purpose in life may briefly be discussed.

Self-esteem. Self-esteem has been found to correlate with well-being in many studies, with a correlation of .50 or more (Veenhoven, 1994). It is often measured by

Rosenberg's scale (1965), with items like "on the whole I am satisfied with myself". In individualistic countries like the USA, the correlation between self-esteem and life satisfaction is very high. In collectivist countries like India, such correlation, even if positive, is not very high. It can be postulated that the "self" in individualistic countries is basically an "independent self". In contrast, the self in collectivist countries is primarily an "interdependent self". This explains the difference between levels of correlation.

Vanderbilt University psychotherapy professor Hans Strupp notes that unhappiness, frustration, despair are basically impairments in self-acceptance and self-esteem. In experimental manipulation researchers Cialdini and Richardson met Arizona State University students who were walking alone in the campus. With students' consents, they asked a few questions only for 5 minutes and gave false feedback that their answers were not satisfactory. This was followed by questions about their school.it was shown that students receiving negative feedback did poorly (on test questions) compared with a control group. This reflects the damaging effect of the loss of self-esteem.

Myers (1992) reports a similar experiment where self-esteem of Canadian students was temporarily wounded by bogus-feedback method. Subsequently it was shown that their performance was depressed.

The University of Michigan study of well-being in America reports that the best predictor of general life satisfaction is not satisfaction with family life, friendship, or income but satisfaction with self (Myers, 1992). People who like and accept themselves feel good about life in general.

Self-serving bias is an additional evidence in the context of our cravings for self-image. We remember and justify our past actions in self-enhancing ways. We exhibit an inflated confidence in the accuracy of our beliefs and judgments. We are quicker to believe flattering descriptions of ourselves than unflattering ones. We shore up our self-image by overestimating the extent to which others support our opinions.

Self-esteem is consistently found to be a powerful predictor of happiness and life satisfaction. In a study of over 13,000 college students representing 31 different countries, Diener and Diener (1995) reported positive correlation of .47 between self-esteem and life satisfaction. The correlation was even stronger in individualistic countries ($r=.56$).

Many psychologists believe that the need for positive self-regard is one of the strongest human motive. People go to great lengths to protect and promise their self-esteem.

Myers (1992) contends that life satisfaction may begin with self-satisfaction. A positive view of self may colour our view of life in general.

High self-esteem may also have value as a buffer against stress and anxiety. Self-esteem acts as a coping resource that affirms the self. People high in self-esteem are not so easily overwhelmed by negative events and are better able to endure and maintain positivity. They have more "reserve" self-esteem, which helps them absorb blows to self-regard without caring in. The buffering effect is a major reason why high self-esteem is considered an important resource for mental and physical health. According to terror management theory, self-esteem may also buffer the anxiety caused by the ultimate threat to self – our own death. According to another prominent theory, self-esteem plays an important role, maintaining social relationship that are so vital to our health. **Sociometer theory** posits that the purpose of self-esteem is to manage social inclusion.

Control. The control-related beliefs have a number of

research tradition. Rotter's (1966) use of 'internal control' has been extensively used in research. According to Rotter, people with internal locus of control (ILC) are those who believe that the environmental changes are brought by their own efforts or strategies. In contrast, people with external locus of control (ELC) are those who believe that changes are the products of chance factors such as fate and luck. Briefly these people are categorized as *"internals"* versus *"externals"*, respectively.

Many studies have found a correlation between scoring high on internal control and subjective well-being. Control does not appear as a factor in Big Five Factors, but it is quite close to the dimension of Conscientiousness. The facets of dutifulness, achievement, self-discipline, and deliberation in the Conscientiousness Factor are aspects of control. Lu et al (1997) used a sample of 494 adults in Taiwan and found that internal control correlated with happiness (using a Chinese version of the Oxford Happiness Inventory).

Seligman's construct of "learned helplessness" explicates the effects of perception of uncontrollability. The theory of learned helplessness shows that depressed individuals tend to perceive that they cannot prevent bad events happening to them and these events would be repeated in future affecting many domains of their lives.

Some researchers have conducted experimental studies to demonstrate the positive impact of perception of control (Langer, 1983). The experiment was conducted in two equitable extension care units where elderly people are taken care of. The researcher suggested to the residents that a group of volunteers would visit them and the volunteers would provide services (cleaning the bed & washrooms, changing beds, offering other services). The researcher gave a routine day-wise one hour per day. It was arranged that the volunteers would arrive at scheduled hours. In the second extension care unit, the residents could call the team-leader and the team-leader would send volunteers as and when necessary. However, the total service period would be limited to 7 hours per week (as with the first unit). It is important to recognize that the resident of the first unit did not have any control over the use of service, since volunteers would come and go as scheduled. In contrast, residents of the second unit had control over the time. The health indices both in the physical terms (weight gain/loss) and psychological terms (worries, anxiety, zest for living) were recorded for two months. Result indicated that residents in the second unit (experimental setting) exhibited health improvement both on physical and psychological indices.

Increasing people's control can enhance their well-being. Rodin encouraged nursing home patients to exert control – to make choices about their environment to influence policy. The result showed that 93 per cent became alert, active and happy. Similar results were obtained after allowing prisoners to move chairs and control the room light and TV, and after enabling workers to participate in decision making (Rodin, 1986).

The sense of control that comes with effective management of time is a valuable resource. Unoccupied time is unsatisfying. Sleeping late, hanging out, watching TV leave an empty feeling. For happy people, time is filled and planned, they are punctual and efficient. One way to manage time is to set big goals, then break them down into daily objectives. For example, writing 500 pages manuscript may be formidable; but writing 3 pages a day is not difficult. It has been observed that we often overestimate our daily work but underestimate our annual productivity. Given that we are making small progress every day, meeting each mini deadline gives us positive feeling – pleasant and confident feeling of personal control.

Purpose in life. Purpose in life is one of the components in Ryff's six-dimension eudaimonic concept of happiness. It appears that this component fills an important gap in existential vaccum of person's life. Although religions and spirituality do this function, purpose in life is a potent source of happiness.

Viktor Frankl (1959), the renowned psychologist and psychiatrist, was the leading light to highlight the value of this mind-set. He survived Hitler's worst concentration camp at Auschwitz (Austria) and spread the message of logo therapy for suffering humanity. He set up the clinic for logo therapy and helped the depressed to get rid of it and maintain purposeful lives. His message for people was to cultivate three types of values: experiential, creative, and attitudinal values. In essence man's greatest goal is to discover meaning and purpose.

A few other psychologists have stressed purpose and meaning as ingredients of happy life.

Battista and Almond (1973) developed a measure of purpose in life. Their Life Regard Inventory is a good example. It measures purpose in the sense of having a set of life goals and the extent to which they had been fulfilled. A representative goals-related item reads: "I have found a really significant meaning for leading my life". The fulfillment item reads: "I have a real passion in my life". Investigators have used this test for a variety of populations.

Cantor and Sanderson (1999) posit that participation in valued activities and working towards personal goals is crucial for well-being. They broadened the concept of purpose and goals to include "valued activities". These goals and activities enhance well-being by giving a sense of agency and purpose, giving structure and meaning to daily life, giving help for coping and strengthening effect on well-being when activities are freely chosen.

McGregor and Little (1998) report a way of studying goals by asking people to list "personal projects" and rate them on scales. Sheldon and Elliot (1990) proposed that "goal self-concordance" would be important. This refers to the importance of the goal and its psychological proximity to life. The researchers believed that goal self-concordance would generate sustained effort which would lead to goal attainment resulting in satisfaction and well-being.

In sum the personality components along with its cognitive aspects provide a more adequate predictive basis than personality per se.

Role of Gender

A much-studied demographic predictor of well-being is gender. What is the role of gender in the context if human happiness. Psychologists have examined the issue with multiple perspectives. Although a vast amount of findings has been generated, a synthesis of major formulations appears to be challenging.

The overall pattern of results from meta-analyses and other independent studies suggests that men and women report approximately the same level of happiness. Woods, Rhodes and Whelan from Texas A&M University carried out a meta-analysis of 93 studies, done in USA. They found that women were on average a little happier than men (not much, 7% of a standard deviation), had a little more positive affect (also 7%) and life satisfaction (3%). However, for a group of "general evaluation" men were more positive. These weak positive effects were a little stronger for married people (8%).

Other national surveys support the general conclusion that there are few (if any) significant differences in overall happiness (Diener, Suh, Lucas & Smith, 1999). Men and women are on average equally likely to report feeling happy and satisfied with life. Another study of 18,000 college students representing 39 different countries found no significant differences (Michalos, 1991). Inglehart (1990) also reported similar findings. Even studies that report differences also indicate that the differences are small in magnitude. It appears that, knowing a person's gender won't tell much about his or her happiness.

Data sampled from 1980s sixteen nation studies illustrate that men and women are equally likely to report being "very happy" and "satisfied" or "very satisfied" with life (Myers, 1992). But does the overall result obscure any important difference? One obvious possibility is the status of employed women. In fact, employed married women are only slightly more likely than those not employed. This rough equivalence has persisted even as women's attitudes and employment rates have changed dramatically. One explanation is that the psychological costs and benefits are roughly equal. On the negative side, housework can be repetitive, boring and socially isolated. But employed women may be having low-paying jobs and they have to shoulder the housework when they get home.

Actually middle-class house-wives who feel less free – whose lives feel full and rushed rather than free and easy – express greater feelings of happiness and fulfillment. Their lives are filled with challenges; they run families, but they also give volunteer leadership to faith communities and organizations. It adds time pressure but life becomes richer.

From their studies at the Wellesley College Center for Research on Women, Baruch and Barnett (1986) concluded that what matters is therefore not which roles a woman occupies – as paid worker, wife, mother – but the quality of her experience in these roles. Happiness is having work that fits one's interest and provides a sense of competence and accomplishment.

This echoes Freud's proposition that the healthiest adult enjoys both love and work. For most people, love is centered on family relationship. Work is any activity, whether for pay or not, that enables one to feel competent and productive. Having both is a big step towards well-being.

Difference in emotional experience. While men and women are surprisingly similar in their average well-being they are as surprisingly different in the experience of their misery. Depressives preporiderate in women's population. In developed countries, there are two depressive women for one depressive man. In developing countries, there are 18 depressive women for 10 depressive men.

There is a much stronger effect for depression, anxiety and negative emotions in general. Women are twice as likely to become depressed as men, 50% more likely to suffer from anxiety or neurosis, and they experience more negative emotions in everyday lives. The gender difference is less for members of traditional cultures (Nolen-Hoeksema & Rusting, 1999).

Research reviewed by Nolen-Hoeksema and associates (Nolen-Hoeksema, 1991, 1995; Nolen-Hoeksema & Rusting, 1999) clearly shows **internalizing disorders** (depression and anxiety) appearing early in girls. These disorders typically appear between the ages 11 and 15. No such early onset is found in boys. The review also indicates that the difference is not limited to boys and girls; this is also found in adults. Women report experiencing more fear, sadness, anxiety and depression. Women not only experience, but also express these negative emotions more than men.

In contrast to internalizing disorders, **externalizing disorders** and behaviours involve the acting out of emotions. These emotions are directed towards objects, situations, and people. The review documents that men display a greater degree of externalizing than women (Nolen-Hoeksema & Rusting, 1999).

In contrast to the experience and expression of greater degree of negative emotions on the part of women, the experience of joy and more intense positive emotions are also reported by women (Nolen-Hoeksema & Rusting, 1999). One consistent finding is that women express more positive emotions than men. For example, hundred of studies indicate that women smile more frequently than men. Women also are more skillful in empathy, in reading nonverbal cues and assessing emotional states of others.

These two contrasting mind-sets provide useful clues as to why men and women have similar degree of happiness. The range of affectivity is higher for women, with greater negative emotion and greater positive emotion. Despite greater sweep (range) for women, the mean (average) of affectivity for men and women becomes approximately the same. This eliminates gender difference in well-being.

Resolution of the paradox. While two sets of findings (greater negative emotion and greater positive emotion in women) appear contradictory, the resolution of the paradox is conceivable.

In view of the complexity, Fujita, Diener, and Sandvik (1991) proposed that gender differences in affect intensity can explain the paradoxical presence of both the greater prevalence of negative affect and the equal overall happiness reported by women.

Fujita et al (1991) posit that women are affectively intense than men. This allows them to experience both more joy and more sorrow. These greater difference in affective experience can be used as a basis for explaining the gender difference in depression,

In order to provide empirical support for the construct of affect intensity, Fujita et al (1991) carried out a study. They measured positive intensity, negative intensity and global happiness in different ways. Three affect intensity measures and three hedonic level measures were used. Affect intensity was measured with the self-report of Affect Intensity Measure (AIM). The AIM is a 40-item instrument that measures how intensively participants feel emotion. The AIM asks participants to answer questions like "When I feel happy it is a strong type of exuberance" and "When I am nervous I get shaky all over". It is important to note that these items do not assess how frequently the participant experiences an emotion, but rather the intensity of the emotion experienced. The AIM yields both a positive and negative affect intensity score.

In addition to the self-report AIM, the AIM was also modified for the Fujita et al study for observer use by changing the instruction so that the observer answered the questions as he or she imagined the participant would answer them. Furthermore, participants were asked to recall positive and negative emotional experiences in a timed period. In each memory category, participants were given 2 to 3 minutes to write down as many memories of events as they could. The four memory category tests were lifetime happy events, lifetime unhappy events, last year happy events and last year unhappy events. A simple count of the number of positive memories recalled in the fixed time period was used as the positive affect intensity measure. Similarly, the negative affect intensity measure was noted. Thus, affect intensity was measured in three different ways: AIM, modified (observation) AIM, and memory preference.

The findings of the study supported of the basis propositions of Fujita et al (1991). On five of the six inventory measures (both positive and negative), women's mean level was found to be more intense than man's mean level. In contrast, the only one of the six hedonic level measures did women differ from men. This difference was on the self-report affect measure on which women reported more positive affect than men did.

The pattern of correlation also was in line with the prediction. In the complete sample matrix, a significant positive correlation was found between the positive intensity and negative intensity measures. This implies that people experiencing high levels of positive emotion also experience high levels of negative emotion. Further significant negative correlations were found between the hedonic level measures within measurement method. This finding was expected because affect intensity has been found to be unitary across valences, whereas positive and negative hedonic level makeup a bipolar affect balance dimension. All affect intensity measures correlated positively with each other across valence and methods. In addition, all of the hedonic level measures correlated in the hypothesized direction.

The result of the study offers support for the proposition that women experience emotion more strongly than do men. The statistical comparison of groups (men versus women) provided evidence that women differ from men on the intensity of their emotion. However, there is little evidence of affect balance difference between the genders. The principal component analysis used as a condensation of the complete sample correlation matrix, provided evidence that affect intensity is unitary across valence. This means that if a person experiences strong negative emotion, that person is more likely to experience strong positive emotion.

The result of these studies clarifies past anomalies. Although women scored significantly higher on almost all of the intensity measures, they did not differ from men on most of the hedonic balance measures. Based on these findings, one would predict that, if researchers only collect negative emotion data and the items tap both hedonic level and affect intensity, they would find women experiencing more negative affect (more depression) than men. One would also predict that, if researchers collect data that balance the positive affect against the negative affect, then the gender differences would disappear. Thus, the paradox of past research is replicable, women score higher on negative affect even though they are not lower on global happiness. It appears that more intense positive emotions tend to counterbalance the more intense negative emotions when women report their overall happiness.

Another explanation may help us to understand the apparent illusion of paradox. Despite tremendous growth and development across the globe, **gender stereotypes** persist Women are believed to experience extreme emotions. Because of stereotypes and expectancies, women may respond in a particular way while answering on the measures. It is interestingly found that there is not much gender difference while participants record their moment-to-moment experience of moods (Experiential Sampling Method or ESM). But a significant difference emerges when participants recall their emotional experience. The difference increases with the lapse of time for the recall (Nolen-Hoeksema & Rusting, 1999).

Finally, it is important that the detection of difference is sensitive to the method of measuring well-being. When hedonic measures are used, differences with respect to emotional experience across genders emerges. When eudaimonic measures stressing healthy functioning are employed, no difference surfaces. Women are found to be as healthy as men are; men have advantages in certain domains while women have benefits in other areas (personal growth and social relation with others).

A seminal point with respect to gender-linked strength and weakness relates to the complementary process. In both men and women, the strength has a down-side and the vulnerability has an upside. For example, women's greater empathy and social contact provide them positive elements of well-being. At the same time, it has "pressure-cooker effect", an empathetic woman feels disturbed at workplace if her neighbour's son/daughter is ill on that day. Similarly, men may be having some deficits in their interpersonal sensitivities. Yet, this deficit may generate emotional stability for a longer period. Thus, each gender appears, on average, to have a unique contradiction of strengths and vulnerabilities. These strengths and limitations may offset each other resulting in equivalence of happiness.

Marital Status

Many demographic variables indicate only small relationships to happiness. One major exception to this trend involves the marital status. About 90% of people eventually marry and the vast majority of people are happier as a result of marriage (Myers, 2000).

The *United Nations Demographic Yearbook* reports that

9 out of 10 people worldwide state 'the need to belong' as a fundamental need and marriage is viewed as the closest friendship bond. A vast amount of literature shows that people are happier when attached than when unattached. Surveys in Europe and America have provided supportive findings. Compared with those who never marry, and compared with those who are separated or divorced, married people reported being happier and satisfied with life (Myers, 2000). The *National Opinion Research* Center in the USA surveyed 35,024 people during 1972 and 1996. A consistent picture supporting marriage-happiness linkage emerged. It was shown that 40% of married adults reported themselves "very happy" compared to 24% of never-married adults (almost half). Pooling data from national surveys of 20,000 people in 19 countries, Mastekaasa (1992) found similar pattern. Married people were also less vulnerable to depression.

In a landmarking meta-analytic study involving 93 samples, Wood, Rhodes and Whetan (1989) examined whether men are relatively more benefited by the positive association between marriage and happiness. However, the married versus not-married happiness gap was similar for men and women. Of course, bad marriages were found to be more distressing to women than to their husbands.

Although the positive effects of marriage have been greatly supported across cultures, *two* critical issues have complicated the inference. These are **selection effects** and **adaptation issue**.

The term selection effect refers to the possibility that people who marry are simply happier people, before they get married, than those who don't marry. Since premarital happiness level is not same and comparable, the later comparison (after marriage) may not reflect the positive impact of marriage. The happiness of married people seems inflated.

However, studies to examine selection effects have provided mixed results. A longitudinal study in Norway found selection effects in the marriage–happiness relationship among 9000 people (Mastekaasa, 1992). But, a 12-year longitudinal study found negligible effect (Johnson & Wit, 2002). Myers (2000) raises another question with respect to selection effects. If happy people are more likely to marry, and to do so earlier in their lives, then as people age, the happiness of married people as a group would go down, as older and less happy people begin to marry. The addition of less happy people to the married group would pull down the average. A similar change would occur in the never-married group. As less-happy people eventually get married, the most unhappy people are increasingly left in the never-married group, reducing the average level of happiness. As Myers (2000) argues the data on well-being and marital status do not support these predictions based on selection effects. In contrast, difference in happiness among married and never-married groups remains unchanged across age groups.

The other critical issue in marriage-happiness relation concerns **adaptation**. Adaptation refers to a return to a set point and longer-term happiness, and people adjust to emotional impact of the marriage. The issue of adaptation raises the question of whether the increase in happiness after marriage is a long-term effect or short-term effect. A longitudinal study of 24000 Germans provided evidence for adaptation as well as for individual variability (Lucas, Clark, Georgellis & Diner, 2003).

In Lucas and colleagues' study, participants were interviewed annually over a 15-year period. Two marital transitions were studied: getting married and becoming widowed. The effects of these events were evaluated by comparing pre-marriage and pre-widowhood happiness to the levels of happiness shortly after the event and in subsequent years of the study. To better isolate the effects of these marital transitions, only those persons who stayed married for the total study period (1,012 participants), and only those who remained widowed (500 participants) were used.

The study produced a small short-term boost in happiness and the increase faded during subsequent years. The findings provided strong effects for the process of adaptation to the emotional consequence of getting married. The result for widowed individuals showed much longer-term effects and much slower adaptation. Eight years after losing their spouse, participants' average happiness ratings approached pre-widowhood levels, but did not recover completely. Many widowed individuals showed stable and long-term decline in life satisfaction and did not show complete adaptation to the loss of their spouses.

The longitudinal design of the study revealed many interesting features. The data revealed that many people increased their happiness after marriage; interestingly, an equal number of participants decreased their happiness. Those who reacted positively to marriage increased their happiness; those who had negative or less positive attitude towards marriage either showed no change or became less happy than they were prior to their marriage. Lucas et al called the phenomenon **hedonic levelling**.

Hedonic levelling explains some of the differences found in the study. The most satisfied people had the least positive reactions to getting married, but they had the strongest negative reactions to divorce and widowhood. As suggested by hedonic levelling, they have already satisfied their needs (prior to marriage). An unhappy or lonely person may have much to gain.

Hedonic levelling appears to be influencing individual reaction to marriage. If marriage has little effect on happy people and big effect on unhappy people, the difference between two groups are reduced or leveled out. The same process may affect the impact of widowhood. People who are happy with life because of their marital status may experience a heavier sense of loss. In contrast, people who are unhappy may experience less sadness.

While Lucas and colleagues' study provide some useful clues with respect to adaptation to life's transitions (marriage and widowhood), the generalizations may not be considered definitive. The study was conducted in Germany and there may be cultural bias creeping in. More cross-cultural studies are needed to clarify the issue of adaptation.

Gender difference in benefits. Two other issues are pertinent in the context of marriage – happiness relation. The first one concerns the issue of gender. Who gets more benefit? : man or woman. Some studies indicate that men get more benefits in terms of positive emotions and protection from depression (Nolen-Hoeksema & Rusting, 1999). However, other studies find no difference. Yet, the effects of divorce or separation are clear-cut. Women experience a greater degree of depression and men resort to drinking and drugs. Myers (2000) opines that the gap in happiness between married and unmarried people remains almost the same for men and for women.

The other related issue is the question of the strength of marriage – happiness relation. Because of the rising rates of divorce across the globe, the popular myth may suggest a picture of declining happiness. Yet research presents the picture otherwise. While there has been increased conflict in younger couples compared to older couples, there is no decline in the benefits of marriage (Mastekaasa, 1993). Divorced individuals have higher rates of divorce in subsequent years of marriages, perhaps because they are less able to make a marriage work. Cohabitating couples undoubtedly benefit from relationships even though they are not counted as married.

The association between marital status and happiness has been found in studies of 40 nations around the world regardless of the divorce rate or the effects of living in an individualistic country (Diener, Suh, Lucas & Smith, 1999). However, the effects of unmarried cohabitation on happiness is affected by culture. In individualistic cultures, cohabiting couples are happier than even married couples, but in collectivist cultures they are more unhappy than married or single individuals. This unhappiness may be due to the stresses generated because of the violation of social norms in the collectivist countries.

Dynamics of marriage-happiness relation. Despite television images of pleasure-filled single life and caustic comments about "yoke" of marriage, most people are happier attached than unattached. There are compelling reasons why marriage promotes happiness.

Marriage–happiness relation is a two-way traffic. Happy people are more appealing as marriage partners. Depressed people more often stay single or suffer divorce. Happy people are more fun to be with. They are more outgoing, trusting, compassionate, and focused on others. Depressed persons induce hostility, depression and anxiety in others and get rejected. For such reasons, happy people readily form happy relations.

But marriage also enhances happiness. First, married people are more likely to enjoy an enduring, supportive and intimate relationship. They are less likely to suffer loneliness. Medical students in the University of California at Los Angeles surveyed a large number of married couples. They found marriage buffers the misery. A good marriage provides each partner a dependable companion, a loved a friend.

Myers (1992) observes: "For me, neither single life nor cohabitation could be at the intimacy and security of this lifelong companionship with my best friend".

Second, marriage enhances happiness by providing compensatory roles. Marriage offers the roles of spouse and parents. These roles provide additional sources of self-esteem and self-satisfaction. Multiple roles may bring additional loads. Yet each role provides rewards, status, avenues to enrich. When there is stagnation or burden associated with a role, the person can enrich the other domain(s)and compensate the loss.

Seligman (2002) offers an exciting explanation of why marriage is a potent predictor of happiness. Seligman cites the Cornell University psychologist Cindy Hazan saying that there are three kinds of love. First is the love of people who give us comfort, acceptance, and help, who strengthen our confidence and guide us. The prototype is children's love of their parents. Second, we love the people who depend on us for these provisions. The prototype of this love is parents' love for their children. The third prototype is romantic love – the idealization of another's strength and virtues and downplaying their limitations. Marriage is a unique arrangement where all these three kinds of love are superbly blended.

Seligman (2002) argues that marriage was "invented"

by natural selection, not by culture. In pair-bonding such as marriage, people learn styles of loving as well as styles of being loved. That makes marriage a unique arrangement.

While marriage has many happiness-promoting features, additional steps may also be taken to enhance happiness further. Harker and Kiltner (2001) found that middle-aged women whose college yearbook photographs showed them displaying a Duchenne smile had lived happier lives and had more fulfilling and long-standing marriages than women who showed a false smile in their college yearbook photos. Smile plays.

John Gottman, a professor at the University of Washington in Seattle is an expert on marriage counselling. By watching hundreds of couples interact for twelve hours each day for an entire weekend in his "love-lab", he derived both the predictors of divorce and predictors of successful marriages. The negative list includes the following:
- A harsh startup in a disagreement
- Criticism of partners, rather than complaints
- Displays of contempt
- Hair-trigger defensiveness
- Lack of validation
- Negative body language

On the positive side, Gottman also lists promoting factors (Gottman & Silver, 1999).
- Reunion conversation (At the end of workday)
- Affection
- Admiration and Appreciation
- At least one common activity each week

In summary, marriage appears to have many potential benefits for individual health and happiness. However, while evaluating the benefits, it is important to recognize the distinction between the hedonic and eudaimonic views of well-being. Some factors that promote health may mortgage happiness. For example, Ryff and Singer (2000) point out that conflict in marriage which is bad for happiness may promote future well-being (say, personal growth – an eudaimonic component). In other words, unhappiness at one point in a marriage may be the basis for greater happiness in the future. In short, health and happiness, though related, are not the same thing. The emphasis on healthy functioning and hedonic happiness would stress different, though related factors. The promotion of health vis-à-vis happiness may accordingly be planned.

The Effect of Age

Growing older is an inescapable part of our existence. When asked which period of life is least rewarding, people often say that adolescence and old age are the worst period. Many people have the stereotypic belief that adolescence is a period of stress and strain. The fluctuations in moods and constant demands from the external world take away the pleasures in adolescence. Similarly, people believe that the decline in health conditions and loss of control over environment complicate the aging process. Actually, people of all ages report similar feelings of well-being (Myers, 1992).

Arizona State University psychologists William Stock, Morris Okun and their associates integrated the results of more than a hundred of studies and found that age accounts for less than 1 percent in well-being. Inglehart (1990) interviewed 169,776 people from sixteen nations and found similar results.

It is plausible that life span development presents elements of compensation. At each phase of life, we acquire some resources and lose others. During old age also, the mechanism of balance operates. However, there are predictable ups and downs in well-being.

Transitional effects. Many people believe that women get into depression during and after menopause. Yet, systematic studies show that a large number of women develop right kind of attitude towards it and go ahead with their healthy living. To learn women's attitude towards menopause, University of Chicago developmental psychologist Bernice Neugarte and her colleagues conducted extensive interview. They asked a wide variety of questions regarding their handicaps, worries, anxieties, freedom, vigour and work habits. Only a small proportion of middle-aged women expressed their deep concerns during and after menopause. Many women were calmer and happier after the change of life than before.

A similar issue involves the **empty nest phenomenon**. Grown-up sons and daughters get married and leave home. It is believed that parents experience loneliness and become depressed. This also appears to be a myth. Many surveys confirm that the empty nest is generally a happy place. Compared to middle-aged parents who still have children at home, those whose nest has emptied report greater happiness. Sometimes married sons and daughters return; the revolving door phenomenon may bring both pain and pleasure. With greater acceptance of empty nest lifestyle, many parents maintain ties with their children and stay happy.

The third talked-about crisis during adulthood is the mid-life crisis. Because of the stagnation at the workplace and expanded family obligations at home, some people's distress peaks anywhere at the middle age. Generally, it is found that some people get into financial or sexual offenses to get away from their mental stresses. But this is not a normal feature in every home or organization. If people and organizations work proactively, it can easily be handled.

There are several reasons why moderation effects work during old age. As our years go by, our feelings become moderate. We do not go to the upper extreme, nor do we go to the lower extreme. Our feelings become stable. Our elation and dismay remain limited. We do not crave for praise, nor do we scare for criticism.

National Institute of Aging (USA) researchers Robert McCrae and Paul Costa devised a special measure "Middle Crisis Scale" to gaudge domain-specific crises during midlife phase. It measures stress as well as meaningfulness in job, family, and leisure pursuits. They administered the scale to 350 thirty-to-sixty-year-old men. They found no evidence of turmoil. To re-check it, they administered to a new group of 350 and a measure of emotional instability to 10,000 men and women. There was no evidence of mid-life crisis. Many researchers believe that it is not age that marks the transition from one life stage to another; it may be significant life event that signifies the transition. Such events may include child birth. child leaving, occupational change, divorce, illness, retirement, and widowhood.

The stability of well-being across the lifespan is maintained because of several reasons. In an interesting experiment, University Chicago psychologist Mihaly Csikszentmihalyi and colleagues provided electronic pagers to a large number of individuals and requested them to record their moods and activities. They had to record whenever they are beeped. There were two interesting findings. First, adolescents' moods were more extreme whereas elders reported low intensity moods. When adolescents report negative mood, they feel as if the sky is falling on their heads. Adolescent moods are also transitory; it changes very rapidly. In contrast, the elderly reports moods that are less extreme and more enduring.

The stability of well-being across the life span is very likely. The elderly experiences slightly more satisfaction at their home, work and leisure pursuits. But they accept both success and failure with certain amount of moderation. Although they feel happy with a big success and somewhat low by failures, their sense of acceptance does not push them neither to euphoric height nor to depressive bottom. By the time people reach late adulthood, their accumulated life experiences help them to adjust their ambition in congruence with their achievement. The impossible dreams they had in the past become sober and their aspirations are more realistic. This is helpful for adaptation.

Finally, it is important to recognize that each phase of life (infancy, childhood, adolescence, adulthood, old age) has its own priorities. Goals change and preoccupation also alters. As long as there is commitment and strivings towards its preoccupation, stability is likely to be maintained. However, the only complicating factor during old age is the element of physical fitness and health. Its significant role deserves discussion elsewhere.

The shifting bases of emotional experience. Happiness, especially hedonic happiness, is basically rooted in emotional experiences. As outlined earlier, happiness is defined in terms of frequency of positive affects, infrequency of negative affects, and balance affect (positivity minus negativity). Further probe into the matter persuades researchers to look into the issue of positive affects more closely. Positive affect appears to be made two types of positive emotions that are relatively independent (Watson, 2005). The independence of these two types of positive emotions presents the possibility that they may be having distinct influences on people's well-being. Kunzmann, Stange and Jordan (2005) labelled these two types as **pleasant affect** and **positive involvement**. Pleasant affect is defined as a positive emotional state involving relatively low arousal. Positive involvement refers to high-arousal states such as feeling inspired, alert, or active. In contrast, pleasant affect or low-arousal states entail feeling satisfied, content, and happy.

According to Kunzmann and his associates, these two types of affective positivity are linked with two kinds of lifestyles. A hedonic lifestyle emphasizes pleasant affect through the pursuit of personal pleasure and consumption. A more eudaimonic lifestyle is consistent with positive involvement. People expressing a growth-related lifestyle would pursue positive involvement.

The Kunzmann research studied pleasant affect, positive involvement, and the hedonic and growth-related lifestyle in a sample of young (15 to 20 years old), middle-aged (30 to 40 years old) and older adults (ages 60 to 70). Their findings were highly relevant for the issue we are discussing. First, these two measures (pleasant affect and positive involvement) have very small correlations with one another. Second, the passive emotions of younger adults included pleasant affects, while positive emotions of older adults included positive involvement. It implied that a more hedonic happiness fits with lifestyle of younger population and growth-related (eudaimonic) happiness fits with older adults.

In this investigation, a seminal question is answered. The question of whether positive affect increases or decreases with age depends on which aspect of positive affect is being considered. Positive affect measured in terms of pleasant affect declines with age (r = -.38). However, positive affect in terms of positive involvement increases with age (r = .42).

In summary, research consistently shows that negative emotions decline with age. Affective positivity shows interesting pattern; pleasant affect declines with age while positive involvement increases with age. Metaphorically it can be said that health is enhanced while happiness is compromised with advancing age. For more enduring and long-term growth-related gains, some amount of pleasant feelings ae compromised.

The discussion leads to the summary conclusion regarding the stability of well-being during old age. Although the focus changes, the well-being remains unaltered. Another group of researchers, while emphasizing growing eudaimonic perspectives in older population, introduce an interesting concept, **"socioemotional selectivity theory"** (Carstensen, Isaacowitz & Charles, 1999). Carstensen's theory provides that older people shift their priorities from the future to their present life circumstance and activities. The shift occurs as a result of their enhanced awareness of the diminished time. They tend to "unplug" themselves from the rat race of getting ahead. They change focus to investing in people and activities that matter most for their lives.

Isaacowitz (2007) employed innovative method to test attentional bias in elderly population. He made modification in Stroop test which is an oft-used test in cognitive research. In conventional Stroop test, colour names are provided on a chart where each colour name is indicated with a different colour (the word 'red' written in green colour). Participants are asked to tell the name of the colour with which a word has been written. The time taken to read out the entire chart is noted. Obviously, the reading reflects interference in attention. The efficient and successful reading requires that the reader ignores the words and fixes his/her attention only on colours.

In a novel way, some clinical psychologists have adapted this Stroop Test for use in clinical setting. They term it as **Emotion Stroop Test**. In this test emotionally loaded word (both positive and negative) are shown on the chart and each word is written with a different colour. As with the Stroop Test, participants are asked to name colours. It is generally found that neurotics (anxious participants) have greater difficulties with colours linked with emotionally-loaded words in comparison of neutral words.

Isaacowitz (2007) used Emotion Stroop to compare young and old people with respect to attentional bias. The socioemotional selectivity theory (Carstensen et al 1999) predicts that aged population would indicate attention bias towards socioemotional stimuli of their environment. Using positive and negative stimuli through television monitor and eye tracking mechanisms. Isaacowitz (2007) examined the role of age and optimism. While he did not obtain the main effect of age as predicted, the interaction effect was clearly observed. With optimism, elderly persons tended to show attentional bias for positive emotional stimuli.

Income, Social Class and Education

Economics are concerned with human welfare. People at large assume that human happiness can be measured by how much money people have. However, psychological research on money-happiness relation shattered the simplistic relationship picture. The United nations consider parameters of health and education along with standard of living, while computing Human Development Index (HDI) for a Nation. In recent decade the King of Bhutan proclaims the *Gross National Happiness* as an indicator of a Nation's progress and prosperity. In such a world scenario, the role of money requires re-examination.

One of the earliest studies was the one by Bradburn (1969). The study examined the relation between money and emotion. A clear relation was shown with positive affects (correlation .32 to .57). The relation with negative affect was much weaker. However, subsequent investigation in terms of both unicultural and cross-cultural investigations looked into more multi-faceted aspects of the issue. It seems the center of gravity has gradually shifted to money-focused view of life. Initial survey affirms a widespread belief that there is more to life than money. People rate money near the bottom of important sources of life satisfaction. In their classic work on quality of life Campbell and his associated (1976) found that money ranked 11th out of 12 listed sources of a satisfying life. King and Nappa (1990) also found similar trend. Both college students and adult community members judged happiness and meaningfulness to the essential features of good life.

In contrast, when focus is shifted to our own lives, we gravitate more towards income and affluence. The National opinion polls in the United States have asked people about the role money plays in their personal happiness and their frequent answers indicate "money" (Myers, 1992, 2000). The leading magazine 'Time' (Jan 17, 2005) and Chicago Tribune reported similar trend (Csikszentmihalyi, 1999). The survey indicated that regardless of their current income, people believed that more money would make them happier.

Ordinarily people would expect that individuals need things other than money when basic needs are met. Yet, that did not happen in the most affluent country like the USA. When University of Michigan interviewers asked what blocks our search for good life, the frequent answer was "more money". According to a 1990 Gallup poll, one in two women, two in three men, and four in five people earning more than seventy-five-thousands a year express their desire for more money. In the American Council on Education's annual survey of over 200,000 entering college students, the proportion indicating the objective of "making more money" rose from one in two in 1970 to three in four in 1990 (Myers, 1992).

At this point, it would be interesting to explore country-to country differences in well-being. Extensive interviews were conducted with representative samples of 170,000 people in 16 nations. In 1990 book Culture Shifts in *Advanced Industrial Society*, University of Michigan political scientist, Ronald Ingelhart presents wealthful data. Year after year, the Danes, Swiss, Irish and Dutch feel happier and most satisfied with life than do the French, Greeks, Italians and Germans.

The national well-being differences correlate moderately with the national difference in affluence. People in the Scandinavian countries generally are both happy and prosperous. But the link between national affluence and well-being is not constant. Germans average more than double the incomes of the Irish, but the Irish are happier. Similarly, Belgians are happier than their wealthier French neighbours.

A more extensive study is a 40-nation cross-cultural investigation on money – happiness relation. Based on this study, a large number of interesting features can be generated. Diener and Oushi (2000) report correlation with income for the 40 countries, and the average correlations are shown below:

Exhibit: Correlations Between Income and Satisfaction

Aspects	Correlations
With life satisfaction	.13
With life satisfaction (students)	.10
Financial satisfaction	.25
Financial satisfaction (students)	.18

Source: Diener and Oishi (2000)

These are modest correlations, which can also be expressed as a difference of 11% on the satisfaction scale between top and bottom income groups. Financial satisfaction has a close connection with income than life satisfaction does.

The cross-national survey involving tens of thousands of adults illustrates several other points. First, there is modest positive correlation between overall national purchasing power and average life satisfaction. Once the gross national product exceeds 8000 US dollars the correlation disappears. The added wealth brings no further life satisfaction.

There are also plenty of exceptions to this wealth–satisfaction relationship. Brazil, China and Argentina are much higher in life satisfaction than would be predicted by their wealth. The Soviet-bloc countries are less satisfied than their wealth would predict, as are the Japanese. The cultural values in Brazil and Argentina and political values in China may support positive emotion in these countries. Similarly, the difficult emergence from communism perhaps lowers happiness in eastern Europe. The explanation of Japanese dissatisfaction is relatively difficult.

In the 40-nation study, India presents an interesting feature. On economic index, it is fairly low (5 while US purchasing power is 100). Yet, on a 10-point score of life satisfaction, India scores 6.7 (reasonably high, though not very high). In addition to India, people in China and Nigeria also display high life satisfaction. These data tell us that *money doesn't necessarily buy happiness*. The change in purchasing power over the last half century in the wealthy countries carries the same messages. Although the purchasing power has more than doubled in the United States, France and Japan, the life satisfaction has not changed a bit. In very poor nations, where poverty threatens life itself, being rich does predict great well-being. In wealthier countries, where everyone has the best safety net, increases in wealth have negligible effects on happiness. Even the fabulously rich with an average net worth of over 125 million dollars are only slightly happier than the average American.

In contrast, Robert Biswas-Diener explored the concept of happiness amongst pavement children in Calcutta (Kolkata). Apart from measuring life satisfaction, he also measured several domain-specific satisfactions in areas such as family, friends, food and a few other domains. For comparison, he also measured satisfaction in University students. Though the overall satisfaction level was low, they continue to search for spots of happiness in the landscape of their lives (Biswas-Diener & Diener, 2001; Diener & Biswas-Diener, 2000).

The Paradox of Plenty is a formidable challenge in the developed world; the increasing wealth does not guarantee happiness enhancement. The United States presents an illustrative case. There has been phenomenal growth of material prosperity in the U.S.A. during last 50 years. A recent review by Diener and Seligman (2004) presents fascinating picture. There has been escalating rise of affluence. The per capita real income has tripled. Consumer statistics reveal astonishing growth in ownership of car and luxury items, expanded living home area and vacation and eating out. During the same period of increased income and consumption, large scale national surveys reveal that American life satisfaction has remained "virtually flat" (Diener & Seligman, 2004).

Reviews of the mental health literature indicates that there are more people suffering from mental disorder and emotional distress today than in the past (Diener & Seligman, 2004). Depression has shown most dramatic increase in incidence. It has shown 10-fold increase, with younger people suffering much higher rates than older people.

The depression-affluence relationship is not limited to the USA; it is also evident in other countries. In contrast, a study of the Amish culture in Pennsylvania suggests that affluence is implicated in depression. The Amish lead simple lives, their communities are close-knit, bound together by religious faith. Amish individuals have only 1/5 to 1/10 the risk of developing depression of those who live in our modern, affluent society.

Diener and his colleagues (1985) carried out a study of 49 rich Americans, as listed by *Forbes*, all earning over 10 million U.S. dollar per annum. Diener et al compared them with 62 chosen at random who lived in the same area. The researchers founded the selected 49 to be only slightly happier than average. Some of them agreed that "money can increase or decrease happiness". One wealthy man said he could never remember being happy. Another woman reported that money could not undo the misery caused by her children's problems. In sum, the affluence-happiness connection is not encouraging.

People wonder as to why there is such poor connection between wealth and happiness. While psychologists are searching for satisfactory answers to explain the mismatch between material well-being and psychological well-being, a number of hypotheses have been formulated.

First, it appears plausible that the rise of "consumer culture" has displaced deeper meaning and values rooted in our family life, social relationship, and religious activities. People's major concerns gravitate towards marketplace. Family is no longer a center of security, nurturance and relationship, it is now primarily a consumption centre. This process has deprived us of our real-self and has created an **empty-self**. This is a misery spot.

Second, with too much emphasis on self-focused life style, public involvement has been eroded. People's participation in schools, community works, social enterprise and group activities has decreased. This erosion in social capitalism is a possible cause of unhappiness.

Finally, proliferation of choices appears to be problematic. In his book, *The Paradox of Choice: Why More is Less (2004)*, Schwartz postulates that people in modern consumer societies have an unprecedented number of alternative choices and that complicates life. Schwartz argues that too many choices create a **"maximizing"** psychology that creates a pressure to choose the best possible option. In contrast, a good number of options encourage '**satisficing**" psychology; it motivates to choose an alternative which is "good enough".

This problem with maximizing approach involves added pressure increased stress and 'rat-race' activities. The satisficing approach is conducive for balance and contentment. It is now easy to surmise as to why maximizing lifestyle in modern affluent societies generate unhealthy competition and ill-health.

The foregoing discussion does not suggest that

poverty needs to be perpetuated and affluence needs to be discarded. The poverty-alleviation programme is a "must" for people struggling for basic needs of life. In terms of Maslow's need hierarchy, the lower-order needs (physiological and security needs) are yet to be ensured. In contrast, the low correlation between income and well-being in affluent countries may stem from the fact that people in affluent countries may be striving for higher-order needs of personal growth and achievement.

However, a seminal point in the money-happiness relationship concerns the varying interpretations and meanings of happiness in different cultures. The role of culture is suggested by the different relationship between income and well-being across countries.

Social class. Social class is sometimes assessed in terms of income. In many western countries including the UK and the USA, hierarchy of occupations (based on skills) in combination of income and education has been used as measure of social class. Studies show curvilinear pattern; occupational class has a greater effect at the bottom end of the scale.

Haring, Okun and Stock (1984) carried out a meta-analysis of American studies, and found that class correlated .20 with satisfaction, more than the effect of income, or job status. The correlation of class and well-being is much greater in some other countries, such as Israel .55, Nigeria .52, India .42, Philippines .44 and Brazil .38. It is important to note that these countries have large class differences.

The effect of class on health is very marked. Mental health is much worse in lower social classes (Argyle, 2001). This is partly due to difference in income and education. Another seminal point contributing to the effect of social class on happiness relates to the level of perceived control. It is observed that people in higher social class enjoy a greater degree of internal control contributing to their enhanced well-being.

Education. Many surveys have found that there is some correlation between education and happiness. Meta-analytic studies indicate that education influences well-being primarily by affecting occupation, not income, and occupation in turn influences both income and well-being. Further analysis shows that education plays important role in getting satisfying work, increased control, better access to marriage and other forms of social support (Argyle, 2001).

In some studies, education has a clear negative effect, when income and occupation had been held constant. This is the outcome of raised expectations.

Chapter 5

Internal Amplifiers

The research scenario with respect to happiness presents multiple efforts to identify correlates and/or predictors of happiness. Such attempts have generated a large number of circumstantial evidences such as gender, personality, marital status and income levels that are dynamically related to well-being. These are valuable research findings. Drawing on the findings, appropriate manipulation of circumstances can be effected. But what about the inner life?

A number of researchers have directed attention towards the underlying triggers. They have focused certain process variables that leverage the well-being potential. The discussions on religiosity, spirituality, meditation, flow experience and savouring are regarded as the internal amplifiers of happiness.

Religiosity and Spirituality

In the beginning, there was resentment to accepting religiosity and spirituality as relevant topics in behavioural research. There were several grounds for such opposition. Many researchers believed that it is very difficult to have operational definitions of religiosity and spirituality. Second, the content areas were considered appropriate for the discipline of philosophy, but not for behavioural science in general and psychology in particular. However, scientific ideas do not constitute a stagnant pool of ideas and concepts; it flows with time. Though the conventional term 'religion' did not inspire psychologists to move forward with research, the health-concerns in the eighties and **positive psychology movement** in the nineties harnessed research motivation for the study of religion and spirituality.

Studies of Religion

Religion is a part of human existence. Its meaning and definitions may vary, but its visibility is conspicuous for long-time past. Obviously when psychologists and behavioural scientists were vigorously searching for who is a happy person, one targeted investigation pointed towards the direction of religion. Many large-scale surveys were conducted in the 1980s and 1990s to find out religion-happiness relationship.

Prior to delineating indicators of religion, the public notion of religion may be considered. Kenneth Pargament is the leading light in the field of religion and spirituality. Pargament and his associates (Pargament, Tarakeshwar, Ellison & Wulff, 2001) wanted to identify criteria of religiousness as perceived by people. They asked college students and clergy members to rate the extent of religiousness. Participants were provided with 100 hypothetical profiles where each profile contained 10 cues in different degrees. The magnitude of each cue varied from profile to profiles. The cues included the degree of church attendance, frequency of prayer, meditation, feeling God's presence, monetary contribution to faith community, personal benefits, and so on. The result showed that the church attendance was the most important cue for rating religiousness.

It is a common experience that religious beliefs and involvement are widespread among people all over the world. Amongst eastern countries including India people's day-to-day lives are intermingled with religious activities. However, more data are available in western settings.

Even in the highly developed countries such as the United States, the role of religion is very prominent. Over last 50 years, national surveys by Gallup and others have found that 90 to 95% of Americans express a belief in God or a high power (Myers, 2000). Two-thirds of Americans belong to a church or synagogue, and 40% attend regularly. Researchers have found small positive correlations between happiness and religious involvement, and moderate to strong association between religion and physical health (Hill & Pargament, 2003).

Other general surveys also show a significant, though weak, effect of religion on happiness. Inglehart (1990) conducted a survey involving 14 European countries taking a total subject sample of 163,000. He found that 85% of regular church participants (going at least once a week) were "very satisfied" with life, compared with 82% of those who went occasionally and 77% of those who never went at all.

Witter, Stock, Okun and Haring (1985) carried out a meta-analysis of 56 American surveys and found modest religion-happiness relation. The overall correlation between religion and well-being was .16. They also found that the effect of religion on happiness was greater for religious activity rather than other measures of religiosity. Some other American studies have included larger national samples. Furthermore, these studies have controlled the effects of confounding variables such as age, education and occupation. Researchers found positive association between religion and well-being, Veenhoven (1994) reported surveys from round the world and indicated that effect of religion on well-being was stronger in America compared with European countries.

Other studies, too, reveal high level of well-being among religiously active people. The summary findings of three large-scale studies may be cited. A 1982 survey of 9000 Europeans found that among the "very happy" were 16 percent of atheists, 19 percent of "not religious", and 25 percent of those who said they were religious. In the United States, where reported happiness is somewhat higher, 31 percent of "somewhat" or "not very" religious people, say they are "very happy", but this rises to 41 percent among those who say their religious affiliation is very "strong". In a 1980s survey of 166000 people in 14 countries, those "satisfied" or "very satisfied" with life included 77 percent of those who never attend church, 82 percent of those who attend occasionally, and 86 percent of those who attend regularly (Myers, 1992).

Morris Okun and William Stock (1987) at Arizona State University found that the two best predictors of well-being among older persons were health and religiousness. Elderly people are happier and satisfied with life if religiously committed and active.

Although it is difficult to pinpoint cause-and-effect relationship linking aspects of religion with components of well-being, a brief discussion on the components of religion may provide helpful clues.

Components of religion

Religion includes several criteria. Religious people engage themselves in a large variety of behaviours. These include visiting the places of worship, prayer, meditation, reading scriptures, company of the holy and many other religious forms of behaviour. As pointed out earlier, visiting the church (or any other place of worship such as temple, mosque, synagogue etc.) is considered as a visible indictor of religiousness.

Many researchers have attempted to directly study the effects of church attendance, Poloma and Pendleton (1991) found that church attendance correlated with life satisfaction, happiness and existential well-being more than other religious variables such as prayers and beliefs, though not as much as "religious satisfaction". *The effect is stronger for the elderly.*

Another study by Moberg and Taves (1965) of 1343 individuals aged 65+ in Minnesota looked into the index of adjustment. The benefits of greater church attendance were evinced for those who were single, retired, old or in poor health. This suggests that the benefits of visiting places of worship maybe due to the social support it provides.

Argyle (2001) has argued that religion has an important social utility. Very close bonds are formed between members because of their shared beliefs, shared rituals and rewarding interactions. Shared experiences have a strong pro-social component. The communal activities may lead to a state of love, harmony, equality and social union among those participating in common religious activity. Obviously, an abundance of social and affective resources promotes health and well-being.

The important component of religiousness involves "closeness to God"; it correlates .16 with happiness and satisfaction when church attendance is controlled. Ellison, Gay and Glass (1989) found that *"devotional intensity"* (regular prayer and feeling closer to God) was the strongest religious predictor of life satisfaction. Poloma and Pendleton (1991) found that peak experiences and prayer experiences were the best predictor of well-being, especially existential well-being. Many researchers believe that existential well-being (meaning and purpose) is the aspect of well-being most influenced by religion (Kirkpatrick, 1992). Kirkpatrick also suggests that the relation with God can be experienced through prayer, personal devotion and religious commitment in much the same way as we interact with humans.

The third component of religiousness is the supportive belief system. Ellison et al (1989) found that having firm beliefs called "existential certainty" correlated with life satisfaction, independently of both prayer and visit to places of worship. They also found that church attendance and prayer are producing positive effects through the mediating mechanism of belief enhancement.

Belief in an after-life is beneficial, especially to those who are old, ill or in danger. However, religious beliefs are more than assent to verbal propositions (" I believe in God"). The belief is indicative of strong emotional commitment and way of life associated with the belief. This is similar to the measures of "meaning and purpose" (a sub-scale of well-being). An example is Battista and Almond's (1973) "Life Regard Inventory". It is this aspect of well-being which is most strongly associated with religion.

An Integration

The expanding interest in religious behaviour in the context of health and happiness stimulated further research. Initially the operationalization of religious behaviour lacked rigour. It was roughly the extent of visiting places of worship (churches, temples, mosques). Though the findings indicated a positive relation between religious behaviour and health, a substantial number of studies reported negative association (showing that people having religious beliefs display psychopathology). This incompatibility generated a paradigm crisis requiring a paradigm shift.

Many researchers closely examined the construct of religion and identified several underlying subtle dimensions. Viktor Frankl was the earliest psychologist and psychiatrist to explicate "search for meaning". Frankl's own suffering in Hitler's concentration camp and his observation that people could survive because of their ability to find meaning gave him an extraordinary insight. He believed that pursuit of meaning is a cardinal principle of human life.

Drawing on Frankl's ideas, Roy Baumeister (1991) in his book *Meanings of Life* described *four* needs that underlie the pursuit of meaning: purpose, value, self-efficacy, and self-worth. These four needs explain the basis for people's motivation to find meaning. The need for **purpose** refers to a desire for direction in life. It specifies personally significant goals. The need for **value** provides justification for the pursuit of goals. The third need **self-efficacy** offers confidence and capacity-building in the direction. **Self-worth** is the fourth basis for pursuit of meaning. It offers positive self-evaluation and self-regard.

Baumeister (1991) argues that the meaning making behaviour of man offers a form of control which is very salient in religion and spirituality. It is **interpretive control**. People acquire some ability to understand why certain things happen. Although people cannot change certain events, they have some understanding. For example, even if they cannot prevent someone's death, they understand and accept the event as a part of a universal cycle. This explains as to how religion deals with what Emmons (1999) call "ultimate concerns". The meaning making role of religion contributes.

At the centre of recent conceptualization is the relationship between religion and spirituality. William James (1985) in his classic work *The Varieties of Religious Experiences* made a distinction between *institutional religion* and *individual religion*. As an institution, religion is an organized set of beliefs, practices, doctrines, and places of worship associated with the different world religions. The individual meaning of religion relates to the personal side of faith, defined by a person's unique belief system, activities and experiences.

In recent years there has been greater urgency to explore the interrelationship of religion and spirituality. Interestingly most people consider themselves both religious and spiritual Zinnbauer (1997) and his colleagues asked participants to choose one of four statements that best defined, their religiousness and spirituality. The 346 participants in the study represented a variety of religious background and ranged in age from 15 to 82, with a mean age of 40. The choices were: I am spiritual and religious; I am spiritual but not religious; I am religious but not spiritual; I am neither spiritual nor religious. A strong majority of the participants (74%) endorsed the religious and spiritual statement, 19% described themselves as spiritual but not religious; 4% as religious but not spiritual; and 3% as neither spiritual nor religious. Participants were also asked about the relationship between religiousness and spirituality.

Only a small percentage (6.7%) indicated that these were completely different. Similarly, only a small proportion (2,6%) noted that they were the same concept. Overall, most people distinguish between the two; a majority of people identify themselves as both religious and spiritual.

Pargament (1997) in his influential book *The Psychology of Religion and Coping* offers a clear definition of religion. Based on his analysis, the defining essence of religion is the **search for the sacred**. The sacred refers to things set apart from ordinary life because of their connection to God, the holy, the divine, to transcendent forces, Universal Truth and Ultimate Reality. The sacred evokes a sense of awe, respect and devotion. It encompasses the beliefs, practices, and feeling relating to a higher being and ultimate truth of existence.

According to Pargament (1997), religion is not limited to a set of beliefs and practices, it addresses the basic questions of our existence. Religious beliefs concern the meaning of life and coping with the inevitable pain and suffering including death. Pargament further combines substance and function in his definition of religion and spirituality. He defines **religion as a search for significance in ways related to the sacred "and spirituality as a search for the sacred"**.

According to Pargament (1997), search incorporates a functional view of religion and spirituality is a means to address life's most fundamental questions. The unique and distinctive function of religion is defined by spirituality.

It appears that Allport's early distinction between **intrinsic** and **extrinsic religious orientation** is very useful in solving the puzzling relationship between religion and spirituality. In empirical terms a person with extrinsic religious orientation uses religion to fulfill certain needs (security, comfort, status or social relation). The person engages in a number of external behaviours such as going to places of worship, praying and following a number of rituals. It is not a value. In contrast, intrinsic religious orientation is not an instrumental device. It does not denote external forms of behaviour such as rituals. It is internalization of certain values, especially human values (love, compassion, nonviolence, humility). Viewed from this angle, extrinsic religiousness is our conventional notion of religion while intrinsic religious orientation is synonymous with spirituality (Allport & Ross, 1967).

Religion in terms of extrinsic religiosity and spirituality in terms of intrinsic religiosity solve the paradox of definition. Now it is conceivable as to why extrinsic religiosity (or simply religion) leads to incompatible findings, sometime positive relationship with well-being and sometimes negative relation. On the other hand, intrinsic religiosity (spirituality), as expected, shows positive association with well-being.

Religion/spirituality and well-being: Given the definitions of religiosity and spirituality in terms of extrinsic orientation and intrinsic orientation respectively, the relationship with well-being emerges clearer.

As pointed out earlier, religion does have a small, but consistent positive relationship to measures of health and well-being (Argyle, 2001; Myers, 2000). The positive connection is somewhat stronger among the elderly. It is also associated with less delinquency, less alcohol and drug abuse. The most consistent results are found for physical health. Results for mental health have been somewhat mixed and some studies have found negative effects.

Researchers have suggested a number of possible mechanisms and pathways. The literature evaluating the possible mediators highlight positive roles of improved health practices, social support and psychosocial resources (self-efficacy, optimism, resilience and positive affectivity).

Finally it is important to recognize the positive health outcomes of spirituality (intrinsic religiosity). The defining properties of spirituality essentially include the promotion of human values that ensure health and happiness.

Meditation: Beyond the Stress-reduction Paradigm

Meditation is now one of the most enduring, widespread and productive area of psychological research and application. However, the evolution of a relationship between meditation and psychology has progressed through three different stages (Walsh & Shapiro, 2006). The first was a prolonged period of *mutual ignorance* in which each tradition remained blissfully or willfully ignorant of the other. Ignorance bred misunderstanding. The second stage was one of *paradigm clash*. Practitioners of each discipline tended to dismiss or pathologize the other. They used the distorting lens of their own unquestioned cultural and paradigmatic assumption – a process sociologists call nihilation. For example, many meditation teachers dismissed Western psychology and psychotherapy as superficial. They claimed that psychology overlooked the deeper level and potentials of mind. Likewise, some mental health practitioner initially pathologized meditation, as well as disciplines such as yoga and shamanism. For example, the classic text *The History of Psychiatry* pointed to "the obvious similarities between schizophrenic regressions and the practice of Yoga and Zen".

However, with greater knowledge has come greater open-mindedness and mutual exploration. Yoga has emerged as one of the world's most widely practiced, enduring and researched psychological discipline. The result is the third and currently dominant stage of growing relationship and *assimilative integration.* Nevertheless, much misunderstanding remains. Contemplatives often still view Western psychology and psychotherapy as limited adjuncts to meditation practice Psychologists usually regard meditation as just another therapeutic technique to be applied and investigated in conventional ways. Unfortunately, research findings on yoga have been interpreted almost exclusively within Western psychological perspectives. This has been widely described as a necessary "decontextualization". In anthropological terms, this is the trap of adopting a purely etic (outsider) perspective rather than both etic and emic (insider) perspectives.

Varieties of Meditation

There are many definitions of meditation. Nevertheless common themes are apparent. Western definitions emphasize that meditation is a self-regulation strategy with a particular focus on training attention. The meditative traditions contend that there are multiple meditations and the main goal is mental development. Patangali's *yoga sutra* emphasizes the control of mind and desires (*chitta* and *vrities* or *vasanas*). Similar emphases are noticed such as *bhavana* (mental cultivation) in Buddhism and lien-hsin (refining the mind) in Taoism. The goal is to cultivate beneficial mental capacities such as calm and concentration and positive emotion such as love and joy. The other goals is to reduce negative emotions such as fear and anger (Goleman, 2003). By integrating these common themes, Walsh and Shapiro (2006) offer a definition: The *term meditation refers to a family of self-regulation practices that focus on training attention and awareness in order to bring mental processes under greater voluntary control and thereby foster general mental well-being and development and/or specific capacities such as calm, clarity, and concentration.*

This definition differentiates meditation from a variety of other therapeutic and self-regulation strategies such as self-hypnosis, visualization, and psychotherapies. In general, these do not focus primarily on training attention and awareness. Rather, they aim primarily at changing mental contents (objects of attention and awareness) such as thoughts, images, and emotions. Likewise, the definition distinguishes related practice such as yoga, Tai Chi, Chi gong. These practices include additional elements such as controlled breathing and body posture (yoga), a body movement and supposed energy manipulation (Tai Chi and Chi gong).

Despite having common features, meditation practices come in many varieties. Walsh and Shapiro (2006) observe the following varieties:

1. **The type of attention**: Concentration meditations aim for continuous focus primarily on one object, such as the breath or an inner sound. Awareness or open meditations aim for fluid attention to multiple or successively chosen objects.
2. **The relationship to cognitive process**: Some practices simply observe cognitions such as thoughts or images whereas other deliberately modify them.
3. **The goal**: Some practices aim to foster general mental development and well-being, whereas others focus primarily on developing specific mental qualities, such as concentration, love, or wisdom.

Although meditation is most often associated with India, it is actually a worldwide practice ground in every major religion and in most cultures. Examples include

Taoist and Hindu yogas, Jewish Hassidic and Kabalistic *dillug* and tzeruf, Islamic Sufism's *Zikr*, Confucian quiet-sitting, Christian contemplations, and Buddhist meditation (Goleman, 2003).

By far the most researched practices are mindfulness, Transcendal Meditation (TM), and Yoga. Mindfulness is an open focus or awareness practice usually identified with Buddhist mindfulness or *vipassana* (clear seeing) insight meditation. TM is a meantra (inner sound) practice that researchers sometimes describe as concentrative, but in advanced stages awareness becomes increasingly panoramic.

Mindfulness and Happiness

While different forms of meditations are linked to happiness enhancements, mindfulness has received special research attention in recent years. Langer's (2005) pioneering work gave it an empirical framework. Mindfulness is a present-centered attention focused on the "here and now" of our experience. Our perception is distorted by our wishes, desires and needs. Mindful meditation is a means of enhancing the clarity of perception by observing and learning about the self. Such meditation increases the accuracy of our self-understanding and provides a basis for self-improvement and happiness (Snyder & Lopez, 2005).

Mindfulness meditation has been extended as a therapeutic practice for people dealing with stress in general and mental disorders in particular. The value of mindful meditation in solving multitude of psychological and physiological problems has been demonstrated (Walsh & Shapira, 2006). The most well-known clinical intervention programme based on mindfulness was developed by Jon Kabat-Zinn, the founder of the Center for Mindfulness in

Medicine, Health Care and Society (CFM) at the University of Massachusetts Medical School. Kabat-Zinn (1990) gives detailed description of his mindfulness training programme in his book *Full Catastrophe Living*. It is asserted that mindfulness practice is an important vehicle for self-change and improved well-being.

What is Mindfulness?

Mindfulness can be understood in terms of its opposite-**mindlessness**, which refers to a state of consciousness marked by little awareness of what is going on in the present moment. It is a state "governed by rule and routine" (Langer, 2005, p. 214) rather than what is happening now. All of us are familiar with mindless states. We may carry out conversation with our friends, but our minds are absorbed in our own thoughts, feelings, worries, and concerns.

In a typical day-to-day activities, many of our behaviours are habitual and automatic; these require little conscious attention (like brushing our teeth). While the automaticity provides us the benefit of releasing us from the burden of continual effortful control, people can become easy victims of their own unconscious habits (undesirable smoking, overeating). Despite its advantage, automaticity is negatively regarded because it contradicts people's view that they "know" why they do things.

Proponents of mindfulness are not resentful to the efficiency of well-learned automatic behaviours. However, they point out that people can easily become victims of their own unconscious undesirable habits (e.g. smoking). An undesirable habit is automatically triggered by many external and internal cues. From the perspective of mindfulness, awareness of when and why you smoke is necessary to control the habit.

Brown and Ryan (2003) assert the potential value of

mindfulness for improving well-being by ensuring attention to the self-regulation of behaviour. Successful goal pursuits require some degree of conscious attention (mindfulness). Mindfulness contributes to more self-determined and autonomous activities. Personal goals that are freely chosen are likely to be satisfying than goals imposed by others and circumstance. Autonomy offers multiple choices whereas automatic behaviours limit our options and enhance unthinking (mindlessness). Therefore, mindfulness is a potential avenue to greater autonomy because it enhances our awareness of choices by unplugging us from reflexive thought patterns and habitual automatic responses.

Awareness denotes all the things that are present on our minds. It continually monitors external cues such as immediate circumstances and ongoing activities. Awareness involves as internal cues such as associated thoughts, feelings and experiences. *Attention* focuses our conscious awareness on a limited set of experiences. For example, we can be conscious of events occurring in our peripheral vision (awareness) and events occurring at the focal visual field (attention). Awareness and attention are linked in the sense attention pulls figure out of the ground of awareness (Brown & Ryan, 2003).

According to Brown and Ryan (2003), **mindfulness** is an open and receptive present-centered attention and awareness that is prereflective and non-judgmental. It entails focusing on the here-and-now, rather than ruminating about the past, or externalizing anxieties about the future. It denotes living in the present-not living for the present. In some ways, it is akin to activity focused attention called "flow" (Csikszentmihalyi, 1997). Further, while mindfulness is a vehicle for self-analysis and self-change, it is simply oriented toward observing rather than evaluating the self. In this respect, it is akin to increasing the sensitivity of a radar which is not programmed to look anything in particular. The main advantage is the ability to see more of what is actually out there. It is this "seeing more" that makes mindfulness a potential antidote for the blunted awareness resulting from modern hectic lives.

Mindfulness Meditation

Meditation denotes a family of self-regulation practices that focus on training attention and awareness with a view to controlling voluntary mental processes. Such practices foster well-being in general and capacities such as calm, clarity and concentration in particular.

Although several valuable books are available on the topic, Kabat-Zinn's (1990) guidelines provide excellent helpful suggestions for practitioners. While mindfulness meditation is an integral part of Eastern philosophy and religion, its adoption in contemporary lifestyles has demystified the process and has made an effective instrument of promoting healthful living.

The constant chatter of one thought after another consumes our mental energy and distracts us from what is happening at the moment. While we live in the present, our thoughts drift off to the past or anxieties of the future. Kabat-Zinn (1990) gives an example of a scenic sunset. Instead of savouring the moment, people filter their experiences through thoughts and description. The actual sun-set is lost in person's thoughts about it. Langer (2005) argues that mindfulness involves an understanding that events do not come with evaluations, we impose them on our experiences, and in so doing create an experience of the event (p. 219). The point of mindfulness is to see the world before we judge, evaluate, and stuff it into preconceived categories and boxes.

Mindfulness as a personal quality is first cultivated in the limited context of meditation, and then begins to transfer to other domains of life. For example, a fisherman begins fishing career with only the enjoyment of the sport and the desire to catch fish. Over time, it grows into the pleasure and expertise of environmental exploration.

Features of Mindfulness

Specificities of practice in mindfulness meditation do vary. Yet Kabat-Zinn (1990) provides the more straightforward description of mindful awareness. It involves setting aside a piece of time (15 to 45 minutes) and a place to quiet the mind down. One might sit on a cushion or pillow with legs crossed in front and hands on his/her knees. One could also sit in a straight-backed chair. The individual should be comfortable and a bit relaxed. The head, back, and the neck should align vertically so that the person is alert to good posture.

Then one should focus one's attention on his/her breathing, following his/her breath in and out without trying to control or change it, but just experiencing its ebb and flow. When one's attention wanders away to something else, one should just note the occurrence and bring attention back to breathing. Beginning meditators find it difficult, an infinite variety of thoughts creep in. With practice, things gradually become controllable. Kabat-Zinn (1990) advises meditators to just acknowledge whatever mind brings to attention and let them go.

> Meditators should not judge or evaluate, they should just accept and return to their breath. The idea is to watch thoughts without trying to suppress them.
> Kabat-Zinn (1990) identifies *seven* interrelated attitudes that are important in mindful meditation.

These are presented in the following exhibit:

Exhibit

1. **Non-judging**: Although we evaluate things in terms of "good" and "bad", such value judgments are relinquished during meditation.
2. **Patience**: Allowing events to unfold in their own time.
3. **Beginner mind**: Have an open-mind. Behave as if you see it for the first time.
4. **Trust**: Take responsibility for being yourself. Do not try to be someone else.
5. **Non-striving**: Striving to achieve a particular result of meditation is not proper.
6. **Acceptance**: Be yourself rather than deny who you are.
7. **Letting go**: Practicing non-attachment to prominent thoughts and feelings.

Overall, mindfulness meditation is a way to observe the process of your mind from the perspective of an observer. It is remarkable that the practice gives a feeling that thoughts are just thoughts, they are not you or your reality (Kabat-Zinn, 1990). The process brings it closer to **psychotherapy** where purpose is to provide healing and health.

Meditation and Health

Several hundred studies conducted over four decades have identified a wide array of meditation-responsive variables that range across psychological, physiological, and chemical parameters in both clinical and nonclinical populations.

Research suggests that meditation can ameliorate a variety of psychological and psychosomatic disorders, especially those in which stress plays a causal or complicating role. For example, cardiovascular disorders responsive to TM include hypertension and hypercholesterolemia. Other medical conditions responsive to meditation include asthma and stuttering, as well as hormonal disorders such as type 2 diabetes, primary dysmenorrtia, and premenstrual syndrome (now called premenstrual dysphoric disorder). Meditation has also proved effective in enhancing immune functions in cancer patients, reducing symptoms of distress in fibromyalgia and cancer patients, and decreasing pain in multiple chronic pain syndromes. Meditation may also enhance treatments for psoriasis, prostate cancer, and atherosclerosis.

Psychtherapeutic effects have been documented (Walsh, 1983). Several clinical populations appear to benefit, the most studied have been those with stress disorders. For example, mindfulness meditation appears to ameliorate insomnia, eating disorder, anxiety, panic, and phobic disorders. Likewise, TM is reported to alleviate anxiety, aggression, and recidivism in prisoners and to reduce both legal and illegal drugs. However, TM subjects are required to cease drug use for several days before training, so they may be a particularly responsive population. Stress-related benefits are consistent with classic claims that a central effect of meditation is "calming the mind and the elimination of anxiety". A similar claim is popularized in the West that meditation is a "relaxation response" (Benson& Proctor, 1984).

Flow: Mechanism of Living in the Present

The present moment is all we are really guaranteed. Enjoying this present moment is a surer way of attaining peace and happiness. Flow is a state of intense absorption and involvement with the present moment. Have you ever been absorbed in what you were doing – painting, writing, conversing, fishing, playing chess, praying, web-surfing – that you completely lost track of time? Perhaps you failed to notice that you were very hungry or your back ached from sitting so long? Did nothing else seem to matter? If the answer is yes, then you have experienced a state called flow.

Coined by a psychologist, Mihaly Csikszentmihalyi (1990), flow denotes a state of complete absorption in what one is doing. You are totally immersed in what you are doing fully concentrating, and unaware of yourself. The activity you are performing is challenging and engrossing, stretching your skills and experience. When in flow, people report feeling strong and efficacious, at the peak of their abilities, alert, in control, and completely unselfconscious. They do the activity for the sheer sake of doing it.

Csikszentmihalyi (1997) argued that the good life, a happy life is characterized by flow, by "complete absorption in what one does". The key to creating flow is to establish a balance between skills and challenge. Whether you are rock climbing, performing surgery, writing a story or driving on the highway, if the challenges of the situation overwhelm your level of skill or expertise, you will feel anxious or frustrated. On the other hand, if the activity is not challenging enough, you will become bored. Flow is a way of describing your experience that falls in just the right space between boredom and anxiety. Your happiness depends on your ability to find the perfect space, to extract flow from what you are doing. The situation can be depicted schematically.

		Perceived Ability	
		Low	High
Level of challenge in task	High	Anxiety	Flow
	Low	Apathy	Boredom

Benefits of Flow

Flow is inherently pleasurable and fulfilling. The enjoyment one obtains is generally lasting and reinforcing. Flow provides a natural high that, unlike artificial highs or hedonic pleasures, is a positive, productive and controllable experience that does not cause guilt or shame.

Second, because flow states are intrinsically rewarding, we naturally want to repeat them. However, there lies a seeming paradox. As we master new skills, our experience of flow diminish because the task at hand is no longer as stimulating. Thus, to maintain flow, we continually have to test ourselves in ever more challenging activities. We have to apply focused mental discipline in ever more challenging activities. We have to stretch our skill or find novel opportunities to use them. This is wonderful, because we are constantly striving, growing, learning and becoming more competent, expert, and complex.

One of the core ideas connected with flow experience is that we cannot allow our happiness to depend on our external circumstances, for every positive event and accomplishment we experience are accompanied by rapid adaptation and escalating expectations. Even as we attain great heights, we begin to want even more. There is no inherent problem in our desire to escalate our goals, we enjoy the struggle along the way.

The experience of flow leads us to be involved in life (rather than be alienated from it), to enjoy activities (rather than to find them dreary), to have a sense of control (rather than helplessness), and to feel a strong sense of self (rather than unworthiness). All these factors imbue life with meaning and lend it a richness and intensity.

Increasing Flow Experience

Flow opens up to a world of a very different kind, a world of thousand possibilities and opportunities. Finding flow involves the ability to expand your mind and body to its limits, to strive to accomplish something difficult, novel, or worthwhile, and to discover rewards in the process of each moment, indeed in life itself.

Control attention: To increase the frequency and length of flow experience in your daily life, you need to become fully involved and engaged, whether it is writing a letter, doing a job-related task, or undertaking leisure activities that engage your skills and expertise. How exactly do you accomplish that? The secret is **attention**. William James, the 'father' of psychology once wrote: "*My experience is what I agree to attend to*". This is a revolutionary thought. What you notice and what you pay attention to is your experience; it is your life. There is only so much attention that you have go around, so how and where you choose to invest it is critical. To enter the state of flow, attention needs to be directed fully to the task at hand. When you're intensely concentrating on doing something, you're essentially directing your attention to the task (e.g., writing poems as opposed to other activities like deciding about breakfast and inquiry about time).

Maintaining the state of flow also involves the control of your attention. If the challenge is too low you become bored; your attention drifts to some other thing. If the challenge is too high, you become self-conscious. Your aim is to gain control over what you pay attention to. Hence choose contents of your task wisely.

Adopt new values: Happy people have the capacity to enjoy their lives even when their material conditions are lacking and even when many of their goals have not been reached. How do they do it? They follow certain paths. They are open to new and different values (cooking, playing, etc.). They learn until the day they die. The state of flow comes naturally to the child, but we may have to work at it.

Learn what flows: Many people believe that the conditions of work and task always generate stress while no-work condition affords pleasure. This is a wrong idea. There are many studies to show that people have negative thoughts when they are not doing anything. Hence it would be proper to select and choose activity that suits you and affords flow. With an open mind, search the task that has potential for flow experience.

Transform routine tasks: Even seemingly boring and tedious activities – waiting for the train, listening to a dull presentation – can be transformed into something more meaningful and stimulating – what you need to do is to create microflow activities with specific goals. For example, you could solve problems in your head, tap melodies to favourite songs. So, when you sit in a doctor's waiting room, your goal might be to draw a project design.

Flow in conversation: Depending on your job and lifestyle, a significant percentage of your days may be spent in conversation with others. Do you usually experience flow when you are talking with another person? Focus your attention as intensely as possible on what the other person is saying and your reaction to his words. Do not be too quick to respond, rather, give him/her the space to expand on his/her thoughts. You may prompt him with brief follow-up questions (And then what happened? And Why did you think so?)

Smart work: One fascinating study of work found that people tend to use their work as one of three ways; as a job, as a career, or as a calling. Those who place their work in the job category essentially perceive it as a necessary evil, a means to an end – the job is needed to support them. People who report having career may see their work as means for promoting their status. Those who see their work as calling report enjoying work and find it to be fulfilling and socially useful. It is important to recognize that people regarding their work as a calling are likely to experience flow during their work process.

While discussing different possibilities of flow experience a caveat needs to be identified. In the process of experiencing flow, some individuals can become addict; they may ignore their primary responsibility. However, with the use of human intelligence and discrimination, people can guard against this addictive practice. Once this caveat is recognized, seeking flow experience is likely to be a source of good life, happy life.

Savouring: An Alternative for Living in the Present

The ability to savour the positive experiences in your life is one of the most important ingradients of happiness. Most people truly understand what it means to savour after overcoming uncomfortable or painful symptoms. When you have a toothache and it's gone, you suddenly are delighted in its absence. When you are overwhelmed by terrible allergies that abruptly dissipate, you truly relish breathing freely (Sahoo, 2013).

You can think of savouring as having a past, present, and future component. You savour the past by remembering about the good old days – your wedding, your appointment letter, and your pleasant vacation. You savour the present by wholly living in, being mindful of and relishing the present moment, whether it's having lunch with a friend, immersed yourself in a book, song, or project at work. This type of savouring overlaps a great deal with flow. Finally you savour the future by anticipating and fantasizing about upcoming positive events. This is an element of optimistic thinking. Although it may appear that the past and future components of savouring are not included in the process of "living in the present", both involve ways of bringing and preserving pleasure of the past and future into the present moment.

Researchers (Bryant & Verhoff, 2007) define savouring as the thoughts or behaviors capable of "generating, intensifying, and prolonging enjoyment". When you stop and smell the roses instead of walking by, you are savouring. When you bask and take pride in your own or friend's accomplishment, you are savouring. There is slight difference between flow and savouring. Savouring requires a stepping outside of experience and reviewing it (e.g., how beautiful is the rose), whereas flow involves a complete immersion in experience.

Strategies to Foster Savouring

If savouring life's joy is one powerful activity for sustainable happiness, people need to use available options to trigger savouring. Any one can select an option and get started right now.

Relish ordinary experiences: The first challenge in using the strategy of savouring is to learn how to appreciate and take pleasure in mundane everyday experiences. Consider as a model what participants were asked to do in recent research aimed at exploring the extent to which making savouring a habit can produce tangible benefits. In one set of studies, depressed participants were invited to take a few minutes once a day to relish something that they usually hurry through (e.g., eating a meal, taking a shower). When it was over they were instructed to write down in what ways they had experienced the event differently as well as how that felt compared with the times when they rushed through it.

Starting tomorrow, consider your daily routine activity and ritual. Do you notice and savour the pleasure of the day, or do you dash through them? If the latter, then resolve to seize the pleasures when they happen and take full advantage of them. Linger over your morning breakfast or afternoon snack, absorbing the aroma, the sweetness (rather than mindlessly consuming). Strive to bask in the feeling of accomplishment when you have finished a task at home or work, rather than distractedly moving on to the next item on your to-do list. Enjoy the little thing, for one day you may look back and realize they were the big things.

Savour and reminisce with family and friends: Often it is easier to savour when you share a positive experience with another. Whether you have visited an interesting place or listening to an inspiring speech, the pleasure of the moment can be heightened to the company of others who similarly value the experience. You might reminisce together about a party you both attended or a vacation you shared. The advantage of savouring and reminiscing with friends and family members bring abundant positive emotions.

Transport yourself: The ability to engage in positive

reminiscence – to transport yourself at will to a different place and time – can provide both pleasure and solace when you need it most. People can travel to mental destinations through recall of positive images and memories. People make lists of happy memories and personal memories (such as photographs, gifts and souvenirs) and then engage in positive memories.

Replay happy days: The practice of repetitively replaying your happy life events serves to prolong and reinforce positive emotions. So think about one of your happiest days – the first day of your school, the first day your child called you papa / mama. Replay it in your mind as though you were rewinding a videotape and playing it back. Think about the events of the day, and remember what happened in as much detail as you can.

Celebrate good news: Sharing successes and accomplishments with others has been shown to be associated with elevated pleasant emotions and well-being. So, when you or your spouse or cousin or friend wins an honour, congratulate him or her (and yourself), and celebrate. Try to enjoy the occasion to the fullest. Passing on and rejoicing in good news lead you to relish and soak up the present moment, as well as to foster connections with others.

Be open to beauty and excellence: The strategy involves allowing yourself to truly admire an object of beauty or display talent, genius, or virtue. Strive even to feel reverence and awe. Positive psychologists suggest that people who open themselves to the beauty and excellence around them are more likely to find joy, meaning, and profound connections in their lives.

Be mindful: Many philosophical and spiritual traditions stress the cultivation of mindfulness as a critical ingradient of well-being. The practice of Zen Buddhism, for example, emphasizes clearing one's mind and grounding oneself in the present moment. A series of studies conducted at the University of Rochester focused on people high in mindfulness – that is, those who are prone to be mindfully attentive to the *here and now and keenly aware of their surroundings*. These people with practice of mindfulness exhibit greater well-being.

Take pleasure in the senses: Pay close attention to and take delight in momentary pleasures, wonders, and magical moments. Focus on the sweetness of a ripe mango, the aroma of a bakery, or the warmth of the sun when you step put from the shade. Take in the cool fresh air after a storm, the brushstrokes of a painting.

Create a savouring album: You may take snaps when you travel. Collect pictures that are likely to give you happiness. Preserve the savouring album and see through the pictures whenever you feel like savouring.

A note about writing: Some psychologists advise savouring through writing, perhaps by keeping a journal in which you describe a memorable past experience or an exciting time in the present. Since writing is a structured activity, some people may not find it very pleasant. Yet, some people may find it to be useful.

Thinking of good times from the past makes you feel better about the present. It helps you appreciate things more. It gives you an idea of where I was then, where I am now and where I ultimately want to be. These memories also give you confidence: "I did it before, I can do it again".

The Buffering Role of Humour

Humour is a topic of central concern in psychology and philosophy. It is observed that an average, children laugh 300 times a day and adults only laugh five times a day. Since children laugh more than adults, it seems that our sense of humour dwindles as we become more aware and educated of the world. Without any central definition of humour utilized in the world of psychology, University of Western Ontario professor, Rod Martin, was prompted to write a unifying book that investigated the role of humour. He defined it as: "**A process (that) can be divided into four essential components: (a) a social context, (b) a cognitive-perceptual process, (c) an emotional response, and (d) the vocal-behavioural expression of laughter.**"

Theories of Humour

A number of theories have been advanced in the context of humour.

Humour incongruity theory: The Incongruity Theory says that humour is the perception of something incongruous – something that violates our mental patterns and expectations. In simple terms people laugh at things that surprise them because of the context in which it is presented: things are incongruent (out of place) within the context of which they are delivered.

One way to further explain the theory, humorous amusement is not just any response to incongruity but a way of enjoying incongruity. The following three features may be noted:
1. A person perceives (thinks, imagines) an object as being incongruous.
2. The person enjoys perceiving (thinking, imagining) the object
3. The person enjoys the perceived (thought, imagined) incongruity at least partly for itself, rather than solely for some ulterior reason.

This approach to joking is similar to techniques of stand-up and the punch (line). The set-up is the first part of the joke: it creates the expectation. The punch (line) is the last part that violates that expectation. In the language of the incongruity theory, the joke's ending is incongruous with the beginning.

Humour superiority theory: The theory suggests that when people make a stupid mistake, they are the victim of an unfortunate situation, or misunderstand an obvious instruction, they look stupid in a social environment. Thus, we laugh at these jokes, people, and situations because it makes us feel superior to the victim and their unfortunate luck.

Simply put, our laughter expresses feelings of superiority over other people or over a former state of ourselves. However, some critics argued that the feeling of superiority is neither necessary nor sufficient for laughter. Sometimes we laugh when a comic character shows surprising skill that we lack. Some people too, laugh at themselves. A gentleman riding a coach who sees ragged beggars on the street, for example, will feel that he is better off than they, but such feelings are unlikely to amuse him. In such cases we are in greater danger of weeping than laughing.

Tension release theory: According to Freud, jokes and laughter's are a way in which people could release their sexual or aggressive thoughts in a socially acceptable way. Freud proposed that it served as a way to cope with the problems and issues in our lives that we are hesitant to confront in another way, thus it provides a source of relief to these thoughts unconsciously. By attempting to cope with varying emotions and thoughts, laughter is a way to release the tension that was built.

The release, Freud said, would be triggered by the dramatic or surprising occurrence in the punchline. But many dramatic surprises are not pleasant at all, and jokes that are neither aggressive nor sexual can work on us regardless of how tense we are.

Humour benign violation theory: This theory holds that humour occurs when three specific conditions are satisfied
  a. a situation is a violation
  b. the situation is benign
  c. both perceptions occur simultaneously

The violations are strictly based on how an individual believes the world should be, thus accounting for the discrepancy between what is reality and what if funny. This theory is also important because it accounts for the thresholds of what is and what is not funny. It explains that a situation may not be funny because the violation isn't simultaneously benign, or because it is beginning without a social violation.

Humour Styles

Over a decade ago, Rod Martin and his colleagues developed a model of humour styles that has since become one of the main theoretical frameworks used to guide psychological research on sense of humour. It describes four distinct styles of humour on the basis of whether it

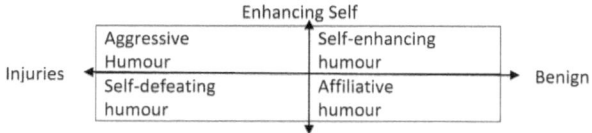

enhances self or relationship with others combined with the effect it has, be it injurious or benign. These styles have differential impact on psychological well-being and psychological functioning.

Affiliative humour: Individuals high in this dimension often use humour as a way to charm and amuse others, ease tension among others, and improve relationships. The goal is to create a sense of fellowship, happiness and well-being.

Individuals who report high levels of affiliative humour are more likely to initiate friendship. In an organizational setting, affiliate humour has been shown to increase group cohesiveness and promote creativity in the workplace. It is also associated with increased levels of self-esteem, well-being, emotional stability, and social intimacy. This style of humour is linked with decreased levels of depression and anxiety.

Aggressive humour: It is a style of humour that is potentially detrimental towards others. This involves put-downs insults, criticism or sarcasm targeted towards individuals. Prejudices such as racism and sexism are considered to be the aggressive styles of humour. This type of humour may at times seem like playful fun, but sometimes the underlying intent is to harm or belittle others.

Self-enhancing humour: This is being able to laugh at yourself, such as making a joke when something bad has happened to you. It entails trying to find the humour in everyday situations and making yourself the target of the humour in a good-natured way. It is related to healthy coping with stress. It is emotion-regulating humour in which individuals use humour to look on the bright side of a bad situation, find the silver lining or maintain a positive attitude even in trying times.

Self-defeating humour: It is the style of humour characterized by the use of potentially detrimental humour towards the self in order to gain approval from others. Psychologically, this can be an unhealthy form of humour. It is sometimes used by targets of bullies to try to avoid attacks – making oneself the buff of jokes before others put you down. Individuals who use this type of humour tend to have higher levels of neuroticism and lower levels of agreeableness and conscientiousness. Self-defeating humour is also associated with higher levels of anxiety, depression and psychiatric symptoms. It is also linked with lower levels of self-esteem, well-being and intimacy.

Considerable research has documented that the increased use of self-enhancing and affiliative humour can facilitate psychological well-being and enhance interpersonal relationships, whereas greater use of self-defeating and aggressive humour can be detrimental.

Humour in Daily Lives

Humour as a defense mechanism: A common response that serves as a defense mechanism. In serious situations humour is an attempt to protect the person from having to face an uncomfortable situation.

- Buffering effect on stress: Stressful experiences, especially those of a chronic nature, may contribute towards a variety of adverse health outcomes. A bulk of research has shown that humour could be a coping mechanism or moderator that lessons the impact of frequent stressors.
- Benefits of humour in workplace: Humour promotes both productivity and creativity in workplace. Companies such as Southwest Airlines have used humour and a positive fun culture to help brand their business, attract and retain employees and to attract customers.

Attitude of Gratitude

It is a truism that how you think --- about yourself, your world, and other people --- is more important to your well-being than the objective circumstances of your life. "The mind is its own place, and in itself Can make a Heaven of Hell, a Hell of Heaven", John Milton wrote in *Paradise Lost*. Philosophers, writers, and great grand-mothers of times past have long highlighted the benefits of positive thinking. While there are several ways to boost positive thinking, the expression of gratitude is an effective strategy for achieving well-being.

Gratitude is many things to many people. It is wonder: it is appreciation; it is looking at the brighter side of a setback; it is fathoming abundance; it is thanking someone in your life; it is thanking God; it is "**counting blessings**". The average person, however, probably associates gratitude with saying thank you for a gift or benefit received.

The world's most prominent researcher and writer about gratitude, Robert Emmons, defines it as "a felt sense of wonder, thankfulness, and appreciation for life". You feel grateful by noticing how fortunate your circumstances are. By definition, the practice of gratitude involves a focus on present moment, on appreciating your life as it is today and what has made it so.

Expressing gratitude is a lot more than saying thank you. Emerging research has recently shown multiple benefits. People who are consistently grateful have been found to be relatively happier, more energetic, and have more frequent positive emotions. They also tend to be more helpful and empathetic, more spiritual and religious, more forgiving and less materialistic than others who are less predisposed to gratefulness. Furthermore, the more a person is inclined to gratitude, the less likely he or she is to be depressed, anxious, lonely, envious and neurotic. All these research findings are correlational; we cannot know whether being grateful causes all these good benefits or possessing good things make people grateful.

In the very first set of studies, one group of participants was asked to write down five things for which they were thankful --- namely, to count their blessings --- and to do so once a week for ten weeks in a row. Other groups of participants were asked to think about other five daily hassles or five major events that occurred to them. The findings were exciting. Relative to the control group, those participants counting their blessings tended to feel more optimistic and more satisfied with their lives. Even their health received a boost; they reported fewer physical symptoms.

In another study the effect of strategy of counting one's blessing was investigated. Participants were asked to keep a sort of gratitude journal – to write down and contemplate five things for which they felt grateful. The exact instructions were as follows: "There are many things in our lives, both large and small, that we might be grateful about. Think back over the events of the past week and write down on the lines below up to five things that happened for which you are grateful or thankful". Five lines followed, headed by "This week I am grateful for".

The participants were engaged in this intervention over the course of six weeks. Half of the participants were instructed to do it once a week (every Sunday night), and half to do it three times a week (every Tuesday, Thursday, and Sunday). As expected, participants involved in intervention showed greater happiness than control group participants.

There are several explanations for positive effects of

counting blessings. First, grateful thinking promotes the memory and positive life experiences. By taking pleasure in some of the gifts of your life, you will be able to extract the maximum possible satisfaction and enjoyment from your current circumstances. Second, expressing gratitude bolsters self-worth and self-esteem. When you realize how much people have done for you or how much you have accomplished, you feel more confident and efficacious. Third, gratitude helps people cope with stress. Expressing gratefulness during personal adversity can help you adjust move on and perhaps begin anew. Fourth, the expression of gratitude encourages moral behaviours. Fifth, gratitude can help build social bonds, strengthening existing relationship and nurturing new ones. Sixth, expressing gratitude tends to inhibit insidious comparisons with others. Seventh, the practice of gratitude is incompatible with negative emotions and may actually diminish or deter such feeling as anger, bitterness and greed.

Practice of Gratitude

It is advisable to practice gratitude. There are several ways. People can choose a strategy that fits with their personality and attitude.

Gratitude journal: If you enjoy writing, choose a time of day when you have several minutes to step outside your life and reflect. It may be the first thing in the morning, or during lunch, or before bedtime. Ponder three to five things for which you are currently grateful. The events may range from the mundane (your TV set is fixed, your flowers are finally in bloom, your spouse got you a gift) to the magnificent experience (your children received awards).

Paths to gratitude: Some of you may not enjoy writing. You may contemplate. Choose one thing each day. You may think of a particular goal and try to recollect the help and assistance you have received in the context of this goal fulfillment. This strategy would help to count your blessings in an effective manner.

Keep the strategy fresh: If you have been practicing a strategy for a long time (say, writing the events), you may become bored with the routine and may cease to extract much meaning from it. You should now change the strategy. Talk to a friend, express gratitude through art (photography, wall magazines) you may purposefully vary the mode of communicating the gratitude messages.

Direct expression: Express gratitude directly to another. The use of phones, letters, emails and face-to-face communication is recommended. Express your appreciation in concrete terms. The target persons may be your parents, favorite uncle, or old friend, old coach, teacher or supervisor. Write him or her a letter now. If possible, visit and read the letter out loud in person, on either a special day (birthday, anniversary). Describe in detail what he or she has done for you and how it has influenced your life. Some people find it uplifting to write gratitude letters to individual whom they don't know personally.

Have you ever written letters of gratitude to your teachers/professors who have impacted your life in a significant way? Have you written letters of thankfulness to writers / poets who have made an impact on your taste and temperaments? Have you expressed gratitude to artists whose contributions you adore? *If you have not done it in the past, do it now.*

There are multiple ways to practice the strategy of gratitude, it would be wise to choose what works best for you. *Select atleast one option and give it a go.* When the strategy loses its freshness or meaningfulness, don't hesitate to make a change in how, when, and how often you express yourself.

Fostering Creativity

Marks of creativity are effective dividers between ages. A creative literary movement separates one period from the other in literature. A creative trend in painting leaves indelible marks for distinguishing one period from the other in art. The creative scientific achievement marks the beginning of a new era in science. Although historians use events as bases for labeling historical periods, they essentially choose events that have characteristics of creativity.

Although creativity is seminal, it has not received research attention proportional to its utility in our lives. It was only J.P. Guilford (1950) who made a fervent appeal for research on creativity. In 1950, Guilford was elected as the President of the American Psychological Association and his presidential address was titled *creativity*. In fact, his research article provided impetus to subsequent works on the problem of creativity.

Guilford's (1950) early work served two important purposes. First, it provided an operational definition of creativity. Second, it explicated the process nature of creativity by specifying interactive components such as content, process and the product. Guilford received the American Psychological Association's Distinguished Contribution Award for his seminal work.

It is generally agreed that creative products are novel and useful. It is novel in the sense that it is original. Since original or novel products are not ordinarily expected, these products generate surprisingness. However, all unusual and uncommon products are not considered creative. The products must be having utility factor. The delirium of a madman may be uncommon, but it is not regarded as a creative product.

In addition to originality, the other indices of creativity were also identified. These include fluency, flexibility and elaboration. These parameters are explicit when specific tests of creativity are considered. A classic illustration involves Guilford's Usual Unusual Test. The test requires individuals to indicate multiple uses of an usual thing. When used for children, the test requires children to indicate several ways of using a piece of brick. In this case, the child may provide such an answer: brick can be used to construct a house, a temple, a store, an office and a school. However, another child may offer a different answer; brick can be used to construct a house: brick can be used as a paper weight: brick can be used to write something on a wall; brick can be used to drive away a cat: brick can be used as a door block.

The analysis of the responses of these two children reveals the difference. Fluency refers to the amount of ideas generated per unit time. Since both of these children have produced five ideas, each should get the credit of 5 marks for fluency. Flexibility defines the number of thought categories. The first child has produced ideas that belong to the single category of "construction". On the contrary, the second child has offered ideas belonging to five separate categories. Consequently, the first child is entitled to a score of 1 whereas the second child is entitled to a score of 5 with respect to flexibility. Originality is not difficult to quantity. If a large number of children are asked the same question, the statistical computation can be made with respect to the unusualness of a particular response. Greater is the unusualness, higher is the originality score. The creativity indices (**fluency, flexibility and originality**) produce test scores separately; these scores can be summed to generate an overall creativity score. In many domains such as science and literature, the person has to elaborate the creative ideas produced. The elaboration gives out implication and inputs for evaluation.

A representative sample of tests of creativity are likely to offer ideas that are helpful for evaluating the psychometric approach. One such test involves Flanagan's Ingenuity Test. This requires subjects to offer insightful solutions for certain social problems. Guilford's Consequences Test is also an oft-used measure. It requires respondents to imagine the consequences of some unusual happenings. Children may be asked to indicate consequences in the context of several hypothetical situations. They are asked to tell what would happen if schools have wheels. What would happen if lions could speak? What would happen if humans would not require food? What would happen if birds could talk? Getzels and Jackson suggested a test called Fable Ending. Children are asked to read an incomplete fable. They are asked to complete it by adding themes. The analysis of the inclusion reveals creativity of children. Similarly, the Plot Title Test requires children to provide a title for a short story. Torrance popularized Project Improvement Test. Children are given a material such as a toy car. They are asked to improvise it. All these tests generate responses that can be scored in terms of fluency, flexibility and originality.

During the 1950s and 1960s, the basic approach in the field of creativity was essentially a psychometric orientation. Children and adults were tested on creativity and creative individuals were identified. The objective of such measurements was to identify the creative individuals and to expose then to creativity training programme.

The creativity training programmes essentially involve the stimulation of divergent thinking. It was postulated that divergent thinking is the process variable in creativity. As has been illustrated, the child indicating the flexibility of thought responds divergently. On the contrary the child replying in terms of a single thought category such as constructing a house and a constructing a school gives evidence of convergent thinking. Since divergent thinking was thought to underlie the creative process, the training programmes gravitated towards the development of divergent thinking style.

Training for Creativity

During war periods, a number of psychologists attempted to formulate specific training programme that would stimulate creativity. Osborn (1963) devised and popularized a method called *brainstorming*. It was argued that the method of brainstorming would be very helpful in stimulating creativity in individuals. It would provide a situation where individuals should be prompted to generate creative solutions. The method is basically used in a group context. A problem is posed and individuals are encouraged to generate solutions. The process consists of two sequential stages: green light stage and red light stage.

The first phase of the brainstorming is labeled green light stage. This is an evaluation-free stage where participating individuals are encouraged to suggest all possible solutions. Assurances are given that no answer would be subjected to criticism and evaluation. People should present as many solutions as possible. They should not be hesitant to offer remote and far-fetched solutions. For instance, children may be asked to suggest the method of preparing a cup of tea. A child may offer a very unusual answer in terms of pouring the milk from the roof top. The child may add that a pot placed on the stove on the ground would prepare the tea. Apparently this solution is a ridicules one. However, the climate of the training session is shaped in such a fashion that the solutions are not rejected at the first instance. It is called brainstorming because there is total freedom on the expression of the thoughts that are crowding a participant's mind.

However, the brainstorming slowly switches over to a second phase called red light stage. All the solutions are considered one by one. Solutions are evaluated in terms of certain specific criteria such as desirability and feasibility. Naturally the quality solutions are identified and selected.

The past research has shown that brainstorming is successful in inculcating creative orientation in participants. The method has been extensively used in decision making sessions of managers in organization. This has also been used to stimulate creativity in children. Sometimes, the criticism is leveled that some participants may feel hesitant to express their ideas because of the contradictory solution offered by their revered persons. With a view to getting around this problem, the modern practice is to use *electronic brainstorming.* In electronic brainstorming each of the participants is provided with a computer terminal where he or she enters his or her ideas. Since the ideas are simultaneously pooled, there is no apprehension that a person's response would inhibit another individual. However, the red light stage evaluates all the solutions generated in this process.

Another training method is based on the similar concept of analogical thinking which is considered central to the creative process. The divergent thinking has sometimes been termed *remote association.* Poincare, the celebrated nuclear mathematician, remarks that creativity is a process of establishing intimacy between two or more strange ideas. In other words, a creative person discovers some form of similarity between two or more dissimilar ideas or objects.

With this rationale, the **method of** *synectics* is used. This method encourages participants to imagine similarity between themselves and some other objects. For instance, participants are encouraged to contemplate similarities with other objects and living beings. It may take the form of *direct analogy*. The person is encouraged to imagine similarities between two or more apparently different objects or animals. Graham Bell, the inventor of telephone, thought of the similarity between the membrane in the inner ear and wire. He reasoned that if the soft membrane could cause vibration in the bone, it would be possible for the wire to cause vibration producing sound. This gave rise to the invention of Bell's telephone system.

Another form of analogy involves *personal analogy*. The participants in synectics are asked to imagine themselves as other objects or living beings. It is important to indicate that the chemist Kekule was pondering over the molecular structure of Benzine. He dreamt of a snake holding it's tall in its mouth. This was helpful in solving his problem.

Similarity, participants are trained to develop *biological analogy*. They are asked to imagine themselves as different parts of a human body. They may also be asked to imagine themselves as other living beings or any limb of other beings. Thus, people are trained to stretch their imagination, shed inhibitions and use *fantasy*. It is assumed that an extended use of analogical *thinking* paves the way for creative process.

More recently, Sternberg and his associates have

popularized another technique called *"thinking hats"*. In the training session, hats of different colours are used. The entire group is randomly divided into a small number of subgroups. Members of each subgroup put on caps of a particular colour. Then a problem is presented. Members wearing blue hats are asked to solve the problem by analytical method whereas members wearing red hats are asked to solve it by employing synthetic method. In essence, different groups are asked to solve problem by using different methods. Following the solution of the problem, hats are exchanged. Now a subgroup attempts solution by using different procedure. Thus, participants are trained to free themselves from the fixed pattern of problem solving style (Sternberg & Lubart, 1996).

The Creative Process

Although these training methods have varied degree of success, a better understanding of creativity involves the analysis of creative process. As pointed out earlier, many psychologists have stressed **divergent thinking** in creative process. The divergent thinking is exemplified by a child's divergent answer to the question. How can you use a piece of brick? The answer in terms of using the brick to build a house, to write something on the wall, to use it as a paperweight, and so on. It is indicative of divergent thought, as thought categories do not converge on a single point. However, emphasis on divergent thinking raises a fundamental question. Is convergent thinking unrelated to creative process?

Kuhn (1966) offers an interesting answer Kuhn was originally a physicist, but later developed interest in the study of the history of behavioural and social sciences. His study gave him an insight. His concept of *paradigm crisis* has become a standard reference in the philosophy of science. He observed that it is unlikely to meet Mr. Novelty if a person makes random wanderings. It is better to concentrate on normative practices and methods initially. If a person follows established practices and methods, it is also likely that some deviate cases would be encountered. It the person considers this deviate case seriously; novel method and product would emerge.

Kuhn (1966) offers several examples. For instance, at one point of time people considered the shape of the earth as a flat surface. They were carrying out navigation. Things were going well till a point when their computation decided one destination, but they actually arrived in a different place. This generated what Kuhn calls *essential tension*. The paradigm crisis causes tension and the solution leads to *paradigm shift*. Kuhn adds that paradigm crisis and its resulting paradigm shift have brought about major breakthrough in scientific and creative thought. In this process Kepler was outdated by Newton; Newton's laws were again eclipsed by laws of quantum-physics. Newton's laws were fine so far as objects were concerned. But these were rendered inapplicable when subatomic particles were thought upon.

In other words, Kuhn stressed the cycle of convergent and divergent thought process. Initially convergent thinking may be necessary. But an encounter with a deviate case needs to trigger divergent thinking. Fleming's invention of penicillin is an exemplary case. Fleming was conducting bacteria culture. One-day Fleming observed that all the bacteria's on the pot had been destroyed and there was fungus formation. Ordinarily Fleming would have dismissed the case with the consideration that it was a faulty experimentation. He would have repeated the experiment again. But Fleming pondered over the cause of fungus formation. This gave rise to the invention of life-saving drug of penicillin. Thus, convergent and divergent skills seem to be necessary at different phases.

Phases of Creative Process

In order to specify phases where divergent thinking is preferable to convergent thinking, psychologists have conceptualized *four stages* of creative thinking. These include: preparation, exploration, incubation, and evaluation.

Preparation: The first stage of creative process is designated as the preparation. The individual sets his or her goal and arranges preliminary materials irrespective of the domain of creativity, the person has to have goal clarity. Scientists must know what they are looking for. At this stage convergent thinking is helpful. The convergent thinking is known as vertical thinking. It is comparable to the process of digging a specific place intensively, whereas divergent thinking is comparable to the activity of digging several places. Needless to say, convergent thinking is effective in delineating the main goal and specific subgoals. The problem must be properly identified.

Exploration: During the phase of exploration, the creative activity takes a different form. An active exploration reflects divergent thinking. In this phase, there are two important characteristics. First, there is a remarkable difference between a coping personality and a creative personality. For solution of the problem at hand, individuals with creative personalities search for alternatives by making use of divergent thinking. However, copers select alternative on the basis of learning experience. They select the alternatives that have been rewarded in the past. The creative person, on the other hand, selects alternatives on the basis of novelty and surprisingness. The unusual and original alternatives that are likely to generate surprisingness are selected. Thus, a poet selects diction that would surprise readers. A painter selects the colour that would move a critic. It is important to recognize that an intense form of divergent thinking facilitates successful exploration.

Incubation: This is a period of no apparent overt activity. It is quite possible that the artist or the scientist is either unable to solve the problem or he/she is not fully satisfied with the obtained outcome. The task remains unfinished. In such situation, they abandon the search process temporarily and get themselves engaged with other pursuits.

Although this is a period of no overt activity in the domain of specific creative area, it cannot be designated as a period of vacuum. In the absence of conscious efforts, the person incubates and continues with it at the subconscious and unconscious levels. While they are busy in performing their day-to-day activity, the latent thought content is centered on problem solution. In a number of cases, the solution is achieved during this incubation period.

Everyone is familiar with the case of Archimedes who got the insight while taking bath in his home. His euphoric Eureka (I have got it) is a vivid illustration of problem-solving in an incubation phase. Recently the world-famous mathematician, Poincare, has indicated an evidence. Despite much effort, he could not solve a mathematical function. Then he gave up and went on a geological tour. As he was getting into a bus during his tour, the geometric pattern of the climbing steps gave him an instant insight. He came home and solved the problem.

Many creative persons have stressed the role of unconscious process in creativity. They have explicated as to how certain novel and bright ideas surfaced during a dreamlike state. Poet S. T. Coleridge speaks of his composition of the famous poem *Kubla Khan*. The three hundred line poem took its form when he was asleep.

Evaluation: The last and fourth stage of creative process is designated evaluation. Having solved the problem, creative persons elaborate the ideas. They think about its implications. More importantly, they evaluate the creative product prior to its dissemination. A poet reads out his poem before his or her spouse, close relatives, intimate associates, and a few chosen readers. The poet also considers possible reception at the end of critics. Needless to say, this process of examination and evaluation entails convergent thinking.

Thus, the analysis of the creative process is linked with stages of creativity. It is clearly shown that creative process requires the cycle of convergent-divergent-convergent thought process. The preparation starts with convergent thinking whereas exploration is based on divergent thinking. Convergent thinking is again repeated at the evaluation phase. Compared to scientific creativity, the cycle has to be repeated a greater number of times in artistic and literary creativity.

Relevant Factors

During the creative process, the relevance of certain specific factors has been identified. Creative persons have spoken about the role of inspiration in their work. The Greek poets describe how divinity inspired them to write poems. Indian poets in the past have admitted the role of divine inspiration. British poet Blake spoke of many mystical experiences in his life. It is quite plausible that the justification of inspiration is surely a manifestation of their *self-motivation.*

Contemporary research on creativity clearly redefines "talent" Renzuli offers a graphic description. According to Renzulli, there are three clusters (motivation, intelligence, and creativity) which overlap each other. This pictorial representation depicts several types. Some people have only one of these three attributes.

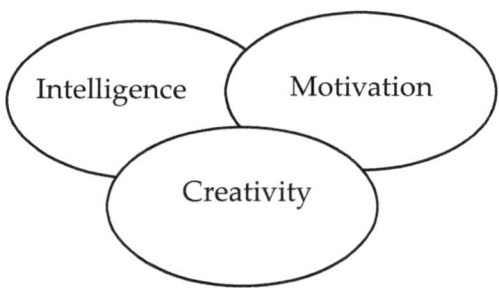

For instance, they may have creativity but it is devoid of motivation and intelligence. Without motivation, it does not last for long; without intelligence, it does not reach high level. Similarly we would expect people who have two of these attributes. For example, with intelligence and creativity, people can generate creative idea, but the lack of hard work does not give it a tangible form. On the contrary, a small number of people possess all these three attributes. Needless to say, their motivation, intelligence and creative ability bring out the creative products on a lasting and tangible manner.

At this point, it is logical to comment on the relationship between intelligence and creativity. Empirical studies examining this relationship has indicated low positive correlation between the two. It implies that all creative individuals have moderate to high intelligence. But all intelligent persons are not creative. It appears that intelligence functions as a threshold for creative activity, but it does not predict creativity beyond certain level.

More recently, the significance of emotional intelligence has been highlighted. Of course, the role of self-motivation implicitly signals the value of emotional intelligence. The word "emotion" is also derived from the fact that it enhances motion (motivation). It appears plausible that emotion in general and emotional intelligence in particular accelerates the creative process. This view is consistent with the contemporary recognition that human brain has two distinct structures "feeling brain" and "thinking brain". Furthermore, from evolutionary point of view, feeling brain is older than the thinking brain (Goleman, 1995).

The Theoretical Position

In view of these recent evidence relating to creative process, contemporary theorists offer a component analysis of creative process. Major components of creative process include domain-relevant skills, the creativity-related process and intrinsic task-relevant involvement. The domain-relevant skills, according to this component analysis, comprise cognitions and abilities which Guilford termed talent in 1958. Included are also acquired learning and skills. Finally, the intrinsic task-relevant motivation is characterized by interest, enjoyment, satisfaction and challenge of the work. Although creative persons are motivated by external reward conditions such as prizes and recognition during the preparatory phase (first ten/fifteen years), these external awards lose importance for them as they advance.

Sternberg uses another expression *resources theory*

for the components of creativity. Sternberg lists cognitive resources, motivational resources and environmental resources. In component analysis, the creativity-relevant process includes not only intra-individual factors such as personality and work habits it also includes extra-individual factors such as social environment.

Sternberg has further specified the components in a new rubric termed *confluence theory*. Creativity is a confluence of six basic elements such as intelligence, cognitions, personality, thinking style, intrinsic motivation and supportive environment. Although a common man with some of these resources can exhibit mundane creativity – the kind of creativity we come across day-to-day life – these resources are needed for *exceptional creativity*. Similarly, some creative persons exhibit creativity within the normative practices of the society. This is boundary-touching creativity. On the contrary, a few other creative persons present products which contradict existing norms. This is called *boundary breaking creativity*.

The Creative Person

A comprehensive understanding of the creative process is incomplete without explication of person-relevant factors. In the past, the research on creativity basically adopted psychometric methods. Children and persons were classified into creative and non-creative on the basis of standardized test scores; comparison of groups revealed certain information. However, a more dynamic method called *evolving system approach* (ESA) has been adopted during last two decades. This system involves an intensive study of the life histories and life span development of creative personalities. In this process, the personal notes, writings, diaries, and activities of creative scientists like Darwin, Linus Pauling and Thomas Young have been examined. Similarly, observations have been made with respect to the noted authors like John Irving and Donaldson and Painter Monet. The ESA method has provided wealthful information.

The person variables associated with the creative process include studies of intelligence, cognitive style, personality, psychopathology and development spurts.

Intelligence: Many investigators have been interested in the extent to which creativity requires superior intelligence. Using performance on standard IQ tests as the gauge of intellectual capacity, the early research indicated that a certain threshold-level of intelligence was required for the manifestation of creativity, but that beyond that threshold, intelligence bore a minimal relation with creative behavior. As pointed out earlier, Renzulli's concept of three overlapping clusters of abilities (creative ability, motivational ability and intellectual ability) provides a better conceptualization of creative person. A creative person, in this scheme, is considered as one having all three clusters of abilities whereas other persons do possess none of these abilities, or two of these abilities or one of these abilities. More critical is the realization that simplistic, exclusive and unidimensional concept of intelligence is to be replaced by a more complex, inclusive and multidimensional constructs. Examples are Guilford's structure of intellect model, Sternberg's triatchic theory of intelligence, and Gardener's multiple theory of intelligence. The last theory is especially provocative in the sense that it includes abilities which are not a part of standard psychometric tests (e.g., musical, bodily-kinesthetic, interpersonal and intrapersonal intelligence). Moreover, each intelligence is associated with a specific manifestation of creativity, such as painting, choreography or psychology.

Cognitive Style: As indicated earlier, creativity involves analogical thinking. Sometimes this is called "remote association". Studies using evolving system approach offer some useful information regarding the evolution of creative product. For instance, a close examination of writings of Stephen Donaldson suggests a geneplore model of relative cognition.

According to this model, the creative person explores and generates a large number of ideas. Some ideas take the form of candidates for creative work. This "preinventive form" is used for further exploration. While screening preinventive types, the person adopts the criteria of novelty, surprisingness, and aesthetics. This is followed by a process of combinations. Combinations generate new cognitions. The convergence of discrepant ideas become the hallmark of creativity.

Creative-ideas can always be analyzed into perception of an analogy between old ideas, previously thought to be strangers to one another. Thus, capacity for analogical thinking is necessary for creative inspiration. Thomas Young, the noted physicist, linguist and psychologist, propounded his wave theory of light on the basis of this insightful observation of waves of water. Darwin's constant use of the metaphor of "tree of life" reflects his analogical thinking in conceptualizing multilinear evolution of living organisms. However, the insightful problem solving, and analogical thinking styles are product of the interaction between creative persons and supportive environment. Although there is some evidence of innate cognitions, expertise acquisition has been clearly shown in the evolving system approach.

Personality: Many researchers have attempted to generate personality profile of a creative person. The first and foremost is the habit of hard work. Edison categorically asserted "Genius is ninety-nine per cent perspiration, only one-percent inspiration". More recently, the noted American novelist, John Irving has said that seven-eighth portion of his success is a product of hard work, one-eighth a product of inspiration. During formative years of creative work, the creative persons spend almost ten hours a day.

The other personality traits include high self-confidence, autonomy and independence, wide range of interests, love of novelty and distaste for traditional dogmas, greater openness to new experiences, a more conspicuous behavioural and cognitive flexibility, risk-taking behaviour. Particularly interesting is what the research has concluded to the longstanding "mad-genius" controversy. These is now significant evidence showing that creativity tends to be associated with certain amount of psychopathology. At the same time, this association is not equivalent to the claim that creative individuals must necessarily suffer from mental disorders. On the contrary, research has shown that (a) numerous creators have no apparent tendencies towards psychopathology, (b) the incidence varies according to the domain of creative activity, (c) many creators who seemingly exhibit disorders possess compensatory characteristics that enable them to control and sublimate abnormality, and (d) some apparent disorders may be quite adaptive to the creative process in the life of the creators.

Life Span Development. Developmental psychologists have examined longitudinal transformation in creative persons. Broadly, two issues have been addressed. The first one involves the study of early experiences during childhood and adolescence. The second one involves the actualization of creative potential during adulthood and later years.

It has been shown that certain elements of early years influence creative potential. The birth order, parental loss, marginality and challenging experiences are important ones. An interesting finding in this context shows that creativity does not spring from the highly nurturing home. Rather diversity of experiences, challenging situations and adversity generate perseverance and resilience in creative children. These difficulties trigger efforts to master the environment.

The actualization of creative potential has been studied from developmental perspective. Psychologists have considered creativity as a function of age during adult and old age. Previous research indicated a curvilinear (inverted backward) function. This implies that creativity declines during old age. However, recent evidence does not fully support this conclusion. It is likely that elderly and old people use several compensatory mechanisms. The continuation of vigorous activity may prevent the decline of creative process. The possibility of resurgence of creativity during old age presents an optimistic picture. Furthermore, cognitive aging for Indian population seems to be slower. Although there is no empirical study to show the age-wise creativity in Indian context, the existing hunch favours an optimistic view of elderly persons' creative spurts.

The discussion on creative process entails the role of socio-cultural milieu in which creative persons grow, blossom and disseminate their contributions.

The Creative Environment

The original research on creativity tended to adopt

an exclusively intra-individualistic perspective. Creativity was viewed as a process that took place in the mind of a single individual who possesses the appropriate personal characteristics and developmental experiences. Beginning in the 1970s, more psychologists began to recognize that creativity takes place in a social context. These investigators have looked into the diversity of external conditions including interpersonal environment and disciplinary environment.

Interpersonal Environment: Although there has long existed the popular image of the lone genius, it is clear that much creativity takes place in interpersonal setting. The particular nature of the interpersonal experiences may serve to either enhance or inhibit the amount of creativity shown by the individual. A good illustration of the possibilities may be found in the research of Amabile (1983) and her associates on the repercussions of rewards, evaluations, surveillance, and other circumstances. Particularly, valuable is the impact of intrinsic and extrinsic incentives for performing a task. Creativity usually appears more favoured when individuals perform a task for internal enjoyment. However, rewards and external incentives may be useful at times especially during initial phase of creative work.

Disciplinary Environment: Most creators do not function in isolation. Creativity requires dynamic interaction between three sub-systems, one of which entails the individual creator. The second subsystem is the domain which consists of the set of rules, the repertoire of techniques, and any other abstract attribute that define a particular mode of creativity. The third sub-system is the field, which consists of those persons who work within the same domain, and thus have their creativity governed by the same domain-specific guidelines. These colleagues are essential to the realization of individual creativity, according to systems view. It is because creativity does not exist, until those making up the field declare that the work represents an original contribution.

Sociocultural Environment: The larger sociocultural environment influences the process of creativity. It has become increasingly clear that certain political environment affects the degree of creativity manifested by the corresponding population. Some of these political influences operate directly on the adult creators, such as when workforce depresses the output. Other political effects function during the developmental stage of an individual's life, either encouraging or discouraging the creative potential. Many nations have experienced golden ages after winning independence from foreign rule with ancient Greece providing a classic example. It is plausible that nationalistic rebellion encourages cultural heterogeneity rather than homogeneity. Cultural diversity seems to facilitate creative process. However, analysis of the sociocultural milieu is only part of the story. For example, the general milieu may explain why the Renaissance began in Italy, but it cannot explain why Michelangelo towered over his Italian contemporaries.

Conclusion

Psychologists have registered tremendous progress in the understanding of creative process. The initial notions in the 1950s and 1960s were centered on the intra-individual processes. Following a lull in the 1970s, research in the 1980s, or 1999s have identified many relevant factors and has stressed interactive position. Furthermore, evolving system approach has offered many insights that were not available by using only psychometric method. However, a number of issues remain unattended. It seems logical that creativity research requires techniques that are really "creative".

Chapter 6

Environmental Boosters

The promotion of health and happiness is not a solo activity. It requires as much as environmental support as it needs individual initiative and efforts. The pursuit of religion and spirituality, the mindset of generating flow experience, personal habits of savouring, attitude of expressing gratitude, temperament of humour and the cultivation of creativity require individual attention and involvement. These elements within the individual amplify the possibility of health and happiness. Yet, certain environmental boosters take these possibilities forward. These boosters include physical activity and exercise, social relation, leisure pursuits, and positive life events.

Physical Activity and Exercise

It is a common observation that most of our health-related threats come from lifestyle diseases. As reported by Marks, Murray, and Estacio (2018), the World Health

Organization (2004) has identified the decreasing level of physical activity as a major cause of death and chronic diseases worldwide. WHO also identifies the following diseases stemming from physical inactivity: cardiovascular disease, colon cancer, Type 2 diabetes, stroke and breast cancer. Conversely greater amount of physical activity is associated with greater levels of health.

The relationship between physical health and psychological well-being is reciprocal (Diener & Seligman, 2004). Improved physical health enhances psychological well-being; higher levels of psychological well-being leverage a wider network of physical activity. One meta-analytic review found significant correlation ($r = 0.30$) between *self-reported health* and well-being (Okun, Stock, Haring, & Witter, 1894). However, when researchers obtained *objective measures* of physical health, such as doctors' report, the correlation between physical health and well-being dropped. In Okun and colleagues' study, the correlation dropped from .30 to .16. Other studies affirm this finding (Brief, Bucher, George & Link, 1993).

The lower correlation between physical health and well-being may also indicate the subjective nature of people's assessment. People with poor physical health, as defined by doctors and medical professionals, may subjectively feel happy. Furthermore, people encountering illness and negative health conditions may also adapt. However, if the illness and negative health condition is very acute and chronic, adaptation may not be pronounced. Despite these confounding variables, the positive association between physical activity and well-being is significant.

Exercise

Exercise is a major form of planned physical activity. The short-term exercise induces positive mood states and long-term regular exercise leads to greater happiness (Argyle, 2001). The short-term exercise leads to the release of endorphins, morphine-like chemical substance produced in the brain. The long-term exercise reduces depression and anxiety, enhances the speed and accuracy of work, improves self-concept, promotes fitness and improves cardiovascular functioning. In addition, regular exercise, in the company of others, promotes social contact and relationship.

Lyubomirsky (2007) cites an experimental study published in the Archives in Internal Medicine in 1999. The researchers recruited men and women fifty years old and over. All of them were suffering from depression. They were randomly divided into three groups. The first group was assigned to four months of aerobic exercise. The second group was assigned to four months of anti-depressant medication (Zoloft). The third group was assigned to both arrangements. The assigned exercise involved three supervised forty-five-minute sessions for week of cycling or walking/ jogging at moderate to high intensity. At the end of four-month intervention, all three groups reported their depression down, experienced less dysfunctional symptoms and showed increased happiness and self-esteem. Interestingly exercise was as effective as medication. In addition, the exercise programme was less expensive; the participants did not have any apprehension of side-effects. The study was termed the Standard Medical Intervention and Long-term Exercise study, SMILE.

The proverbial feel-good component of exercise is well-known. But the finding that the psychological benefits of physical activity could effectively work as medicines in reducing depression, anxiety and stress was quite surprising. The SMILE study stimulated similar investigation for other samples.

Thayer (1989) found that a 10-minute brisk walk resulted in less tiredness, more energy and less tension 2 hours later. Other studies found that after an hour's exercise, such as aerobics, those involved felt less tense, depressed, angry, tired or confused. Regular exercise, such as four times a week, for 10 weeks, has produced more enduring positive states. Steptoe (1998) found an effect for solitary exercise. Hills and Argyle (1998) found that those who were members of sports clubs had higher scores on the Oxford Happiness Inventory than those who did not belong to sport clubs.

In a study, Klein, Greist, Guttman (1985) allocated 74 depressed persons to 12 weeks of either running, group therapy or meditation. Nine months later all had improved the same amount. In another study, they found that counselling and running had more effect than counselling alone. A number of such studies have shown clearly that exercise is good for depression, that the results last for at least a year, and that this is as good as counselling or psychotherapy, for the less severe cases at least. Many doctors and psychiatrists are now prescribing exercise for their depressed patients, though these may be a problem in persuading them to do so.

Mediating mechanisms: There are several explanations for activity-happiness linkage. First, regular exercise programmes boost self-esteem and self-efficacy. People taking up sports and games perceive themselves as capable individuals. The perceived capability brings positive feelings. Second, the habit of physical activity offers potential for flow. It also provides distraction from worries and ruminations. It essentially serves as a time-out from stressful events of everyday life. Many people are inclined to compare the benefits of exercise with those of meditation. Researchers have also compared the benefits and found similar results. Both the processes show identical effects. Interestingly the processes are different. Exercise and physical activities produce high-arousal emotions such as vigour, energy and enthusiasm. In contrast, meditation induce low-arousal emotions such as calm, serenity and peace. Yet the results are identical.

It is also important to recognize that physical activity performed with others promotes social contact. It bolsters social support and friendship networks. Thus, the feel-good component of physical activity has both physiological and psychological effects. Physiologically it improves physical fitness including cardiovascular health. It has been shown to elevate serotonin levels, similar to the effects of anti-depressant, Prozac. Psychological effects are of two types: short-term and long-term. Certain positive effects are experienced after a relatively short time interval. Other psychological benefits are more enduring and they induce positive effects across extended lifespan.

Exercise experts have advised to calculate one's maximum heart rate (most simply defined as 220 minus one's age) and work out at a level between 65 and 80 percent of that figure. It is advisable to start aerobic exercise within that range.

Related Activities

Alternate forms: There is increasing challenge to the dominance of the functional approaches to promoting physical activity with its attendant emphasis on physical health. Alternative strategies consider such issues as the more social, emotional and aesthetic aspects of physical activity. Three such alternative forms are dance, walking groups and lifestyle sports.

Dance is a very non-intrusive means of promoting physical activity. India has a long-standing heritage of maintaining and promoting various forms of classical dance as well as folk forms. It is attractive to men and women from different social backgrounds. Apart from the cultural and aesthetics value of various dance forms, its contribution for physical fitness is immense. It is gradually becoming popular especially for younger people.

Walking especially in natural, semi-rural, or rural setting, can be both physically and mentally rewarding. Researchers term it *"healing balm effect"*. The walking group induces positive feelings. This is a preferable form for the elderly.

Lifestyle sports are activities that can be planned in tune with the climate, culture and interest. It is difficult to list such activities. For example, there would be wide variation across climate zones (winter games vs summer games). Many of these sports are frequently termed *extreme sports*, these are especially popular among young people. Interview with young people taking up these sports maintain that these sports offer them a flow-like experience.

Social Capital

It is a great paradox that both happiness and headache have their origins in relationship. Social relationship is perhaps the greatest single cause of happiness and other aspects of well-being. When managed well, relationship builds social capital that enriches individual and collective life. In contrast, troubled relationship generates threats and challenges for well-functioning life. While David Myers (1992) refers to the contribution of relationship to health and happiness a deep truth, the celebrated philosophers Jean-Paul Sarte observes: "Hell is other people".

Despite bivariate dimensions (positive and negative) of interpersonal relationships, the importance of relationship has been recognized by psychologists and nonpsychologists. Further to Aristotle's remark, that man is a social animal, evolutionary psychologists have greatly stressed the human bondage (Buss, 2000). Social bonds are needed for boosting our survival chances. Human babies take long time to grow independent; they need the protection from their caregivers. Adults form attachments and these attachments provide mates, offer security for daily living, give assistance for hunting and other livelihood, and arrange togetherness for joy. In-fact, different forms of social and cultural functions are reinstatement of this social bonding.

At an empirical level, psychologists have observed the saliency of relationship as perceived by human groups. People typically list close relationship as one of the most important life goals and a primary source of life satisfaction. In one study 75% of college students expressed that they were willing to forego another important life goal (e.g., career, higher education) in exchange of a satisfying romantic relationship. Similarly, most people point to relationship as a preferred choice in the context of "**deathbed test**" (In the last moment of your life what would you like to have?). The value of close relationship is one of life's most important needs. Baumeister and Leary (1995) provide an extensive review of this human need of belongingness. They describe it "as a pervasive drive to form and maintain quality of lasting, positive, and significant interpersonal relationship" (P. 497).

Recent evidence from neuroscientists has identified the causal pathways relevant to love and affiliation. It appears that evolution has provided an in-built mechanism within human body to mediate connectivity. **Oxytocin** is a pituitary hormone that has physiological and psychological effects. It destresses the organism; hence psychologists label it as a "cuddle hormone". There is copious flow of oxytocin in mother's body when the mother breast feeds the baby. Secretion of oxytocin is also evinced during sexual union, pleasant interaction and even during mutual appreciation. Obviously close physical contacts such as touching, hugging and kissing stimulate its release. Oxytocin is responsible for the release of milk in nursing mothers. The calm emotional state and feeling of safety are the resulting outcomes. These findings indicate that evolution has provided a biological foundation for developing and maintaining good interpersonal relationship (Reis & Gable, 2003)

Theories of human motivation and development typically present some sort of innate process by which people seek to establish and maintain connectivity with others. In addition to Baumeister and Leary's (1995) "need to belong", Deci and Ryan (1985) proposed a need for relatedness. According to Deci and Ryan's "Self-Determination Theory (SDT)", autonomy competence and relatedness are the three most important motivations in human functioning. They further posit that the satisfaction of these three needs predict daily fluctuations in affective well-being, but relatedness is specifically associated only with positive affect, not with negative affect.

Parameters of Closeness

A number of researchers argue that relationships are intrinsically positive. What sort of interactions produce feelings of relatedness? Reis, Collins, and Berscheid (2000) asked participants to describe the extent to which their three longest interactions of each day involved seven different types of social activity. Feelings understood and appreciated was the strongest predictor of relatedness (Reis, 1990).

Intimacy theory identifies several parameters that are relevant to feeling close. These include revealing central aspects of the self, genuine concern for the other, interdependence (mutual influence), a sense of "we-ness", and commitment (intention to stay in the relationship through its ups and downs). The theory includes both affective and cognitive components.

Among people's diverse social goals, intimacy tends to have high priority across the lifespan. From early adolescence on, people selectively choose friends and limit it to a selected few. The choices are patterned in terms of the match between their own goals and the goals of their selected friend(s).

In one study (Gable, 2000), married couples were asked to keep diaries indicating positive and negative behaviours they have received and enacted towards their partners. They also noted whether their partners had enacted the same towards them (expression of love / criticism). They also described their feeling on the day. The results showed that positive and negative interactions made independent contributions.

Aversive Dimension

Relationships are people's most frequent sources of both happiness and distress. People treat happiness and distress in relationship as opposing outcomes on a bipolar scale (happiness is simply the absence of distress and distress is absence of happiness). However, current research posits that positive and negative processes in relationships are functionally independent; these are not opposite of each other.

The fundamental distinction concerns rewarding (positive and desired) and punishing (negative and unwelcome) aspects of social environment. Technically researchers refer to these dimensions as **appetite** and **aversion**.

The fundamental question concerns: Is bad stronger than good? Relationship scientists have long been concerned with the relative impact of positive and negative factors. Once a relationship has been formed **conflict** is the most important potential factor affecting satisfaction in relationship and ultimately its course. There has been strong evidence in favour of negativity bias. Gottman's series of studies have identified negative affect reciprocity as an indicator of marital dysfunction.

In a series of field studies, Gottman and Silver (1999) made arrangements for recording and videotaping day-to-day conversations of family members. They took participants' consent and recorded live-in communication for an extended period of time. The major objective was to assess the impact of positive and negative communications. The couples discussed difficult issues, argued, solved problems and generated inferences. The participants also had discussions with their children. The effects were analyzed quantitatively and qualitatively.

The findings were highly interesting. The results clearly showed negativity bias; the negative had stronger impact compared with the positives. The question can be addressed differently: How many positives would neutralize a single negative? **Gottman's proportion was 1:5**. For example, if a partner makes one negative comment and it produces damaging effect, then the same partner has to offer *five* positive comments to neutralize the bad effect. In other words, Gottman advises the principle of **capitalization**.

In order to build and promote positive relation, we have to impart more and more positive communication (appreciation, acknowledgement). According to Gottman and his associates, this principle of capitalization (building our live on the foundation of positives) is essential for satisfying life in general and sustainable marriages in particular.

Later researchers have studied the issue of this golden ratio: What would be the limit on capitalization. Should we go on imparting the positives without any limit. Barbara Fredrickson has generated a rule: Good is good within a limit. The upper limit on this golden ratio is suggested at 1:11 (Fredrickson & Losada, 2005).

Friendship

Friendship is a major source of joy. Larson (1990) carried out a study in which participants were bleeped on random occasions and asked to report their mood. The results showed that they were in the most positive mood when they were with friends, followed by family and being alone. Some of these friends may have been of the opposite sex. The benefit is not limited to adolescents, but also for older populations.

The benefits of being with friends may be due partly to the enjoyable things they do together. Argyle and Furnham (1982) found that the things people do with friends more than with others are like playing, going out, having intimate conversation and other fun-giving activities.

Friends brings benefits in another way. People learn the art of altruism. While helping friends, they learn how to help others. This is a naturalistic way of going beyond self-centric life and deriving pleasure out of prosocial activities.

People cultivating "communal relationship" develop

mindset to give help to others and receive help. This generates a lot of positive emotions. This is a potent reason why extraverts are relatively happier than introverts. The social and interpersonal skills of extraverts in terms of undertaking cooperative activities, befriending others and keeping themselves engaged with various activities help extraverts to promote happiness (Carr, 2004; Meyers, 2000).

Thus, social relation influences all aspects of well-being. Friendship promotes strong positive moods, happiness and health and prevents loneliness. Falling in love brings great joy. Marriage and happy family life is a potent source of happiness.

Building Flourishing Relationship

The capacity for love is a central component of all human societies. Love in all its manifestations, whether for children, parents, friends, or romantic partners, gives depth to human relationships. Specifically, love brings people close to each other physically and emotionally. When experienced intensely, *it makes people feel expansively about themselves and the world.*

While love has been depicted in classical literature in the past, contemporary behavioural scientists have attempted to identify its various components at an empirical level. Love for a companion is considered central to life well lived. Romantic love may not be essential in life, but it may be essential for joy. Life without love would be for many people like a black-and-white movie full of events and activities but without the colour that gives vibrancy and provides a sense of celebration.

A step-wise conceptualization of romantic love may foster an understanding of how it develops between two people.

Stage 1: Passionate and Companionate Aspects.

Romantic love is a complex emotion that may be best *parsed* into *passionate* and *companionate* forms. Passionate love (the intense arousal that fuels a romantic union) involves a state of absorption between two people that often is accompanied by moods ranging from ecstasy to anguish. Companionate love (the soothing, steady warmth that sustains a relationship) is manifested on a strong bond and intertwining of lives that bring about feelings of comfort and peace. These two forms can occur simultaneously or intermittently rather than sequentially.

Romantic love is characterized by intense arousal and warm affection. During this stage partners seek knowledge about each other, they also use this knowledge to further their relationship. In a study of college students who were probably in the early stages of romantic relationship, nearly half named their romantic partners when asked to identify their closest friend. This suggests that passionate and companionate love can coexist in the new relationships of young people. Likewise in a study of couples married for as long as 40 years, researchers found that companionate love and passionate love were alive, and that passionate love was the strongest predictor of marital satisfaction.

Stage 2: The Triangular Components of Love.

In developing a triangular theory of love, psychologist Robert Sternberg (1986) opined that love is a mix of three components: (1) passion, or physical attractiveness and romantic drives, (2) intimacy, or feeling of closeness and connectedness, and (3) commitment, involving the discussion to initiate and sustain a relationship. Various combinations of these three components hold eight forms of love. For example, intimacy and passion combined produce romantic love, whereas intimacy and commitment together constitute companionate love. Consummate love, the most durable type is manifested when all three components (passion, intimacy and commitment) are present at high levels and in balance across both partners.

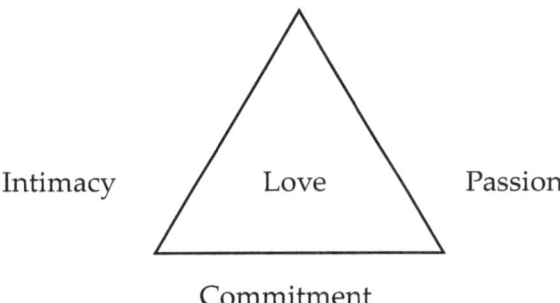

Consummate (Couple) Love = Intimacy + Commitment + Passion
Romantic Love = Intimacy + Passion
Friendship = Intimacy + Commitment
Infatuation = Passion only
Empty Love = Commitment only
(Commercial Relation)
Fatuous Love = Passion + Commitment

Intimacy refers to mutual understanding, warm affection and mutual concern for the other's welfare. **Passion** means strong emotion, excitement, and physical arousal, often tied to sexual desire and attraction. **Commitment** is the conscious decision to stay in a relationship for a long period. It includes a series of devotion to the relationship and a willingness, to work on maintaining it – by putting together different combinations of the three ingredients, Sternberg's (1986) model describes several varieties of love and the specific components of romantic and companionate love.

High intimacy and passion describes romantic love in Sternberg's (1986) model. It may seem strange not to include commitment, but Sternberg argues that commitment is not a defining feature of romantic love. A winter romance, for example, may involve intimate mutual disclosure and strong passion, but no commitment to continue the relationship at winter's end.

Companionate love is a slow-developing love built on high intimacy and strong commitment. When youthful passion fades in a marriage, companionate love, based on deep, affectionate friendship provides a solid foundation for a lasting and successful relationship.

Both **fatuous love** (passion + commitment) and **infatuated love** (passion only) types might be regarded as forms of immature, blind or unreasonable love built on passion. Fatuous love combines high passion and commitment with an absence of intimacy. This would describe people who hardly know each other, but are caught up in a whirlwind passionate romance. Their commitment is based on passion and sustained solely by passion. Because passion is likely to fade with time, fatuous love relationships are unlikely to last. The same can be said for infatuated love, based only on passion, without intimacy or commitment. This might describe a teen romance in which sexual passion is taken for love. Infatuated love may also describe the sense of awe, adoration, and sex-related feelings that some people have for their favorite. Bollywood movie or music celebrity.

Empty Love (commitment only) includes no passion, no intimacy, just a commitment to stay together. Appropriately called empty love, this would describe an emotionally "dead" relationship that both members find some reason to continue. Reasons might include things such as convenience financial benefits, a sense of obligation or duty.

Consummate or complete love (intimacy + passion + commitment) is marked by high intimacy, passion and commitment. It is a form of love that many people desire. As in romantic love, the passionate component typically decreases over time. Yet, other components remain strong and grow. Sternberg's three-component model of love has received good empirical support. People's understanding of love's primary features and the differences among various types of relationships appear to fit well with the intimacy / passion / commitment conception. It is obvious to surmise that these components grow as love becomes more and more mature and sustainable.

Stage 3: The Self-Expansion of Romantic Love

Humans have a basic motivation to expand the self; the emotions, cognitions and behaviours of love fuel such self-expansion. People seek to expand themselves through love.

According to self-expansion theory, relationship satisfaction is a natural by-product of self-expressive love. Being in a loving relationship makes people feel good. They then associate these positive feelings with the relationship, thereby reinforcing their commitment to relationship. The positive consequences of being in love are clear. Researchers find that those who fall in love experience increased self-esteem and self-efficacy. On a more cognitive level, self-expansion means that each partner has made a decision to include another in his or her self. This investment in each other adds to relationship satisfaction. Each of the partners makes a greater use of the expression "we" instead of "I". This inclusivity is a prominent feature of flourishing relationship.

Another relationship involves a culture of appreciation. Generally, it is a human weakness that we tend to explain our success in terms of internal (dispositional) factors and explain failure in terms of external (environmental) factors. For example, we consider ourselves as bright if we complete a work successfully. In contrast, we blame the situational (environmental) difficulty if we fail. But we do not use similar yardsticks to explain others' success / failure. If others succeed, we give credit to situational parameters. If others fail, we blame their dispositional (personality) inadequacy.

What about the explanatory style in the context of flourishing relationship? If a wife fails in fixing the dinner in time, how does the husband explain the event? Is it because of the carelessness of wife or because of some unexpected arrival of guests in home. Needless to say, as relationship flourishes, each of the partners takes an adaptive explanatory style. For success, he/she appreciates the other's positive disposition. For failure, he/she looks at the environmental constraints. This kind of explanatory style is a mark of maturing relationship.

The *scholarship* on love also describes the meaning of "I love you". In a number of studies, the meaning of the statement, "I love you" has been analysed. When participants are asked to describe exactly what they meant when they say "I love you", a variety of answers are generated. Some of the answers include: I understand; I support you, I am thankful to you. Ours is a good life; It is good to be with you. The variability in the meaning of these expressions suggests the complexity and richness of the emotion of love.

Well-minded relationships are healthy and long lasting. The following exhibit depicts the sequence in flourishing relationship.

Adaptive	Nonadaptive
• An in-depth knowing process: both partners seek to know and to be known by the other	No special effort to know or to be known by other
• Both partners use the knowledge gained in enhancing relationship	Knowledge gained is not used
• Both partners accept what they learn and respect the other for the person they learn about	Acceptance of what is learned is low
• Both partners in time develop a sense of being special and appreciated in the relationship	One or both partners fail to develop a sense of being special and appreciated in the relationship

Cultural Factors

The particular meanings of happy life are rooted in specific cultures. However, this does not imply that no uniform scientific knowledge about happiness is possible. Consistent with scientific temper, we can analyze and generate commonalities as well as specificities with respect to optimal functioning in life.

Culture refers to the symbolic aspect of environment. An inclusive definition of culture is provided by Corin (1995).

a system of meanings and symbols. This system shapes every area of life, delivers a world view that gives meaning to personal and collective experience and frames the way people locate themselves within the world, and believe in it. Every aspect of reality is seen as embedded within webs of meaning that define a certain world view and that cannot be studied or understood apart from this collective frame. (p 273).

In simple terms, it refers to the shared attributes of one group. It represents common heritage or set of beliefs, norms, and values. Because of shared beliefs resulting in commonalities of behaviours, cultural factors are given importance for analysis of human happiness.

All cultures feature strengths (adaptive coping and resilience) that may buffer people from developing disorders. Consumers of mental health service naturally carry these cultural diversities directly into the treatment programme. The culture of the health service providers influences many aspects of the delivery system including diagnosis, treatment and health care. This interaction of beneficiaries and health professionals requires a compatibility of understanding.

In the United States where people from different cultural backgrounds live and aspire for healthy functioning, David Satcher, Surgeon General of the U.S.A. presented a report titled "Culture Counts" in the year 2001. The main message contained two basic elements. First the cultures that patient come from shape their mental health and influences the quality of services they receive. Second the culture of the service providers affects the delivery system. what is essential is a kind of compatibility and mutual understanding.

Health belief systems have gone through several phases of evolutions. There have been much transformations. Yet, the origins can be traced to their cultural roots. In the west the classical view of health derived from the Graeco-Arabic medical system. *galenic* medicine provided an expert system developed from the Greeks, in particular the work of Hippocrates. A central concept is Galen's formulation was *balance*. Balance was conceived as a balance of bodily fluids or humours. They identified four main fluids: bile, phlegm, blood, and black bile. Health entails balance; any imbalance causes illness and lack of health.

Christianity drew upon different traditions. Galenic medicines dominated in Europe for almost two millennia. During the middle ages, Galen's work became confined to the learned few and religion became more commonplace. Illness was viewed as a punishment for sinfulness. Implicitly righteous living was stressed. **Biomedicine** arrived during the Enlightenment. Two streams of thought dominated during this period. The first was the acceptance of role of reason. The second was the emergence of *positivism*, which stressed science-based observations. Professional understanding of health and illness became linked with the understanding of individual human body.

Chinese views of health was greatly influenced by the religion and philosophy of Taoism. It was believed that two basic power of *yin and yang* governs the entire universe including human body. Yang is considered to represent the male, positive energy that gives light and fullness. The Yin is considered the female, negative force leading to darkness and emptiness. A harmony in yin and yang represents health while disharmony defines illness **Confucianism** also influenced Chinese views on health. Human suffering is traditionally explained as a result of destiny.

Islamic views on medicine was influenced by religion. During sickness, Muslims are expected to seek Allah's mercy and help through prayer.

Ayurvedic medicine represents a system based upon *veda* (science). It is practiced extensively in India. The body is defined in terms of the flow of substances through channels. Each substance has its own channel. Sickness occurs when a channel is blocked, and the flow is diverted into another channel. When all channels are blocked, the flow of substances is not possible, and death occurs. The aim of Ayurvedic medicine is to identify the blockages and to get the movement again. The different forms of imbalance can be removed by therapeutic interventions based on diet, yoga, breathwork (pranayama), bodywork, meditation and herbs. The used herbs play a major role.

African health beliefs make use of a wide range of a mixture of herbal and physical remedies intertwined with various religious beliefs.

Herbal medicine involves the use of plants and plant extracts to treat illness and promote health. Homeopathy involves the use of highly diluted substances to trigger the body's natural healing system. it is based on the principle "let like be cured by like". This means that a substance that can cause symptoms when taken in large doses can also be used to treat the same symptoms when taken in smaller doses. Its origin can be traced back to the work of the German physician Samuel Hahnemann (1755-1843).

Aromatherapy involves the use of oils from plant extracts for therapeutic purposes. The practice dates back to ancient Egyptian, Chinese, and Indian traditions. French chemist and scholar Rene-Maurile Gattefosse (1881-

1950) is regarded as the father of modern aromatherapy. He discovered the healing properties of lavender when he accidentally burned his hand while working in his laboratory. He continued the experiment on essential oils. In recent years, aromatherapy is being used for stress and pain relief.

In sum, various cultural streams containing health belief systems have contributed towards an evolution of modern health system. in the midst of modern health practices, various systems of indigenous and alternative health practices also exist (Marks, Murray & Estacio, 2018).

Taxonomy of Cultures

A careful transition from a historical and analytical description of culturally embedded health belief system to a more systematic consideration of culture-health linkage requires a taxonomy of culture.

As stated earlier, culture entails shared beliefs, attitudes, values and meaning. Culture also denotes social roles, norms, and practices that are shared by a social group or society (Triandis, 2000). While types of dress, food and rituals are all included in a culture, the language is the most distinguishing feature of a culture. Infact, anthropologists posit that two or more groups constitute separate *cultunits* when they use mutually *unintelligible* languages. In this sense, Americans and Japanese belong to two different cultural groups because Americans do not understand Japanese language and Japanese do not understand American English.

In order to have valued cross-cultural comparison, it is essential that a taxonomic system is needed. Psychologists have made several attempts to classify cultures. There are three fundamental bases of classifying cultures:

individualism vrs collectivism, high context vrs low context culture, and tight culture vrs loose culture.

Individualism–collectivism is a basic classificatory scheme. Many cultures can be characterized according to the relative value they place on individuals vis-à-vis collectivities (Kitayama & Markus, 2000; Triandis, 2000). Another way of distinguishing these two categories of cultures involves the level of awareness of individual needs (Sahoo, Sia & Panda, 1987). In individualistic cultures, people are acutely aware of their own needs and goals as distinguished from needs and goals of other people. In contrast, in collectivist countries, people subordinate their own goals to give priority to their group needs and goals. An example would clearly demonstrate the difference. Let us imagine that a simple question is asked: Why do you work? A typical American's answers would involve: I want to have a decent happy life. I wish to have a holiday resort. I would be able to own a car. In contrast, answers from a Japanese or Indian would contain these elements: I wish to provide good education for my children. I want good living conditions for my family. The emphasis on self vis-à-vis group is evident.

Gert Hofstede (1980) attempted to identify pancultural dimensions of work behaviour. His mega-project involved 40 countries ranging from industrially underdeveloped nations to highly industrialized prosperous nations. The survey instrument used for 116000 participants yielded *four* transcultural dimensions including individualism–collectivism. The study was repeated later with 50 countries and the findings were similar.

In Hofstede's (1980) study of global work values, the individualism–collectivism dimension reflects the relationship between the individual and the group of which he or she is a member. People in individualistic cultures place emphasis on individual initiative and achievement. They are self-oriented and tend to look after their own self-interest. In contrast, people in collectivist cultures consider themselves as basically group-members and they look after each other's interest. In Hofstede's rank-ordering of countries (from most individualistic to least individualistic), the USA is highest on individualism and lowest on collectivism. Gautamela is lowest on individualism and highest on collectivism. India ranks 30 out of the 50 countries; it indicates that India is slightly more collectivist than individualistic, if we categorize the top 25 countries as tending more towards individualism and the bottom 25 countries as leaning more towards collectivism.

In the context of our discussion on culture-happiness linkage, there are two major implications of this cultural dimension of individualism-collectivism.

First, the concept of self is distinctively different in individualistic and collectivist countries. **Individualistic cultures** include industrialized countries of North America, Western Europe and Australia including New Zealand. The self experienced in these countries is primarily an **independent self**. The focus is on the self, there is emphasis on individual rights, responsibility and freedom. The cultural values endorse self-direction, self-reliance, and assertiveness.

Collectivist countries mostly include Asian countries, Middle east, South America and Africa. These collectivist countries emphasize group norms. The self experienced in these countries is basically an **interdependent self**. In these cultures, personal identity is defined rationally, according to connections with others (family peers, workplace, religion, country). Collective cultures attach importance to social roles, social responsibility, social harmony and cooperation with others.

One way to look about the distinction is in terms of personal identity versus social identify (Tajfel, 1982). Personal identity prompts people to respond in a self-referenced manner (I am a dancer; I am sociable). People tend to give self-descriptions in terms of their individual characteristics. In contrast, people in collectivist countries stress their social identities (I am a girl; I am a student in a college). This is clearly revealed with the use of a test called **"I am Test"**. The test requires participants to write (or say) 20 sentences starting with "I am". The analysis of responses illustrates personal identity vrs social identity.

The second major implication of cultural dimension of individualism–collectivism involves the relative **salience of self-esteem**. Because self-esteem is given priority in the scheme of self-concept in individualistic cultures, it is natural that self-esteem plays relatively a greater role in subjective well-being in individualistic countries.

Another classification scheme for cultures is in terms of high-context versus low-context cultures. Supposing that a person brings an envelope carrying a letter for Mr. Ravi. The person says: "Sir, there is a letter for you". Mr. Ravi collects the letter and forms several hunches: Who has brought the letter? What is his status? What kind of dress he has put on? Where did he come from? Prior to opening the cover and reading the contents, Ravi (from a collectivist country like India), would spin several thoughts on the basis of contextual factors (physical form of the letter, the person carrying it, etc). In contrast, an individual from a low-context culture (USA or Canada) would be influenced by the contents inside.

People in individualistic countries tend to describe

themselves in terms of internal traits where *no context* is specified. They appear to have greater need for self-consistency across situations. People in collectivist cultures appear comfortable with self-descriptions when the context is specified because this fits their interdependent view of self. People in collectivist cultures have a more flexible and context-dependent self and are less concerned about being consistent across situations.

The third classification scheme "**tight versus loose cultures**" is mostly designated by anthropologists. Tight cultures or societies are those where cultural norms are greatly stressed and any deviation from the norm is punished in some form or other. A great deal of stratification / segregation (role segregation, status segregation) is found in such cultures. On the other hand, a loose society or culture endorses flexible norms. Although this scheme of culture taxonomy has not yet been extensively used in behavioural research, it may receive attention in future.

Culture and Happiness

Despite the complexities in the definition and classifications of cultures, the relationship between culture and happiness has received research attention. Both cross-cultural and uni-cultural investigations have been undertaken (Argyle, 2001; Baumgardner & Crothers, 2009).

A representative international happiness study is the World Value Study Group (1994) of 41 nations. Life satisfaction was measured by a single item 10-point scale. There were approximately 1000 participants in each country. Positive and negative affect experience were assessed with the help of five questions for each category. Hedonic score was computed from positive affect (PA) minus negative affect (NA). The life satisfaction on the scale had a large sweep. On one extreme Bulgaria showed the least (5.3) while Switzerland indicated the highest (8.39). With respect to positive affectivity Sweden scored highest (3.03) and Japan the lowest (1.12). Negative affectivity was lowest for Switzerland (0.24) and highest for Turkey (2.5). The picture lacked some amount of consistency in the sense some of the findings were paradoxical. Switzerland had the highest satisfaction but quite low on positive affectivity. Similarly, Turkey had highest positive affectivity but low satisfaction (Diener, 2000; Diener, Oshi, & Lucas, 2003; Diener & Suh, 2000).

Another international survey of 54 countries, using one-item happiness measure (Worcester, 1998) Provided similar findings as with the World Value study. The happiest countries were Iceland, Sweden, Netherland, Denmark, Australia, Ireland, and Switzerland. The least happy were Bulgaria and parts of former USSR.

The Eurobarometer has conducted survey involving European countries. The results covering the period 1974 to 1983 indicate that the Netherlands and Denmark appear to be much happier than Italy, France and Germany.

However, there are some surprising observations. Why are the Icelanders so happy despite terrible harsh weather in that county? Why does Scandinavia always fare so well while Italy, France and Germany lag behind? In the Eurobarometer survey, 45% of the Dutch were very happy while only 5% of the Italians were very happy. Similarly 55% of the Dutch were very satisfied with life while only 10% of the Italians and 15% of the French were satisfied with life.

It is important to recognize that an extensive use of EPQ (Eysenck Personality Questionnaire) offers information regarding wellness status, though EPQ is not a direct measure of well-being. Its Neuroticism scale is a measure of anxiety. Hence it may provide information regarding negative affects. Extraversion is correlated with happiness; it may be regarded as an index of happiness.

The survey employing EPQ shows that extraversion is very high for the USA and a little less for Australia, Britain and Canada, but also for the European countries. However, Nigeria, India and Israel came out even higher. China is very low as in other studies. Neuroticism is high in all industrialized countries though lower in Germany and Canada and lower still in Israel and Nigeria (Argyle, 2001).

Lynn (1981) tested several hypotheses pertaining to cross-cultural differences. He opined that neuroticism, which is accepted as an index of negative affect, is higher in Middle Eastern Arab countries as well as South American countries excepting Brazil. This is primarily because of the socio-political disturbances in these areas. He also found that countries defeated in the World War II experienced disturbed emotionality (neuroticism) till 1965 though subsequent political stability permitted a gradual return to affective positivity. As expected, extroversion (taken as an index of happiness) is high in the USA, Canada, and Australia. The level of affluence is a key contributing factor for these countries. The Indian scenarios are satisfactory and conceivable. India scores high average (6.21) on a ten-point scale of life satisfaction in the World Value Study Group record. This is higher than the level predicted on the basis of affluence and purchasing power.

The major task of explaining cultural differences may take two different forms: **functional explanations** and **structural explanations**. Functional explanations refer to certain functional properties of the culture (such as emphasis given on self-esteem) that may boost happiness. The other causal dynamics may denote the structural feature. These entail stylistic dimensions the ways happiness is experienced and expressed. These may be called **hedonic styles**.

Functional Dynamics

A number of functional features such as wealth, individualism and human rights and interpersonal trust appear to be relevant.

Income and wealth: Income has consistently been found to correlate with average satisfaction. Argyle (2001) reports that average life satisfaction is correlated with average income at about .70. It is much higher than within-country correlation. The within-country difference is confounded by individual differences. In contrast, between-country difference considers collective arrangements such as food supply, health facility and education.

Diener et al's (1995) data from 41 countries covered in the World Value Survey provided a high correlation of .69 between mean purchasing power and life satisfaction. Rich countries such as Switzerland, Canada and USA indicated higher correlations while poor countries displayed lower correlations (e.g., Bulgaria). However, the effects of income level off about middle-income level. This happens primarily because adequacy of income fulfills needs. Diener (1995) combined 14 objective indicators of domains of well-being. He found that the size of this index increased with income, but only up to a value of $3000 per month in 1981 U.S. dollars, after which further increase makes no additional contribution. Diener and Diener (1995) posit that icomemay bring other good things. Yet, its contribution has an upper limit.

Another way to look at the contribution of income is in

terms of **income equality**. Income equality can be computed by assessing the ratio of average incomes of the richest 20% and the poorest 20%. The ratio is 26:1 for Brazil followed by Botswana and Costa Rica. The most equal countries are Hungary (3.0), Poland (3.6), Japan (4.5) and Sweden (4.6). Equality has a quite strong correlation with subjective well-being. Diener et al (1995) found this to be .48.

There are other features of nations that correlate with satisfaction such as individualism and human rights.

Individualism: The individualism–collectivism as a fundamental basis of cultural taxonomy has been explicated in the foregoing section of this chapter. Triandis (2000) has developed and validated several forms of measures to scale individualism-collectivism. Hofstede (1980) also has devised method to gaudge individualism in work context.

Diener et al (1995) used additional measures of individualism along with Triandis scale. They found the correlation between individualism and well-being very high (.77). If income is held constant, the correlation between individualism and well-being decreased. Veenhoven (2000) separated rich countries from poor countries and computed correlation. The findings were interesting. For affluent countries the correlation between individualism and well-being was positive. In contrast, poor countries showed negative correlation between individualism and well-being. This implies that the freedom of individualism is best for affluent nations, but mutual help and social support is desirable for collectivist countries.

As pointed out earlier, **self-esteem** is valued in individualistic cultures, where it is more strongly related to life satisfaction. In collectivist cultures, correlation is much lower and for women in some culture there is no relation (Diener & Diener, 1995).

Human rights: Diener et al (1995) found that combined measure of several kinds of human rights correlated .45 with satisfaction. Yet this correlation disappeared when income was held constant. Diener et al (1995) argued that this happened because rich countries offer human right. However, Veenhoven (2000) argued that although political and personal freedom could be explained by wealth, economic freedom is a distinct factor.

Frey and Stutzer (2000) compared the 26 Swiss cantons, which vary a lot in how much the residents can take part in democratic institutions. This had quite a strong effect on average happiness reported in those cantons. Similarly one study has assessed interpersonal trust across some nations and found positive correlation between trust and well-being.

Structural Dynamics

Hedonic styles: Cross-cultural differences can be explained at functional levels as well as structural levels. At the functional levels, certain cultures permit and facilitate specific types of need gratification whereas other cultures encourage another kind of need satisfaction. For example, affluence opens some opportunities while blocking other needs. As a result, differences in happiness and well-being emerge.

At another level the culture differences induce a typical mind-set in people. Just as an individual has personality, similarly an environment (cultural environment) takes on a model personality. People in specific cultures internalize that modality and experience accordingly, in the context of happiness and well-being this can be termed *hedonic styles*. Two such styles may be discussed: independent-interdependent styles, and affectivity bias.

Independent-Interdependent Styles: People in individualistic countries like to United States, Canada, Australia and other Western European countries display a characteristic mode of experiencing happiness. Feeling good about the self is the central component of their happiness. Even if a group of friends go to a hotel to have dinner and finish the dinner together, the waiter / waitress would ask the question: "Sir / Madam! Individual bill or collective bill?" It is very likely that individual bills would be collected and paid, unless one of them has had told categorically that he or she is hosting the dinner because of his or her birthday. For the sake of convenience, one may say "collective" and the collective bill is paid. But the person would put an empty pot and the participants would calculate their individual portions and put it there. The friend placing the empty pot would collect all money and put in personal purse. This is natural, no sense of guilt is felt.

The individual model of self is the focal point in individualistic cultures. From an early age children in individualistic cultures ("me" cultures) are taught how to feel good about your self. Happiness results from finding out who you are, in terms of your individual identity. As an individual, you must know your own needs, goals, aspirations and pleasures as opposed to goals and attributes of others. The socialization imparted to children also takes this form. Happiness results from being "true to yourself".

A remarkable feature in this style of happiness experience is the **self-serving bias**. In any segment of human population, when a question is asked about performance, bias is observed in answer. Where would you place yourself in math-test? Where would you place yourself in test score? What would be your happiness level? Do you expect your position above the neutral (median) level or below the neutral point? Although theoretically 50% are above the neutral and 50% are below the neutral, a common observation shows that more than 50% of the participants respond in self-affirming ways: they say they would be above neutral points. This self-serving bias is common in any population.

Interestingly a number of studies have examined this self-serving bias across cultures (Diener & Diener, 1995; Diener et al 1995). It was shown than 83% of American men, 82% of American women, 78% of Canadian men and 79% of Canadian women indicated themselves to be above the neutral point. In contrast, 40% of Japanese and 50% of Koreans give such answer.

It is conceivable that this tendency to boost self-serving bias is linked with motivation for self-esteem in individualistic cultures. Self-esteem is more strongly associated with well-being in individualistic countries. This is in harmony with the individualistic belief that happiness is important and it springs from individual satisfaction.

Another feature visible in individualistic cultures is orientation towards self-enhancement. Self-enhancing tendencies are commonly observed in the attribution styles of people in individualistic countries. When explaining academic achievement, a typical American student would be inclined to say: "I got high grades, because I am hardworking" or I am bright (would not say: I got high grades because the question was easy). The focus on individualistic model motivates people in individualistic countries to promote and develop their self-image. They tend to perceive themselves as "better than averages", exaggerate the amount of control they have over life and take credit for success.

In contrast, the collectivist style of happiness as we

find in Japan, China and India, is different. The central value around which happiness revolves state: I am happy when others are happy. Individual goal is subordinated to group goals.

In Asian cultures, children are encouraged to moderate their emotion, fit in with others, take pride in the achievement of their groups, and to adopt a self-critical and **self-effacing** attitude towards themselves.

A large number of studies (e.g., Suh, 2000) conducted in Asian countries such as Japan, Korea, China and India clearly show collectivist bias in happiness styles.

Affectivity bias. Research on emotion (both positive and negative) has clearly distinguished emotional expression from emotional experience. Different **social norms** regulate the expression of emotion. In other words, each culture has its own **display rules** and emotions are expressed or suppressed depending on the culturally governed display rules. This is very important while making culture-wise happiness statements.

In general, it is important to recognize that some countries and groups display a positive happiness bias while other countries or groups tend to show negative happiness bias.

It has been suggested that the high satisfaction and happiness scores in the USA are primarily due to this social norm that encourages the expression of cheerfulness. As indicated earlier, North Americans harbor more positive self-view, display greater self-serving bias and engage in greater self-enhancement than Asians. American's self-presentational styles stress "rosy outlook".

In Japan, it is not socially acceptable to show negative facial expression in public Friesen has conducted many experimental studies where films depicting different types of emotions are displayed. It has been indicated that Japanese exercise a strict control over, they inhibit the negative expression such as disgust.

In another study English boys starting boarding schools at age 8 or 13 were actually feeling homesick and depressed. Yet it was rarely reflected in their overt behaviour because of the social norm that demands the suppression of negative emotion.

In parts of Africa and India, depression is rarely reported. People generally do not report depression, sadness, guilt and inadequacy, though certain bodily symptoms are observed. The self-report measure of their happiness may be misleading.

In contrast, there are countries and groups where negative happiness bias is visible. **Negativity bias** is visible in the Ifaluk tribe (in a small Pacific Island) where looking happy is not acceptable. In China, people focus more on negative events. They are less optimistic than Americans. They consider it important to have a modest demeanour (Lee & Seligman, 1997).

Issues of Comparability

The foregoing section has offered a substantial amount of information regarding cross-cultural differences in happiness. However, the fundamental issue remains unsolved. Cross-cultural psychologists posit that **equivalence** is a major problem in cross-cultural comparison. For valid cross-cultural comparison, three forms of equivalence must exist. These are *functional conceptual* and *metric equivalence* (Sahoo, 1983).

Functional equivalence exists when the objective of the research is geared to same goals or functions. Since the present goal or objective concerns happiness/well-being, this requirement is met. The second issue involves conceptual equivalence. Research method in cross-cultural psychology posits that conceptual equivalence exists when the concepts, materials, stimuli and tasks used in different cultures are equitable. Hence a seminal question involves: Is happiness similarly understood across cultures?

In the context of happiness, the conceptual equivalence is still a debate. Many professional including Seligman and Diener view it **"culture free"** whereas others consider it **culturally embedded"**.

Given that the definition and measuring instruments were developed by researchers in Western cultures, critic would apprehend a cultural bias built into the process. Hence cultural differences found in studies are not real cultural differences but procedural artifacts.

However, Diener and his colleagues argue that happiness/well-being is a universal concept. People give their own personal appraisal of lives. The concept is not *imposed* on the subset of population, it is *derived* from their responses. Further analysis has shown that the universality of the construct is not unduly affected by diversity of the languages. Veenhoven (2000) showed that Swiss report much higher well-being the French, Germans or Italians even through each of these languages is spoken in Switzerland. If the rating of life satisfaction depended on the particular meaning of the word "satisfaction" as translated into different languages then the Swiss might have well-being levels similar to German, French and Italian individuals living in their respective countries. The fact that this does not happen proves that well-being primarily would fit anybody's idea of a good life.

The *metric equivalence* or cross-cultural validity of well-being measures has received research attention. Ratings of life satisfaction, rating of happiness or ratings of "worst to best possible life" show nearly the same identical rank (Veenhoven, 2000). Researchers have employed a variety of measures such as experience sampling method, rating scale, observation, and rating on positive and negative affects. With multiplicity of measures, it is possible to cross-validate the assessment.

Resolution and Resources

A number of issues have been identified; some cross-cultural concerns have been expressed. It is important to note that the wave of positive psychology came only at the end of twentieth century. It has greatly influenced research on well-being. Many innovative ideas have been generated and many more refinements are in the process.

There is no problem in accepting the proposition that well-being contains both universals as well as culture specific-features. Culture does have predictable influences. Diener and his associates assert that 15% of the variation in life satisfaction is associated with between-culture differences in the World Value Survey of 43 nations.

Since happiness includes both transcultural features and culture-specific elements, happiness-promotive programmes need to contain both the elements. The art, dance, literature and a lot variety of cultural stuffs may provide valuable resources along with universal capital such as wealth and human right.

Chapter 7

Social Ecology of Happiness

Happiness, like humans, is embedded in a social ecological context. Bronfrenbrenner (1989) describes social ecology in terms of nested systems such as *microsystem, mesosystem, exosystem and macrosystem*. The microsystem is represented by the family where human development makes a significant visible beginning. Subsequently the influences from school represent the mesosystem and neighbours and parents' colleagues in form of exosystem shape the growing child. The effects by the broader environment, the macrosystem, comes later. The growth of happiness encounters similar contextual influences. Although a large number of significant life events (both positive and negative) mould the anatomy of happiness, some specific domains play important roles. As with human development, the family as microsystem paves the way for future changes. The early socialization of family moves forward and gathers ingredients at workplace and community setting.

Family Happiness

Family is an evolved institution that provides security, comfort and happiness. More specifically close supportive relationship between husband and wife, between siblings, and between extended family members enhance the social support available to all family members (Carr, 2004). The social support enhances and forms an evolutionary perspective. We are 'hard-wired' to derive happiness from this contact with our kinship network (Argyle, 2001; Buss, 2000; Myers, 2002). In addition to buffering stress, family offers a bounty of benefits that multiply human happiness.

Adaptive Benefits of Family

There is a striking parallelism between evolution of family and evolution of happiness (Buss, 1994, 1995, 2000). In an excellent analysis, Buss (2000) adopts an evolutionary perspective and explicates major obstacles to achieving happiness. He further explains how people evolved mechanisms of family that provided deep sources of happiness. Family offered mating bonds, deep friendship, close kinship and cooperative coalitions. Current mechanisms of mind are basically end-product of a selective process. Whatever features have been proved successful in the selective process, those features have been transmitted to the subsequent generations (Buss, 2000).

According to Buss (2000), the big discrepancy between ancestral and modern environments places severe adaptation demands on the selective process. The ancestral environments consisted of small groups (50 to 200 individuals), limited mating choice, and restricted social hierarchy. Modern environments changed all these features. People typically live in a massive urban metropolis surrounded by millions of humans. Modern humans are surrounded by thousands of potential mates. They are bombarded by media images of attractive models. Some empirical evidence suggests that men exposed to multiple images of attractive women tend to lower their ratings for their regular partner compared with men exposed to average looking women (Kenrick, Neuberg, Zierk, & Krones, 1994). This *contrast effect* generated by media exposure is a barrier to happiness.

Similarly ancestral humans relied on their friends and relatives to seek justice, to correct social wrongs, and to deal with violence inflicted on them. Modern humans rely on police and a legal system that does not ensure a time limit for the end of the problem. This adds to the misery of humans.

Another barrier to human happiness involves a number of subjective distress (anxiety depression, fears and phobia, anger and upset). All these negative tendencies, Buss argues assertively, are evolved psychological mechanisms developed to deal with the adaptive problem. For example, sexual jealousy function to alert a person to a mate's possible or actual infidelity. Anger and upset are evolved psychological mechanisms to prevent *interference*. These negative emotions function to draw attention to the source of threat, alert the individual to take steps and help to retrieve relevant memory. These findings support the hypothesis that many apparently negative emotions may be quite functional for humans. These are helpful for solving adaptive problems in social living.

The negative emotions are not limited to sexual situations. People experience distress when someone blocks their goals. Another impediment to happiness springs from the competition inherent to evolution by selection. Empirical evidence supports that people do take pleasure in the downfall of others. It raises a fundamental question: If a person's happiness depends, in part, on another's misery or failure, then how can people design lives to improve the quality of all, not just those who happen to get ahead?

Despite the obstacles to happiness, evolved mental mechanisms provide conditions to bridge the gap between modern and ancestral environments. Modern environments may deprive people of closeness of extended kin. Yet individuals can take steps to remain in closer proximity or to maintain greater closeness to existing kin. Modern electronic communication, including E-mail, telephone, and video calls might be used to this end when physical proximity is not possible. With people living longer, opportunities to interact with grandparents and grandchildren expand.

In certain developing countries including India, *functionally joint families* do exist in certain forms. Although husband and wife do live in nuclear family setting they make periodic visit to places where their elderly parents live. They spend some days or weeks there. This happiness especially during festive occasions or at a time when parents are sick requiring medical help. This kind of proximity provides some positive psychological support.

Within the framework of extended kin, certain abuses such as child abuse and wife battering may be greatly reduced or eliminated. Although protective properties of extended kin have not yet been extensively studied, this is a task that lies ahead.

When properly managed, families are conducive to flow experience (Csikszentmihalyi & Csikszentmihalyi, 1988). Some families offer socialization experiences that allow children to develop personality traits that make it easier for children to have flow experience.

Rathunde (1988) attempted to identify families where the experience of flow is more likely. The findings are valuable. In such families, children and adolescents are characterized by optimal levels of clarity, choice and commitment. Goals and feedbacks are unambiguous, children know clearly what is expected of them. Children also know that their parents are interested in what they are doing and experiencing.

In addition to creating flow in relationship with our children, conditions for flow in all facets of intimate relationship can be created. By caring deeply for our partners or companions, by sharing valued interests, hopes and dreams with them, by taking on joint activities with them, by raising children jointly, and by facing life's stresses and challenges, it is possible to generate flow in intimate relationship. However, we must be familiar with psychodynamics of close relationship and living together for a successful navigation of family life.

Features of Close Relationship

We meet a lot of people every day as we step outside our door. We exchange greetings, give and collect telephone numbers, and promise to call as and when necessary. We also meet many people in different places, at school, work, market, bus, train and aeroplanes. While many such relationships are formed, all relationships do not take the form of close relationships. Casual relationships come and go, yet some relationships are solidified into close relationships. These may be the bonds of friendship, romantic partners or married couples.

Close relationship can be distinguished from casual relationship in many ways, but the degree of intimacy is the central distinction. Intimacy grows with interaction.

Intimacy is not necessarily a sexual relationship. The term intimacy can apply both to friends and to lovers. It captures mutual understanding, depth of connection, and the degree of involvement.

Some psychologists have identified *six* characteristics of close relationship. These include knowledge, trust, caring, interdependence, mutuality, and commitment.

Knowledge: Our closet friends and intimate partners know more about us than anyone else. They have extensive knowledge of our personal history, deepest feelings, remarkable achievements, strengths, and weaknesses. Intimate knowledge is shared through a process *of* **self-disclosure**. Self-disclosure refers to the act of revealing the information of the self to others. As we tell more and more about us, our friends and intimate partners are also inclined to tell more and more about themselves.

The mutual sharing of information, especially personal and private information, through the process of self-disclosure takes the shape of an exchange activity. If we do not disclose our personal information for a long time, our friend or romantic partner may also reduce his or her self-disclosure activity.

Researchers have found that (a) we disclose to people we like; (b) we like people who disclose intimate self-information; (c) we like people to whom we have disclosed.

Another interesting pattern is observed in the context of self-disclosure. This is called **disclosure reciprocity**. Disclosure begets disclosure. It is found that the degree and diversity of disclosure increases with time. Initially we share mostly neutral information such as name, residence, etc. Gradually we enter into personal domains. Secrets and confidential matters are disclosed only after relationship takes a solid form.

Trust: Mutual trust is another distinguishing feature. Reciprocal disclosure brings people together and they are inclined to develop trust in each other. They believe that the secrets they have disclosed to their friends or romantic partners would not be opened up to others. They also expect no harm from their friends and romantic partners Trust is a necessary condition for self-disclosure. We don't disclose to people we don't trust.

Caring: Care means concern and attention for others We respect others' feelings. In the context of casual relationships, our conversation is limited to formal exchanges such as "How are you" or "I am fine". Questions that reflect care and concern are more personal and deeper. We may inquire about detailed aspects of health, finance and education. We may also delve into areas in which our friends are experiencing problems. We may also make use of nonverbal cues such as physical closeness, touch, and eye contact. Care and concern is also indicated in several forms of activities such as visiting a sick friend, extending greetings on birth-days, congratulating on achievements and expressing sadness at the time of others' misfortune.

Interdependence: The lives of people in intimate relationship are deeply interwined. The mutual influence of each person on the actions, feelings, and thinking of the other is immense. We typically care more and attach greater priority to the suggestions, opinions and judgments of our family members, friends and spouses. We may consult a doctor when there is a specific health problem. We seek advice from an expert. For many other personal problems, we depend on people with whom we have close relationship.

Mutuality: In the context of close relationship, a visible change in our mind-set is observed. The expression 'I' takes the 'we' form. Instead of saying "I have done it", people in close relationship tend to say – "we have done it". This sense of togetherness reflects mutuality.

Commitment: Commitment is an essential feature of close relationship. It is an intention to continue the relationship into future. Indirectly commitment involves some degree of personal sacrifice and compromise of individual self-interest for the sake of good relationship.

Commitment as a core feature brings a few other elements in its train. These include loyalty, faithfulness, hard work, and keeping promise. Mutual commitment provides the cementing force.

Our most satisfying relationships are likely to contain all six parameters. However, these components may vary in strength. The degree of intimacy and closeness would depend on the relative strength of each characteristic. The difference between a friend, a good friend, and the best friend is largely a matter of strength of these parameters.

Secret of Living Together

Living together happily is both a challenge and an opportunity. Because of many difficulties and problems, the prospect of living together has been clouded. The points that follow would guide us to live together happily. It is expected that our readers would derive great benefits out of these guide-lines.

Marriage and well-being are strongly connected. A successful marriage is one of the most powerful contributors to enriched individual health and happiness. Unhappy marriages have an equally strong connection to unhappiness and diminished health. Since most people marry, the level of well-being within society as a whole would depend on the quality of happy marriages.

Statistics regarding the status of marriage do not

present a rosy picture. Major reviews of census data in the West do present pessimistic scenarios. In the United States, some 50% of all new marriages end in divorce or separation. Other western countries, such as the Netherlands, Sweden, Canada, and England, have also witnessed increases in divorce, but US divorce rates are nearly double those of other developed countries. Divorce rates have always been higher within the first 5 to 7 years of marriages, consistent with the conventional wisdom about the '7-year-itch'. However, today many longer-term marriages also fail (i.e., 10 years and up). There is no 'safe' point beyond which all marriages last, although after 15 years, the divorce rate drops substantially.

The percentage of people who live together before marriage has increased dramatically. Nearly a third of American households are made of unmarried men and women living together. An estimated 50% of college students live with a romantic partner without getting married. Does cohabitation increase the success of a future marriage? The idea that a 'trial marriage' may help partners to know them well is undercut by the fact that these cohabiting couples have higher divorce rate than non-cohabiting couples. It appears that the lack of strength of commitment on the part of cohabiting partners is a possible causal factor.

Although divorce rate in India is not very disturbing, we have to attend to warning signal. The divorce rate is still lower compared to world scenarios. Out of 1,000 marriages in India, 11 marriages terminate in a divorce. These statistics were lower in 1990, when out of 1000 marriages just 7.4 percent marriages ended up in a divorce. The divorce rate is higher in urban areas compared to rural setting. In the 21st century rates in the cities have been shooting up alarmingly. In Delhi, rates doubled in five years. In Bangalore, rates tripled in four years. These are very shocking statistics.

In the Indian context, research has identified a number of causal factors. These include work pressure and stress, monetary security, haphazard working hours, lack of time to spend in the house with family and financial freedom. The Chairperson of Women's Commission has disclosed that in a majority of cases, the marital discord has stemmed from an unsatisfactory physical relationship. The Chairperson's opinion is that as the people are viewing the computer screen for prolonged periods, this has led to impotency. Some psychiatrists have pointed out the role of job stress in marital discord.

It is axiomatic that increased freedom and decreased constraints have played significant roles in the rate of enhanced failures of marriages. In the past, unhappy married couples had to face a number of constraints. First, women did not enjoy much economic freedom and they had to depend on their husbands for day-to-day living. Second, divorce at one time carried a significant cultural stigma for both men and women. Third, the importance of staying together for the sake of children was a strong consideration. Fourth, a belief about the sanctity of marriage was strong. Furthermore, the courts and legal system have greatly reduced the difficulties of divorce and separation.

Uniqueness of Lasting Marriages

Instead of explaining the causes of failed marriages, it is more appropriate to examine factors of uniqueness of lasting marriages. Today, choice and love are playing increasing roles in mate selection. We can think about a question: If a person had all the other qualities one desires, would one marry the person if one is not in love? When American college students were surveyed in 1967, 45% of men and 76% of women said yes to this question. Men evidently had more romantic attitude whereas women were practical. However, four decades later, no was the overwhelming answer to the same question by both men and women. The prominence of love to prevail over differences in social status, religion, background and life events is a regular theme in movies and television programmes.

Large scale surveys indicate the importance of loving and liking in selection of marriage partners. Buss asked over 10,000 people from 37 countries to rate 18 characteristics according to their desirability in mate selection. Despite cultural differences the number one criterion for mate selection was love or mutual attraction.

Despite such positive human bonding, the increasing rate of failures of marriage prompts us to look happy couples. What are the forces that cement the relationship permanently? Psychologists have empirically delineated a number of interesting features of successful marriages.

1. **Be a Mother as well as a Mentor**

Blend of realism and idealism: The value of a good mix of realism and idealization is supported by research. It is found that some degree of idealization contributes to couple's happiness and satisfaction. Couples who have the most positive view of each other's personal attributes are not only happier, but they are less likely to break up. The tendency to view our partners more positively than they see themselves means that we overlook our partners' shortcoming. This is the view that mothers have of their children. They see the best in their kids and downplay faults. The mutuality of this idealization enhances self-esteem and satisfaction.

People desire evaluations that affirm or verify their own self-views. More specifically, people want positive feedback about their positive qualities. We each want verification of our won self-views. Relationships are enhanced when your partner affirms your own self-view because this proves that she or he knows you as you know yourself. The authencity of your partner's understanding of "who you really are" creates strong feeling of intimacy.

The opposing nature of idealization is also needed. Idealization is essential in short-term relationship and at the beginning of marriage. As relationship matures, more accurate information becomes important. To much idealization may do harm for a long-term relationship. If one of the partner is involved in drinking or gambling, it would be improper for the other to remain silent. An accurate understanding of partner's shortcoming and its expression would be needed for the furtherance of long-term relationship. In short, both idealization and reality are to be blended in their combination of differential proportion during the developing course of relationship.

2. **Develop Friendly Attitude**

Friendship mindset. The second powerful determinant of happy married relation is the mind-set reflected in the context of best friendship. The impact of strong commitment is evinced in these cases. With passage of time, passion declines. Yet intimacy and commitment grow. They may stay home by themselves, perhaps each engrossed in a book, as long as they are across each other. Such married couples exhibit attitudes, values and behaviours that are found in two persons who are tied by the thread of best friendship.

3. **Foster Secure Attachment Style**

Attachment styles: It is a common experience that our

primary bonding with our mothers offers us a resource of great significance. For the first-time, we learn that there is some one who attends and cares for our needs. For most of us, our first "love" experiences are with parents – often our mothers. All of us develop an intense attachment with our primary caregivers – most frequently our biological parents. **Attachment theory** tells us that some of our most basic and unconscious emotional responses in intimacy are shaped by the kind of relationship with our parents.

Attachment Styles may take various forms depending on the quality of relationship between the child and mother. If the child experiences sensitive and responsible mothering, the child develops secure attachment style which is appropriate. If there are problems in the relationship the child develops maladaptive styles including avoiding style. The secure attachment style gives child a sense of security and self-worth. It is believed that such adaptive secure attachment style gets transmitted to adolescent and adulthood. Children and adolescents having secure attachment styles are capable of establishing close relationship with others and are capable of sustaining such secure relationship for a longer period of time.

However, some researchers do not agree with this argument. They believe that many events creep into adult's life and may change attachment style induced during childhood years.

4. **Resolve Conflicts**

Conflict resolution style: A great deal of research has focused on how relationship partners deal with conflict and interpret negative behaviours. This is because some amount of conflict is inevitable in our intimate relation. Married couples may encounter differences in their expectations.

Differences with respect to spending habits, managing children, arranging higher education for adolescents, and changing own careers may arise. The approaches adopted by intimate partners for solving these problems may strengthen or weaken the relationship.

An interesting inference derived from relationship research states that *once a relationship is well-established, its success depends more on the absence of conflict (the bad) than on the presence of affection (the good)*. A couple's satisfaction with their marriage is linked significantly more strongly to the level of conflict than it is to the level of positive behaviour. A well-known daily diary study found that a nearly two-thirds of couples' marital satisfaction was related to the occurrence (or lack) of negative behaviours and conflict, and much less to the occurrence (or lack) of positive behaviours. In our intimate relationship the bad seems stronger than the good. A single negative act appears capable of "undoing" countless acts of affection and kindness.

The most extensive studies of marital conflict have been conducted by Gottman. Among his many studies were intensive observation of married couples in the "love lab". This was an apartment set up to video-tape verbal, nonverbal, and physiological responses of couples as they talked about topics posed by the investigator. The topics were controversial, and observations were directed to identify strengths and weaknesses Gottman & Silver, 1999).

It was found that negative communication patterns were more predictive of marital satisfaction level and overall relationship quality than were displays of affection and kindness. In particular, these four factors were very harmful

1. *Criticism*. A high proportion of negative as compared to positive comments, remarks and nonverbal

signals
2. *Defensiveness.* Taking criticism and comments personally ("I am not going to take it any more")
3. *Stonewalling.* Refusal to respond
4. *Contempt.* Showing scorn, anger, and rejection

Interestingly Gottman wanted to determine the proportion of positive behaviour that neutralizes the effect of a single negative behaviour. On the basis of his observations in "love-lab", a ratio of 5 positive interactions to 1 negative interaction was found to the dividing line between successful and unsuccessful marriages. In a healthy relationship, there are five times more positive than negative interaction. Troubled relationships have very low ratios. The 5-to-1 ratio supports the general principle that 'bad is stronger than good'.

The implication suggests that the harm done by one bad thing needs to be offset by five good things for marriages to be satisfying. The 5-to-1 obviously underlines an approach to improve the quality of relationship – *find ways to reward your partner.* Frequent and simple acts of care, concern, affection and kindness can shift the ratios into the positive range. This makes conflict less likely and easier to resolve when it occurs.

5. **Build as many Positives as Possible**

Capitalization. Positive emotions have beneficial effects that are both independent of and beyond those of negative emotions. In addition to offsetting the ill-effects of negative effect, positive emotions independently enhance the quality of our life. It is just as important to receive supportive responses to our positive life experiences as it is to receive support at the time of our adversity. When people celebrate a positive event (e.g., birth-days, felicitation) with others, they derive immense benefits. This process is referred to as **capitalization** (capitalizing on a additional benefits).

In a study, participants kept a daily diary in which they recorded their positive and negative emotions and their life satisfaction. For each day, they also recorded their most important positive event and whether they had shared it with others. Results indicated that on 70% of the days people had shared. It was found that well-being was enhanced on "sharing" days compared to "non-sharing" days.

How do people respond to some positive events (such as promotion, academic achievement, winning a prize) happening to their partners? Research shows four types of reactions in sharing a positive event: (1) *active constructive* (e.g., the person gets the feeling that partner is more happy and excited than person experiencing the event), (2) *active-destructive* (the partner comments on the down side of the event – "you got promotion, but created more enemies for us), (3) *passive-constructive* (the partner says he/she is happy but does not express it enthusiastically), (4) *passive destructive* (the partner does not pay attention to it). The comparison of these four types shows that only active – constructive responses to the sharing of positive life events are related to enhanced relationship. The three other responses types are associated with decreased relationship quality. It clearly posits that capitalization is dependent on an active, enthusiastic, and supporting reaction from one's partner.

6. **Use Moderation Approach**
    Gender-linked problem solving pattern: In the context

of positive reactions, researchers have observed a typical gender difference. Women, who are often more attuned to and concerned about the ongoing quality of close relationship, make more demands to resolve problems and to improve a marriage than men. Relationship problems raised by one partner are sensitive issues because they directly or indirectly imply criticism of the other. In raising these issues, women are generally more emotionally expressive and report more intense emotion than men. Men seem generally less sensitive to relationship problems and less comfortable talking about them.

These differences are likely to produce an interaction pattern in which the woman makes demand to talk about a problem and the man withdraws or becomes defensive (refuses to talk). This frustrates the wife and she makes more demand. It is suggested that a balance is needed between these extreme tendencies. The discussion with an attitude of moderation is helpful for enhanced relationship.

7. **Adopt Useful Explanatory Style**

Supportive explanatory styles: It is natural that bad (negative) events do happen to one of the two partners. As soon as bad things do happen to one partner, the other hastens to explain it. Who is responsible for the event? It is a fundamental question for which immediate causal explanation is offered. Suppose the husband did not secure promotion. Is it because of his negligence of duty or because of some situational factors?

Generally, it is found that we blame others or external situation when we encounter bad events. But we blame the other person when the other person encounters the problem.

In a healthy relationship, partners should consider

the role of external circumstances or situations while explaining the bad events happening to the partner. "My husband / wife has failed to bring a gift on my birthday not because he or she is inattentive to my emotion, it is because of the current pressure of work". Such an explanatory style of explaining other partner's failure would be helpful in promoting cordial relationship.

Exhibit: Faulty Attribution (Explanatory) Style

	Success	Failure
Me	Internal Factor (Trait / Disposition)	External Factor (Situation / Environment)
Other	External Factor (Situation / Environment)	Internal Factor (Trait / Disposition)

8. **Develop Sense of Humour**

Sense of humour. Humour is a buffer to stress. It has immense role in reducing our stress and providing an outlet for the release of pent-up emotion. In married life, our ability to use humour and diffuse strained communication plays a significant role.

While sexual attraction may decline over years, the strength of humour does not decline. Even 50-year-married couples report that laughing together has made marriage a great success. Humour is undoubtedly one major reason as to why happy couples enjoy each other's company. Humour can detoxify conflict and relieve stress in a relationship.

Laughter is an emotional reaction that most people cannot fake. An obligatory and forced laughter is easily distinguished from the real thing. Because it is less subject to conscious control, a genuine laugh is thought to be an honest expression of how a person really feels.

9. **Evolve Commonality of Activity**

In many situations, it is possible to develop some activity where partners conjointly do the work. For example, one of the partners may do the secretarial work of the other partner, if possible. The husband and wife can work as doctors in the same unit. One may be the doctor while other is the nurse. By stretching our imagination, we can contemplate various forms of jobs, activities or hobbies where one's work supplements or complements the other's activity. Such a commonality of activity would be a source of combined pleasure.

10. **Believe in Relationship Growth**

Destiny vrsgrowth: People in a relationship may or may not be having similar implicit theories and expectations regarding marriage. There are two distinct implicit theories defined either by a belief in **romantic destiny** or by a belief in **relationship growth**. The basic premise of the romantic destiny theory is that two people are either compatible or they are incompatible. If a marriage runs well, it signals compatibility. If it runs into problem, it indicates incompatibility. "We are right for each other" or "We aren't right for each other" – This is the typical verbal expression of people believing in romantic destiny.

The growth theory assumes that relationships are challenging and will grow and develop over time. People believing in growth theory feel that obstacles foster development. They assume that obstacles and difficulties in relationship are but natural. Yet partners have the ability to overcome obstacles and to intensify the bonding.

People who hold to the romantic destiny theory endorse items such as, "A successful relationship is mostly a matter of finding a compatible partner right from the start", and "Early troubles in a relationship signify a poor match between partners". Growth theory advocates would agree with items such as, "Challenges and obstacles in a relationship can make love even stronger", or "It takes a lot of time and effort to cultivate a good relationship".

A strong belief in romantic destiny leads to an interpretation of conflict as a sign of incompatibility over which couples can exercise little control. A belief in relationship growth provides a more positive and accepting perspective on the inevitable conflict. From a growth perspective, conflict is a natural part of all relationships and it does not mean that someone has to be at fault. Problems are temporary and solvable. Hence, effort and commitment can make the difference between success and failure.

In sum, the main ingredients of happy couple life include friendship and commitment. Deep and abiding friendship is the top reason of lasting marriages. Both partners agree: "My spouse is my best friend". In addition, couples recognize the importance of strong commitment to making their relationship truly permanent. "Together we laugh" – This is an off-quoted voice of happy couples.

Know Your Explanatory Style

You are given a number of events. Imagine each event happening to you. Each event is followed by two alternative explanations: A & B. Choose the explanation that you consider appropriate for you.
1. Your spouse/ intimate friend forgot to bring you a gift on your birthday.
    A. She / he was neglectful.
    B. She / he was under pressure of work.
2. Your spouse / intimate friend did not congratulate you on your promotion

A. She / he was careless.

B. She / he was too busy with domestic responsibility.

3. Your spouse / intimate friend failed to pick you up at the Railway Station

    A. She / he chatted with her / his friend so long that she / he lost track of time.

    B. She / he faced formidable traffic jam.

4. Your spouse / intimate friend did not give you medicine in time

    A. She / he was unmindful.

    B. Children forced her / him to pay attention to their needs.

5. Your spouse / intimate friend picked up a quarrel with you

    A. She / he is quarrelsome.

    B. She / he was in angry mood that day.

6. Your spouse / intimate friend spoiled your dress while ironing it

    A. She / he is always uncaring.

    B. She / he was very tired then.

7. Your spouse / intimate friend spoke rudely

    A. She / he is impolite.

    B. She / he was in a bad mood that time.

8. Your spouse / intimate friend told you a lie

    A. She / he is very casual.

    B. She / he wanted to save herself / himself from your anger that time.

9. Your spouse / intimate friend could not complete the work

    A. She / he is incompetent.

    B. She / he is not skilled in the work she / he was doing.

10. Your spouse / intimate friend failed to arrange the function in time

      A. She / he lacks in skill.

      B. She / he is poor in organizing event.

11. Your spouse / intimate friend played a game but lost miserably

      A. She / he has no ability.

      B. She / he is weak in the game she / he played.

12. Your spouse / intimate friend went out for shopping, but bought useless things

      A. She / he lacks in intelligence.

      B. She / he is poor in money matters.

13. Your spouse / intimate friend cooked delicious food for you

      A. She / he is competent in cooking.

      B. She / he received cooperation from all family members.

14. Your spouse / intimate friend told a joke and everybody laughed

      A. She / he told the joke properly.

      B. Everybody was in humorous mood.

15. Your spouse / intimate friend accomplished success

      A. She / he is versatile.

      B. People extended support.

16. Your spouse / intimate friend did a good project

      A. She / he has ability.

      B. Luck favoured her / him a lot.

17. Your spouse / intimate friend contested for a post and won

      A. She / he is popular.

      B. Things worked out finely that occasion.

18. Your spouse / intimate friend delivered a nice speech

      A. She / he is usually well-spoken.

      B. People were in a mood to appreciate that day.

19. Your spouse / intimate friend solved a problem

A. She / he is always intelligent.
   B. Others were helpful in extending solutions that time.
20. Your spouse / intimate friend defended her / his position well
   A. She / he is usually knowledgeable.
   B. People supported her / him during the debate.
21. Your spouse / intimate friend invested money and got good returns
   A. She / he is skillful.
   B. She / he is good in monetary matters.
22. Your spouse / intimate friend played tennis and won
   A. She / he is good in games.
   B. She / he is good in tennis.
23. Your spouse / intimate friend chose the right school for your children
   A. She / he is insightful.
   B. She / he is judicious with respect to children's education.
24. Your spouse / intimate friend was appreciated for her / his work
   A. She / he is a deserving person.
   B. She / he is good in the work she / he did.

Scoring Note

- Count the number of B's from item 1 to 12 and the number of A's from 13 to 24.
- Add these two scores.
- This is your adaptive (good) explanatory style scores.
- Interpret as indicated:
  - Below 6: poor relations
  - 7 to 12: fair relationship
  - 13 to 18: good relationship
  - More than 18: very good relationship

Workplace Happiness

The centrality of workplace happiness is well-recognized in theory and application. The classical author Sigmund Freud was the first to make a bold statement that a healthy person must have the capacity to love and work. Since Freud's prophetic statement the research on interpersonal relationship and work behaviour has proliferated. A large number of researchers across the world have attempted to understand the role of job in producing a healthy life.

The accelerated growth of literature on healthy work behaviour stems from two important sources. First, work and family are the two most important domains of human activities. Humans spend a considerable amount of time at workplace. The experiences, happenings, activities and memories related to work influence not only individual's personal life but also his or her extra-organizational life. Second, the theoretical construct and empirically developed valid methods of measuring job satisfaction, job involvement and other related instruments have provided impetus for such growth. For example, Warr (1994, 1999) has explicated a triaxial approach where job satisfaction, job involvement and organizational commitment are considered job-related facets of well-being. Furthermore, recent developments in positive psychology have offered both conceptual frameworks and operationalization to study healthy work focus (Diener & Lucas, 1999).

Job Satisfaction and Happiness

The literature on job satisfaction is huge. Locks (1976) identified more than 3000 published articles on job satisfaction. Further a PsychInfo search of the years 1976 through 2000 yielded 7,855 articles on job satisfaction (Harter, Schmidt, & Hayes, 2002).

Incidentally measures of job satisfaction/ employee satisfaction are also in large numbers. The simplest is single-item scale, such as Hoppock's famous one (1935): "Choose one of the following statements which best tells us how well you like your job". There are seven alternatives from "I hate it" to "I love it". There are longer and more elaborate scales but Wanous, Reichers and Hudy (1997) carried out a meta-analysis of how these multi-item scales compare with single-item measure. They found an average correlation of .63. Despite this satisfactory level of association, many researchers perfer elaborate multi-item measures.

On the other side, there are several measures of health and well-being. More specifically the leading lights of positive psychology movement (Diener, Seligman and associates) have developed some measures while refining other measures. However, management scientists have advocated the inclusion of various physiological measures in addition to self-report scales (Danna & Griffin, 1999). The objective bio-markers include cardiovascular assessment of heart rate and blood pressure, biochemical measures of uric acid, blood sugar, steroid hormones (i.e. cortisol), serum cholesterol, catecholamines (i.e., adrenaline and noradrenaline / epinephrine or noreprinephrine), and gastrointestinal symptoms, especially peptic ulcer. Both self-report and objective measures can be used within the same research. Although studies in organizational context have started using biomarkers, both forms of measures are expected to be used with greater frequency in future.

The evaluation of perceived job stressors, job dissatisfaction and stressful life events can be made on five biochemical indicators of stress obtained through blood or urine specimen: ratio of HDL (high density lipid) cholesterol to serum cholesterol, triglyceride serum, uric acid level, systolic blood pressure, and diastolic blood pressure. Some researchers compute a composite index of stress-related coronary-rise called the **Framington Index** that combines a number of variables (glucose intolerance, and ECG abnormalities) and self-reported psychosomatic complaints such as experienced headaches, muscle fatigue, backaches, chest pains, and sleeping problems. Although correlations between self-reported stresses and biochemical measures have been found to be weak, more and more efforts are now directed towards using multi-method measures of job satisfaction as well as life satisfaction.

Despite some limitations in measurements, the correlation of job satisfaction with overall happiness is about .40 (Diener & Lucas, 1999). Employed people consistently report being happier than their counterparts without jobs (Argyle, 2001; Warr, 1994, 1999). In a survey of 7000 workers from nine European countries, Clark (1998) found that 42% reported having "high job satisfaction". Similarly, Tait, Padgett, and Baldwin (1989) carried out a meta-analysis of studies examining the association between job satisfaction and happiness. They found the average correlation of .44. the strength of this correlation was greater for men, older workers, those more involved in their work, with higher incomes, more education and self-employed (Warr, 1999).

In the context of the relation between job satisfaction and happiness in general, we may be curious to know which causes which. There are *three* possible explanations. The first possibility is positive **spillover**. Spillover is a process whereby experiences in one domain influence the other. In the context of job satisfaction, positive moods, values, skills and behaviours generated in workplace percolate to life and nonwork areas. Hence the relationship surfaces. The other explanatory concept involves **compensation**. Some people may experience deficits in their workplace. Experiencing low at job setting may motivate employees to make up the loss in family and other nonwork domains. They are motivated to leverage energy for satisfaction in family and other domains. There is also a third possibility; work and nonwork (life) domains may be independent in the sense positivity (or negativity) experienced in one domain may not affect the happening in the other domain. Though not relevant for our present context of work-happiness relation, possibility of **conflict** is not ruled out. A number of researchers have studied work-life conflict. These researchers argue that human energy is limited; hence investment of mental energy and effort in one domain creates conditions of deficit and interference in other. Job involvement may interfere with family involvement or vice versa. Conflict may be otherwise labelled as negative spill-over.

A critical factor in the relationship between work and happiness is job satisfaction, and job satisfaction is strongly correlated with life satisfaction. Researchers believe the causal direction of the relationship goes both ways (**reciprocal relationship**). Happy people find satisfaction in their work and a satisfying job contributes to individual happiness (Argyle, 2001). Conversely stress, boredom, fatigue, monotony and interpersonal conflict at work may generate dissatisfaction and unhappiness. These negative experiences may have negative spillover effects. A bad workday may contribute to intensify conflict at home and a good workday may bring happiness in the family (Diener & Seligman, 2004).

Contributing Factors

Several factors cement the relationship between work and happiness. The identification of such contributing factors is helpful in designing work setting to enhance employees' happiness.

Engagement and involvement is a key factor. Engagement is said to occur when employees find that their needs are satisfied. Engagement plays health-promotive role. In a mega-study involving more than ten thousand people, participants were bleeped every half-an-hour starting from 7 a.m. to 10 p.m. They were asked to write what they were doing and how they were feeling. This continued for quite some time. Interestingly it was found that they were feeling fine when they were busy doing something. During idle time they were not fine. This study conclusively prove that engagement reduces negative thinking and brings a sense of being useful.

Engagement reflects conditions in which employees "know what is expected of them, have what they need to do their work, have opportunities to feel something significant with coworkers whom they trust and have chances to improve and develop" (Harter et al, 2002, p. 269). Warr (1999) has reported that the most engaging jobs are those with special duties and in which there is a good match between the required activities and the skills and personality of the employees. For example, Harter and Schmidt (2002) carried out a meta-analysis of positivity reporting of 300,000 employees in more than 50 companies. Their engagement item ("I have the opportunity to do what I do best") was predictive of success and productivity. Harter et al, (2002) also found a significant correlation of .37 between employee performance and several indicators of work engagement.

Employee engagement bears resemblance to the **construct of flow** (Csikszentmihalyi & Csikszentmihalyi, 1988). As discussed in earlier chapters, flow is experienced when there is a matching between job difficulty and perceived ability. As shown by the exhibit, an employee's absorption and engagement is ensured in right kind condition with high level of challenge and high level of perceived skill. A major implication of this flow model demands arrangement of such matching by the work organization and the leader.

Exhibit Level of Challenge

	Low	High
Perceived Skill — High	Boredom	**Flow**
Perceived Skill — Low	Apathy	Anxiety

Akin to the concept of engagement is the construct of **commitment** (Herrbach, 2006). Herrbach observed that employees who experience more positive affect at work are more likely to experience higher level of affective commitment in their respective organizations. This would positively influence employee's motivation to work hard, work productively and stay in the organization for a longer time. Commitment would strengthen the relationship between work and happiness.

Needs and goals. Happiness is not independent of individual needs. Individual employees strive towards needs and goals; successful attainment generates happiness which, in turn, furthers productivity.

Happy workers generally have a sense of efficiency and effectiveness in performing their work activities. A meta-analysis of 300 samples (about 55,000 workers) yielded a significant correlation of .30 between performance on general satisfaction. Similarly, **career self-efficacy**, which is defined as the personal confidence in one's capacity to handle career development was found to be significantly related to both success and satisfaction with one's occupational efforts and decisions (Betz & Luzzo, 1996).

Performing well at work is more likely when workers have clear goals. As shown in relevant literature, lucid goals offer satisfaction when they are met (Snyder, Lopez & Pedrotti, 2011). Most research in this area has investigated the links between happiness and successful work performance by examining success as a predictor and happiness as an outcome (i.e., good work performance leads to a happy life). Boehm and Lyubomirsky (2008) investigated the relationship in the other direction. On the basis of an elaborate review of relevant literature, they concluded that happiness is a precursor to career success (Happy people are more successful at work).

Another construct, **need saliency**, appears to be very relevant in the context of performance satisfaction relationship. Cross-cultural motivational psychologists posit that different needs do have different potential for satisfying different subset of human populations (Kanungo, 1982). Accordingly, some work-related needs (e.g., pay, security, interesting nature of work) are salient (rated very high) for some categories of populations whereas other needs are *nonsalient* (rated low in priority). According to **need saliency theory**, job involvement (also work involvement) is related to salient need satisfaction and unrelated to nonsalient need satisfaction. Kanungo and associates have conducted a number of unicultural and cross-cultural studies; they have found supportive evidence. Sahoo and associates (2014) have carried a number of studies in Indian context; the need saliency is greatly supported. Interestingly the factor of interesting / challenging nature of work emerges as the most salient need in western context. In contrast, security emerges as the most salient need in Afro-Asian countries in general and India in particular. The implication of saliency model is clear. Leaders and organizations need to identify *salient needs* in specific target work population prior to fulfilling these needs for productivity and employee well-being.

In addition to need saliency theory, there are two other well-articulated frameworks that contribute towards an understanding of job-happiness relationship.

Job Characteristic Model

The Job Characteristic Model (JCM) is one of the most influential framework of work redesign in the JCM, five characteristics – skills variety, task identity, task significance, task autonomy, and task feedback – are identified in order to capture the general content and structure of jobs. The presence of these core job dimensions leads to three psychological states – perceived meaningfulness of work, felt responsibility for outcomes, and knowledge of results. In turn, it is posited that employees with a need for personal growth and development, as well as knowledge and skill, will display a wide range of positive personal and work outcomes, including greater work motivation, performance, satisfaction with work, and lower absenteeism and turnover as a result of job quality.

Figure

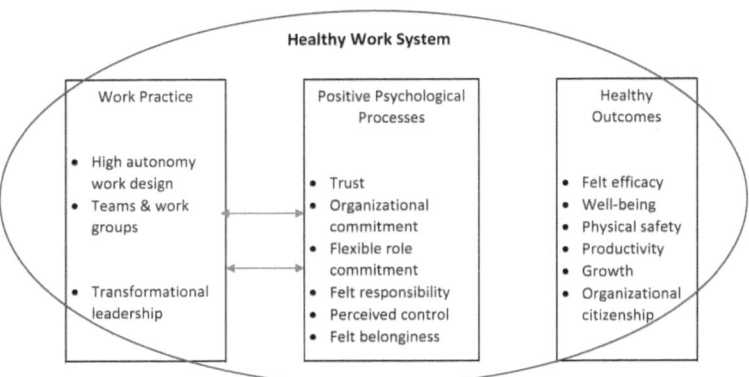

By combining the aspects of the JCM, a Motivating Potential Score (MPS) can be generated to provide a comparative metric of job enrichment. The MPS is calculated as follows: (skill variety + task significance + task identify) ÷ 3 x task autonomy x task feedback. Higher MPS indicates greater job enrichment (Hackman & Oldham, 1976).

Demand/control model: Karasek (1979) has proposed demand/control model to design jobs that enhances psychological and physical well-being. According to this model, healthy work environments are those in which appropriate demands (e.g., production goals) are made of workers who are given correspondingly suitable amounts of decision latitude (e.g., the ability to control the pace and method of work).

Karasek (1979) explains the effects of work design on well-being through a learning and development mechanism. Jobs with high demands and high control (termed 'active' jobs) can inhibit stress by promoting both employee confidence and active learning. Workers with active jobs are more likely to apply coping strategies and seek challenging situations that promote mastery. In contrast, a "relaxed" job (low demands and high control) does not provide employees with much intrinsic motivation. Similarly "high strain" jobs (high demand and low control) are likely to encourage a form of helplessness. Last, a "passive" job (low demand and low control) does not encourage skill development.

Exhibit : Demand / Control Model

	Demand Low	Demand High
Control High	Related Jobs	Active Jobs
Control Low	Passive Jobs	High Strain Jobs

There is a striking parallelism between the Flow model and Demand/Control model. The major implication involves this blending of task challenge and perceived competence. This is needed for enhancing workplace happiness,

An Integrated Approach

The discussion on the role of several psychological factors such as engagement/involvement, commitment, need saliency, intrinsic motivation and so on does not preclude the contribution of other conditions such as pay, safe work environment, respect and appreciation, companionship, and loyalty to coworkers and bosses (Turner, Barling, & Zacharatos, 2005).

Many of the generalizations derived are also moderated by factors such as age, gender and personality.

Moderating variables: A number of individual difference variables moderate the relationship between work and happiness. Researchers find that job satisfaction increases with age. There is a U-shaped pattern. Young workers have greater aspirations, expectations and eagerness to learn. For older workers, job satisfaction also increases. This happens because older workers have better jobs, are paid more, have more intrinsic reward, and have greater commitment. Similarly, many studies have examined gender effect (Clark, 1998). Many studies report that women are more satisfied than men (Clark, 1998). It is expected that male workers would have greater job satisfaction because they have better jobs, receive higher pay, and enjoy higher occupational status. However, women have different expectation of work; they may accept being paid less. Researchers find that personal control is more important for men whereas support from supervisor is more important for women.

Arvy and associates (1994) studied 2200 pairs of twins and found that 30% of the variability in job satisfaction could be explained by genetic factors. In general, positive affect in job is related to extraversion and negative affect in job is associated with neuroticism. Personal control is a desirable feature of job. Employees with internal locus of control report greater job satisfaction (Argyle, 2001).

Effects of job satisfaction. As discussed earlier, happy workers work better. Job satisfaction greatly improves performance. A meta-analysis of 217 studies found an average correlation of .17. Some studies have found a strong correlation for workers at higher levels of skill ($r=.31$, versus .15 for others).

Job satisfaction has been shown to produce other benefits such as organizational citizenship behaviour (OCB), reduced absenteeism and reduced labour turnover. Studies of job satisfaction have reported a positive correlation of .25 between job satisfaction and OCB. Similarly, a meta-analysis of 114studies indicates a correlation of -.15 between job satisfaction and absenteeism. Further job satisfaction is found to predict turnover (intention to quit) by a year later (Argyle, 2001).

Overall, work is good for mental health. Murphy and Athanasou (1999) analyzed 16 longitudinal studies and found positive effect for mental health. It was .54 for starting work and -.36 for stopping work. For some individuals, work is stressful and it can be a source of ill-health. A measure that has commonly been used is the General Health Questionnaire (the GHQ; Goldberg, 1978). It has been found that job satisfaction is predictive of scores on the GHQ and similar well-being measures (Argyle, 2001).

Social support from coworkers or supervisors can do a lot to reduce work stress. It is asserted that job stress is less for those who have atleast one friend at work. Such friends provide tangible help, informational assistance, acceptance, and confidence.

The therapeutic role of work has extensively been reported. Ross and Mirowsky (1995) follows up 2500 individuals for a year, and found that those in full-time work indicated no decline in health. In contrast, all the other groups including housewives had some problems. Being paid explains a part of this, but full-time college (unpaid) is as good as work.

Job satisfaction is a stable predictor of health. Individuals at work rarely complain about psychosomatic problems such as headaches and stomach upsets. They also report fewer illnesses such as heart attacks, arthritis, and a shorter length of life. However, there was a classical study involving administrative grades of the British Civil Service. It was shown that the lowest grades has 3 ½ times the rate of fatal heart attacks as those in the top grades. This was basically due to difference in health behaviours such as smoking drinking, obesity, and physical inactivity. Further factors may be the lack of control and autonomy in low-grade jobs.

Effect of unemployment. While work offers happiness, unemployment may be a source of unhappiness. The level of unemployment varies across time and a high level creates high levels of stress. Unemployment affects every aspect of happiness including positive affects, negative affects and life satisfaction. The unemployed feel bored, experience low self-esteem and sometimes hostile. A basic feature of the lifestyle of the unemployed is the way they use their unstructured time. They use a lot of time in passive leisures such as TV watching.

The unemployed have often been found to be more depressed and anxious. They show other signs of poor mental health. The meta-analytic study of Murphy and Athanasou (1999) clearly shows starting work leads to increasing mental health and unemployment and loss of jobs have adverse effect on health. The condition of employment becomes more distressing if there is lack of money and social support. People with neuroticism are likely to be much more distressed. In order to relieve the unhappiness of the unemployed, a few steps may be undertaken. They may be helped to learn to use unstructured time properly. Social contacts outside the family is a big help. An important step in the direction is to provide broad goals and purposes resulting in involved activities.

Job, career and calling. Like any other goal-directed journey, a purposive work life is also a journey with a destination. It starts with a *job*, gets transformed to a *career*, and ultimately becomes a *calling* where the distinction between the means and ends is lost. Work becomes the means as well as ends. Although the role of money and other incentives is useful in the beginning of one's own work life, it does not take very far.

On the basis of recent development in behavioural sciences, it is asserted that an integration and synthesis of multiple sources of capital is needed for the peak attainment. Luthans and his associates (2015) have stressed the role of positive psychological capital in recent decades. Yet, the following combination is suggested as the multiple source

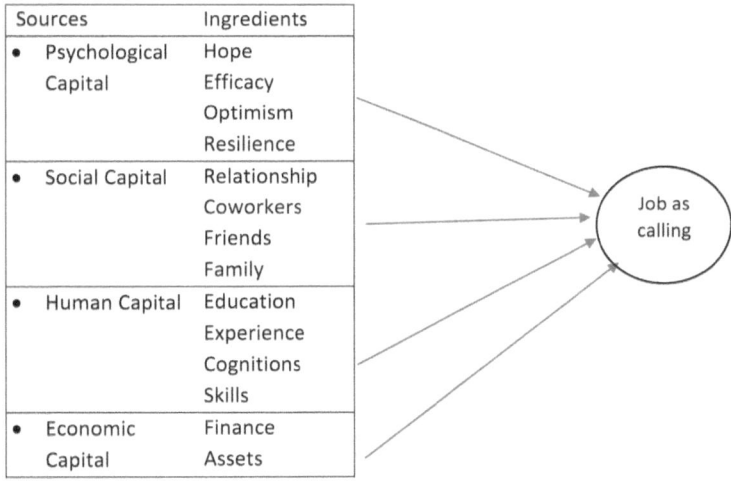

Community Happiness

Man is not an island. Human life is embedded in a community. It is not possible to have sustainable happiness in the absence of community well-being. Personal happiness and community happiness are dynamically related. There is a reciprocal relationship. If an individual is genuinely happy, the happiness flows to other members and groups of the community. Similarly community well-being offers conditions for individual growth and development resulting in authentic happiness (Seligman, 2002).

A basic condition for mutual interactive position is the provision of security. People need to feel secure in a community. They need to carry out day-to-day livinghood and transactions in their community. They must feel safe to walk along during the day and nights. The outbreak of war and various natural calamities (earthquake, floods, hurricane, cyclone, Covid19) pose threat to community well-being. People can strive for other needs once a basic sense of security is fulfilled. In addition to ensured safety, community well-being offers space and places where people can meet, spend time with friends and enjoy interaction. Further, the community must be free of discriminatory practices.

Person–Community Fit

A good community living requires a match between person's personality, goals, ambitions, aesthetics and the offerings of the community. Once people's survival (basic) needs ae met, they look forward to satisfying other needs preferably intrinsic needs.

In the context of need satisfaction, there are two important elements. First, Maslow's hierarchy of needs concept provides that human needs are hierarchically arranged; people make transitions from lower-order needs to higher-order needs: physiological, security, social, self-esteem and self-actualization needs. Viewed from this angle, a community help at each stage of a person's journey is of great help.

Second, the need saliency theory has also some

relevance. A community contains a big chunk of population. Accordingly, different subsets are likely to attach priority to different needs. For example, some people may consider security needs as highly salient (important) whereas other people may view autonomy as salient. Hence potential for community well-being would be high where opportunities exist for satisfaction of multiple needs.

Community Involvement

Happiness requires active involvement in community, groups and organizations. Many people belong to groups that connect them to a wider network of friends and associates. Participating in outreach activities to clean up the community, feed those in need, running night schools helping differentially able children and the care of the destitute provide channels of experiencing joy.

In India, there are many faith communities working for the disadvantaged. An active involvement in the voluntary service activities of these faith communities is a constant source of happiness (Myers, 2000).

The Spirit of Giving

A cardinal principle of community happiness involves the spirit of giving. The spirit of giving back to society is invaluable. Neuroscientists have found that the regions of the brain that are activated when we receive money (based on fMRI) glow even brighter when we give money (Davidson & Begley, 2013). According to Jordin Grafman, a neuroscientist at the National Institute of Health (USA), these reactions in the brain "help us plan into the future, feel emotionally closer to others, and give us a sense of reward after a behaviour – which reinforces that behaviour, making it more likely we will do the same thing again".

We often get a sense of joy from giving a gift to our friends. When we do a thing for others we know how we can make a difference. Rath and Harter (2010) surveyed more than 21,00 people on this topic of giving. Nearly 9 to 10 reported "getting an emotional boost" from doing kind things for other people.

Throughout the course of our lives, well-doing promotes deeper social interaction, enhanced meaning and purpose, and a sense of active lifestyle. Several studies have shown positive links between altruism and happiness. For example, in situations where people donate their organs for others, pleasures of donors and receivers are incalculable. As a part of gallup's global research, people are asked if they have volunteered in the organ donation event. Across 150 countries, researchers find that people who are involved in this donation programme are immensely happy.

Thus, people with high community happiness feel safe and secure where they live. They take pride in their community and believe that it is headed in the right direction. They have the mindset of giving back to community. They have also identified areas where they can make a meaningful contribution for the community and world at large.

Chapter 8

Explanatory Frameworks

Research involves systematic investigations. Research in the area of happiness/well-being has identified a large number of interesting questions. The research has also helped to develop and validate a number of measurement tools. The effective use of instruments both in the unicultural as well as multi-cultural settings has generated sufficient amount of empirical findings. Yet, a basic problem exists with respect to the meaningful interpretation of findings. Although researchers have handpicked their pet theories to explain findings, the lack of robust explanatory model has posed a big problem.

The search for robust theory of happiness continues. While a meaningful category of psychological theories is still awaited, the existing frameworks may be helpful for understanding the process nature of happiness. The identification of predictors of happiness offers scope for increment of happiness. Yet, a search for theoretical frameworks has generated many useful ideas for happiness enhancement programmes. Drawing on the list of theories offered by Diener and Ryan (2009), salient features of major theories of happiness are described.

Telic Theories

Telic or endpoint theories maintain that happiness is gained when some state, such as goal or need, is reached. It is further maintained that satisfaction of needs causes happiness and conversely, the persistence of unfulfilled needs causes unhappiness.

Alternatively, telic theories are derived from different origins of the strivings. In need theories, there are certain innate or learned needs that the person seeks to fulfill. The person may or may not be aware of these needs. Nevertheless, it is postulated that happiness will follow from their fulfillment. In contrast, goal theories are based on specific desires of which the person is aware. The person is consciously seeking certain goals and happiness results when goals are reached. Goals and needs are related in that underlying needs may lead to specific goals. Needs may be universal, such as those postulated by Maslow or they may differ from individual to individual.

It is not just enough to know goal-happiness linkage. It is necessary to identify the attributes of goal strivings that cause happiness.

The Quality of Goals

Goal attainment is a benchmark for experience of happiness. When asked what makes a happy life, people often say the fulfillment of their goals, wishes, desires and ambitions. Researchers go deeper and find that happiness is a by-product of deeper strivings and involvement in worthwhile project and activities.

Although people in general and researchers in particular highlight the construct of "meaning" in human lives, meaning has no meaning independent of goals. Goals are signals that orient people to what is valuable, meaningful and purposeful. All goals are not equal. Some goals are trivial whereas other goals are meaningful. In recent years psychologists are delineating such goals with attribute of personal meaning (Emmons, 2007).

Resent empirical research has demonstrated a strong association between goals with personal meaning on one hand and happiness on the other (Emmons, 1991).

At an empirical level, a great deal of research has been devoted to identify meaningful goals. Incidentally such research has involved diverse methodologies, varied samples and different settings. Gradually a consensual taxonomy of life meaning has emerged. There is much convergence across three major lists. Ebersole (1998) lists life narratives, life work, relationships, religious beliefs, and service, while Emmons (1999) includes personal strivings, achievement, intimacy, religiosity, spirituality, and generativity. Wong (1998) mentions personal meaning, achievement, relationship, religion, and self-transcendence.

Taken together, the literature delineates *"Big Four"* taxonomy of personal meaning dimensions (WIST): work, intimacy, spirituality, and transcendence. It may be noted that transcendence/generativity entails contributing to society, leaving a legacy, and transcending self-interest.

Goal Contents and Happiness

As indicated earlier, not all goals are created equal. People strive for diverse ends in their goal pursuits, and all goals do not contribute towards their well-being. In a meta-analysis of the relation between personality and well-being, DeNeve and Cooper (1998) analyzed the role of 137 personality traits in the context of well-being. Such a systematic review of literature coded personal goals into broad thematic clusters. Twelve thematic content categories were found to be related to well-being / happiness.

Emmons (1999) further categorized them into three broad types of goal strivings (intimacy, generativity and spirituality). These three goal types correspond to three of the four major categories of personal meaning. Intimacy expresses a desire for close, reciprocal relationship (e.g., "Help my friends and let them know I care"). Spirituality goals are oriented towards transcending the self (e.g., Learn to tune into higher power throughout the day"). Generativity denotes commitment and concern for future generations (e.g., "Feel useful to society").

Across several samples of population, the presence of intimacy strivings, generativity strivings, and spirituality strivings within a person's goal hierarchy generate greater happiness. Conversely, power strivings tend to be associated with lower levels of well-being (Emmons, 1991).

Intrinsic versus extrinsic orientation" Another productive line of investigation concerns the relative importance of intrinsic versus extrinsic needs in the context of happiness.

Kasser and Ryan (1996) rated the importance of extrinsic and intrinsic needs as perceived by people and examined this perceived priority with their well-being. They found that perceived importance of extrinsic goals was positively linked with measures of anxiety, depression, narcissism, and physical illness symptoms. In contrast, perceived importance of intrinsic goals of personal growth and community contributions was predictor of well-being. The authors concluded that there is a dark side to the American dream and a relative emphasis on fame, fortune and success to the neglect of intrinsically meaningful goals is likely to lead to psychological and interpersonal problems.

The how of goal-setting: The how of goal-setting is also related to happiness. Two broad ways of goal-setting can be contrasted: approach orientation and avoidance orientation. This orientation refers to individual difference in the mental representation of goals.

Approach orientation corresponds to the degree to which individuals are striving for positive, desirable goals. In contrast, avoidance orientation entails striving to avoid negative, aversive goals. The distinction between approach and avoidance is fundamental and basic to the study of human behaviour and motivation. Approach goals are positive incentives to be sought after whereas avoidant goals are negative consequences to be avoided and prevented. For example, an individual may be trying to "spend time with friends" versus "avoid being lonely". In general, between 10 and 20% of a person goals tend to be avoidance goals (Emmons, 1999). A number of studies have shown that avoidant striving is associated with less positive psychological outcomes compared to approach strivings (Emmons, 1999). Emmons and Kaiser (1996) found that individuals with avoidant strivings experience a larger number of psychological distress including anxiety.

Taken together not all goals but the quality of goal strivings lead to the experience of happiness. Research shows that goal strivings in the area of big four WIST (work, intimacy, spirituality and transcendence) produce meaningful experience. Stated differently, strivings in goal domains of intimacy, spirituality and generativity are associated with happiness while strivings in goal domain of power is negatively related. Further intrinsic goals have positive relation, while extrinsic goals have negative relation with well-being. In addition, approach goal orientation is viewed as a predictor of happiness while avoidant orientation in goal striving is considered as an inhibitor of well-being. In view of this deep linkage between goal strivings and well-being, many researchers categorize Ryan and Deci's (2000) SDT (Self-determination theory) as both a telic theory and eudaimonia theory. It may be added that Ryan and Deci emphasize the relatedness, competence and autonomy in human functioning.

Top-down versus Bottom-up Theories

Both top-down and bottom-up well-being theories conceptualize well-being in terms of its parts. However, bottom-up theories maintain that well-being is simply the sum of many small pleasures. According to this view, when a person judges whether his or her life is happy, some mental calculation is used to sum up momentary pleasures or pain. A happy life in this view is an accumulation of happy moments. In contrast, the top-down approach assumes that there is a global propensity to experience things in a positive way and this propensity (personality trait) influences the momentary world. In other words, well-being is a trait arising from inherited or habitual propensity to experience the world in a specific manner (e.g., optimism).

The concept of the top-down theory approach emerges to avoid getting stuck to the hedonic treadmill. In the context of bottom-up approach, accumulation of pleasant moments is a necessary condition for well-being. For example, a person gets promotion, wins a lottery, and enjoys leisure. The accumulation of pleasant events brings happiness. Gradually holidays are over, money is exhausted and routine life is imposed. The feeling of pleasure ends. The person is back to hedonic treadmill. The lack of pleasant moments has potential to make someone depressed. If we want to be happy every-day we need to find at least two pleasant moments to be accumulated at one time. This is the assumption based on the bottom-up theory of happiness.

In contrast, the presence of the top-down approach is expected to address limitations in viewing well-being as limited by separate dimensions. For example, Andrews (1974) discusses how to assess the quality of life by using perception. Because objective conditions bring many variations, it is relatively dependable to treat person's perception as the behavioural denominator. Gregory (2015) also argues that anything seen can have different meanings and the process of interpretations may vary.

The ability in building perceptions of the quality of life is derived from prior experience and knowledge about the situations and environment. King (2010) posits that perception arises from complex processes based on experience, knowledge, and trust.

The construct of perception as a cognitive mediator plays dynamic role within the person and determines the person's evaluation of life in the past, present and future.

Thus, a significant amount of literature of well-being focuses on top-down approach. Instead of being influenced by the valence (positivity and negativity of experience), maintaining a positive mood within is likely to maintain stability in experience. This would be consistent with the expectation of the top-down theory.

The discussion on top-down theories orients research attention towards various forms of cognitive theories. These cognitive theories are related to top-down conceptualization in that they posit that cognitive processes determine individual happiness.

Cognitive Theories

Cognitive theories focus on processes including bias, attention, memory and present orientation. They indicate the ways in which individuals scan events, remember them and interpret them. They also denote the filter system in belief. SDT (Ryan & Deci, 2000) can be classified as a cognitive theory. The autonomy component of SDT (the belief that the individual has freedom to choose activities) gives SDT the cognitive character.

Similarly, Lyubomirsky and Diekerhoof (2010) posited the construal model of happiness. They contend that happy and unhappy people emphasize differing cognitive interpretations. For example, happy people focus more on human and nonmaterial aspects than do less happy people.

Within the rubric of cognitive theories, there are various forms.

Associationistic Theories

Many theories are based on memory, conditioning or cognitive principles that can be subsumed under the broad rubric of associationistic models. Cognitive approaches to well-being are in their infancy. One cognitive approach rests on the attributions (explanations) people make about the events happening to them. For example, those event bring the most well-being if they attributed to internal and stable factors. (e.g., I am able to please people forever).

One general cognitive approach to well-being has to do with associative networks in memory. Forgas, Bower, and Moylan (1990) have shown that people will recall memories that are affectively congruent with their current emotional state. Research on memory network suggests that persons could develop a rich network of positive associations and a more limited and isolated network of negative ones. In such persons, more events or ideas could be happy ideas and affect. Thus, a person with such a predominantly positive network could be predisposed to react to more events in a positive way.

A related type to theory is based on classically conditioned elicitation of affect. Research has shown that affective conditioning can be extremely resistant to extinctions. Thus, happy persons might be those who have had very positive affective experiences associated with a large number of frequent every-day stimuli Zajonc'(1998) contends that affective reaction occurs independently or/ and more rapidly than cognitive evaluation of stimuli.

There is some evidence that a person can give conscious direction to the affective association in his or her life. Fordyce (1977) offered evidence that a conscious attempt to reduce negative thoughts can increase happiness. It is found that reciting positive statements in the morning leads to a happier day. It is also found that positive thinking similar to that recommended by Norman Peale is correlated with well-being. Thus, explicit conscious attempt to avoid negative thoughts and to think of happy ones may increase happiness.

Certain individuals may have built up a strong network of positive associations and earned to react habitually in a positive way. These individuals are characterized as possessing a happy temperament. A person with a Pollyanna approach to life is perhaps the protype of a person who has formed positive associations to the world. Several studies have found a relationship between happiness, a cognitive bias towards positive associations and high Pollyanna personality scores.

Judgment Theories

Judgment theories maintain that well-being results

from a comparison between some standard and actual conditions. If actual conditions exceed, happiness will result. In the case of satisfaction, such comparisons may be conscious. However, in the case of affect, comparison with a standard may occur in a nonconscious manner.

Judgment theories are classified on the basis of the standard that is used. In social comparison theories, one uses other people as a standard. It a person is better off than others, persons would be satisfied or happy. Sometimes a person's past life is used to set standard. If the individual's current life exceeds this standard, that person will probably be happy.

In social comparison framework, proximal others are usually weighted heavily because of their salience. Wills (1981) showed that downward comparison with less fortunate persons can increase well-being. It was also found that believing others live in poor circumstances can enhance one's life satisfaction. It is argued that whether the amount of income that will satisfy people depends on the income of others in the society. One shortcoming to social comparison theories is that they do not make clear when a person will need to make comparison with others.

Adaptation theory is based on a standard derived from an individual's own experience. If current events are better than the standard, the individuals will be happy. However, if the good events continue, adaptation will occur, the individual's standard will rise, so that it eventually matches the newer events. Thus, according to the adaptation theory, recent changes produce happiness and unhappiness because a person will eventually adapt to the overall level of events. It is shown that lottery winners are no happier and quadriplegias in less happy than normal control. It is suggested that people adapt to all events, no matter how fortunate or unfortunate. It is also found that spinal cord injury victims are extremely unhappy after their accidents. However, their affect quickly begins moving back towards happiness suggesting that adaptation is occurring rapidly even to this extreme misfortune.

Parducci (1968) developed a provocative theory of well-being based on laboratory models of human judgment. The range principle frequency model predicts a precise standard against which incoming events are judged. The model has the most interesting implications for persons, who have skewed distributions of life events. It predicts that the greatest happiness will occur for those who have a negatively skewed distribution of events. A positively skewed distribution of events will produce unhappiness a majority of the time.

One popular form of judgment theory is aspiration level. It maintains that happiness will depend on the discrepancy in a person's life between actual conditions and aspirations. Happiness depends on the ratio of unfulfilled desires to total desires. According to this theory, high aspirations are as much a threat to happiness as are bad conditions. The level of aspiration presumably comes from an individual's previous experience, goals and so forth. Although there is evidence that supports the idea that the discrepancy between actual conditions and the level a person aspires is correlated with well-being, this relationship does not appear to be strong.

A fundamental question related to judgment theories deals with when each type of comparisons takes precedence. For example, when will social comparison be most important and when will adaptation or one's prior conditions be more important? There is some suggestion that social comparison may be more important to many satisfaction judgments. In contrast, one's prior experience may usually have more influence on affect.

Thus, the exploration of the process nature of well-being has identified a number of theoretical routes. Researchers have attempted to substantiate their own viewpoint in terms of supportive empirical evidence. Yet, a crucial examination of their relative standings is a challenging task that lies ahead.

Benefit of Downward Comparison

As indicated in the foregoing section, downward social comparison is an internal cognitive process whereby one compares oneself with worse-off others (Wills, 1981). This type of down ward social comparison enhances application of one's own circumstance and helps sustain, motivation and well-being (Wood, 1989).

Considering the view that it may be useful to train people to adopt downward comparisons, researchers have attempted to study the underlying mechanisms of social comparison. In a study Stewart, Chipperfield, Ruthing and Heckhausen (2013) attempted to examine a boundary condition on the protective relationship between downward social comparison and well-being among older adults.

The study was based on the Heckhausen et al's (2010) the Motivational Theory of Lifespan Development. The theory asserts that striving for control is a vital part of human adaptation, it underlies much of our goal-directed behaviour. Hence it has direct positive impact on well-being. Stewart et al (2013) argued that individuals who effectively exert control in their environment are likely to experience well-being. In contrast, individual who cannot control their circumstances are likely to experience psychological distress. They further argued that advanced age restricts many daily tasks and this task restriction leads to declining control and diminishing well-being.

Stewart et al (2013) attempted to examine whether downward social comparison (comparing oneself with the worse off offers secondary control and prevents the decline in well-being.

Community-dwelling older adults (ages 79-97) experiencing task restrictions were identified. Empirical tests of well-being, perceived stress and older adult adjustment were administered. In-depth interviews were conducted to identify moderating variables of their well-being and adjustment.

It was shown that there is a significant interaction between downward social comparison and perceived control for three outcomes: life satisfaction, perceived stress, and depressive symptoms. However, the analysis revealed that downward social comparison was associated with greater well-being at low levels of perceived control, but was unrelated to well-being at higher levels of perceived control. In other words, older adults have less need to protect their well-being via secondary control strategy like downward social comparison when perceived control is high and goals are still attainable.

Lyubomirsky (2007) was interested in another issue. She was interested to find out what kinds of social comparisons are used by happy people vis-à-vis unhappy people. She singled out "exceptionally happy" and "exceptionally unhappy" people and then interviewed both groups at length. Her initial assumption was that happy people would be more likely to compare themselves with others who were inferior (thus making themselves feel better off), whereas unhappy people would be inclined to compare themselves with others who were superior (thus rendering themselves unhappy). However, the analysis of the interview revealed that happy people did not seem to care. Instead, they appeared to use their own internal standards to judge themselves (e.g., how good they are in swimming or literature). The subsequent research indicated that the happiest people take pleasure in other people's success and show concern in the face of other's failures. In contrast, unhappy persons are deflated rather than delighted about their peers' accomplishments and are relieved rather than sympathetic in the face of their peers' failures.

Lyubomirsky (2007) further investigated this problem in laboratory experimental condition. She involved very happy and very unhappy people as participants in an experiment. She also used "confederate" and the participants were not aware of this arrangement.

In the lab situations, two individuals were seated facing each other. One of them was the real participant and the other was the confederate. The real participant knew that the other person is also another participant. At the central position, the investigator (experimenter) was seated. Impression was given that both the participants are required to play and solve anagram problems.

The investigator holds a large number of cards that are serially numbered. At the beginning of the experiment, the investigator hands over Card 1 and Card 2 to these two participating players. Each card has three problems. Each problem contains 5 randomized letters and each participant is required to make meaningful three-letter word. After the participant completes solving three problems on the card, he/she is supposed to hand it over to the investigator and gets a new card for next trial.

Since the experimenter uses manipulation and the confederate quickly solves the problem. The confederate hands over solved card quickly and gets new card. By the time the participant completes one card, the confederate finishes three cards. Since cards are numbered, the participant could see the rapidity with which other partner's task is completed. In other words, the manipulation was such the participant is placed in the condition of *upward social comparison* (e.g., the other person is superior).

The result of the study was interesting. Happy participants felt more upbeat than they had been earlier and thought better of their ability, regardless of whether they had seen someone performing better. Unhappy people reported feeling more sad, frustrated, and anxious after sitting next to someone who outperformed them. The happier the person, the less attention he/she pays to how others around him/her are doing.

In view of negative outcomes of ruminations and upward social comparisons, Lyubomirsky (2007) offers some useful tips to shake off damaging thoughts. With a view to prevent harmful ruminations, one can follow certain effective strategies. The first strategy is to select a distracting activity (an interesting activity, of course). The second strategy is the "Stop" technique: you may think, say or even shout to yourself, "Stop" or "No" when you find yourself ruminating. The third strategy is to talk to a sympathetic or trusted person about your thoughts and problems.

Apart from these strategies, you need to gain a new perspective on yourself and your problems. Write a list of situations (places, times, and people) that appear to trigger your ruminations. If possible, avoid these situations. Finally carry a big picture of your life. This would help you to free yourself from the tyranny of trifles. These are some of the tips that would help you to shake off harmful comparisons. Remember the Buddhist precept: "A flower does not compare itself with other flowers; it just blooms".

Neuroscience of Happiness

The most recent entry into the domain of explanatory frameworks is the cerebral model of happiness. Although it is still in the process of refinement, the possibility of further exploration and experimentation suggests new directions.

Studies of Brain Mechanisms

Studies of brain mechanisms represent the frontiers of happiness research. Considering the proposition that happiness essentially consists of two major ingredients of *hedonia* (a psychological state of pleasure) and *eudaimonia* (meaningfulness), contemporary brain research has been directed to identify neural correlates of these two ingredients.

Fortunately, the recent advances in neuropsychology have identified the neural correlates of hedonia or pleasure components. In contrast it is relatively more difficult to comprehend brain activity linked with eudaimonia (cognitive and moral aspect of a life lived).

Eudaimonia means essentially a life experienced as valuably meaningful and as engaging. The goal has been to uncover how such experiences are reflected in patterns of brain function.

At the conceptual level, hedonia processing and eudaimonic meaningfulness appear to be different. Yet, empirically, there is a great linkage. High questionnaire scores on hedonia and eudaimonia typically converges in happy people. It is found that 80 per cent of people reporting their lives as meaningful also report their life satisfaction as "pretty to very happy". Similarly, 80% of people reporting higher levels of total life satisfaction view their lives as meaningful (Diener, Kesebir & Lucas, 2008). The tendency of pleasure and meaningfulness ratings to cohere together opens a potential opportunity for the neuroscientific study of both aspects of happiness. If both pleasure and meaningfulness co-occur in the same happy people, then identifying neural markers of one may provide information for the other.

The pleasure aspect is most tractable. Happy people typically feel more pleasure in life. It has been suggested that the best and simplest measure of happiness may be to merely ask people how they hedonically feel right now – again and again – so as to assess their pleasure accumulation (Kahneman, 1999). Such repeated self-reports of pleasure states could be used for identifying stable neurobiological brain *traits* that dispose particular individuals towards happiness.

In the context of identifying happy brain, the pioneering research of Richard Davidson stands out (Davidson & Begley, 2012; Goleman, 2003). Davidson's research has shown that there are regions of the prefrontal cortex (PC) associated with happy and unhappy states (Figure 1).

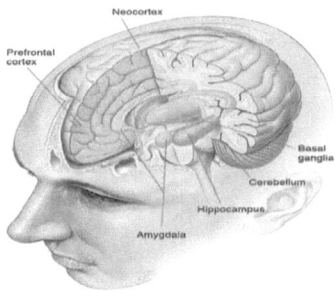

Figure 1. Key Regions of the Brain
Source: From Siegel (2007)

The cortex is the outer layer of the brain, and it is enlarged in mammals, particularly in humans. The areas of the brain that Davidson identified are the middle prefrontal cortex (Figure 2), the left and right middle frontal gyruses (LMFG and rMFG). People with high levels of electrical activity in the LMFG report feeling happy and people with high levels of activity in the rMFG report feeling unhappy (Goleman, 2003). In addition, people with high levels of electrical activity in the left prefrontal region are able to notice and appreciate positive experiences. They are found to be capable of creating a happy life. In contrast, subjects with high electrical activity in the rMFG reported high incidence of emotions such as worry, anxiety and sadness.

Davidson uses the ratio of left to right activity in the MFG as a ratio of brain equation for happiness. He found that the ratio tends to be fairly stable for any individual. While circumstances may change, events affect the MFG ratio only slightly, and it returns to baseline levels quickly. Thus, Davidson's research shows that people have a happiness set point. It is consistent with the proposition that happiness is at least 50% genetically determined.

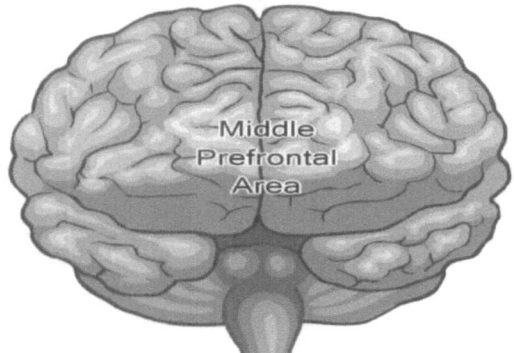

Figure 2. The Key Region Linked with Happiness
Source: From Siegel (2007)

Goleman (2003) reports a number of studies where senior practitioners in the Tibetan Buddhist tradition indicated greater left prefrontal activities. Davidson argues that the MFG ratio is more responsive to inner states than outer circumstances. This is consistent with the Buddhist view that mental happiness is effectively maintained through inner discipline.

Davidson's follow-up studies involve participants in mindfulness-based stress reduction (MBSR) programme. Researchers measured MFG ratios in subjects before and after they participated in a 8-week programme, which required a daily meditation practice of 45 minutes. Results showed that the MFG ratios increased significantly. Participants also reported greater happiness, decreased anxiety. A bulk of studies indicate that meditation can cause a significant leftward shift in MFG ratios.

A related finding is that mindfulness tends to be associated with activity in similar areas of the brain, as the mood centers – the middle prefrontal regions. Initial research suggests that the anterior cingulate cortex (ACC) is centrally involved. Other areas associated with attention include the dorsolateral and orbitofrontal regions of the PC (Figure 3).

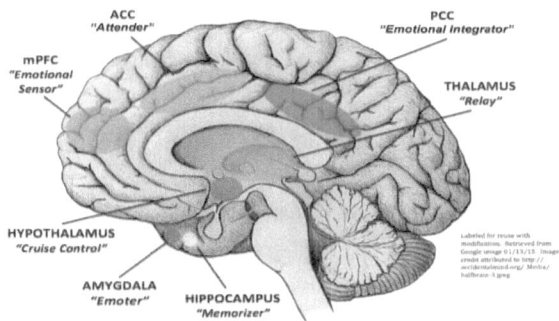

Figure 3. The ACC Region and Other Relevant Areas
Source: From Goleman (2003)

Siegel (2007) evaluated the pertinent literature and concluded that mindfulness uses much of the same brain circuitry as our social engagement system. In empathizing with another we activate the medial prefrontal cortex (MPC), especially the anterior cingulate cortex region (ACC). It appears that mindfulness is a form of inner attunement. This attunement is important during early childhood, when our social engagement system is wired into the brain by the experiences an infant has in relationship with caregivers. The brains of adults who were securely attached as children exhibit mark of the same functions as do brains of those who have practiced mindfulness. It is indicative of the higher integration of body, emotion and thought.

In addition to the significant role of mindfulness and other forms of meditations, the *neuroplasticity* is another feature of the brain that is relevant to happiness. The brain can change through life. Learning a language or playing a musical instrument has been shown to increase in size the corresponding areas of the brain, irrespective of one's age. The key element in such change is not so much the task, but the attention paid to the task. What one attends to over and over is what gets mapped into our brain. It is reflected in the principle: "Neurons that fire together wire together".

Recent research suggests that a happy brain is more plastic and open to change. Depression is associated with the shrinkage of the dentate gyrus in the hippocampus which in the part of the brain that handles novelty (Figure 3). While the brain is always receiving new stimuli, the depressed people are quickly controlled by the old pattern and do not recognize the novelty. The amygdala and the hippocampus accentuate the old, the painful and the negative.

This information about the dentate gyrus applies to all

people not just those who are depressed, because dealing with the freshness of present moment experience improves anyone's mood. Meditators learn to be happy even in the midst of difficulty. In this sense, meditation is preventive against all forms of depression and unhappiness.

Chapter 9

Achieving Lasting Happiness

Almost two thousand five hundred years ago, young prince Siddhartha left luxurious palace, lovely wife and baby son to find answer to the fundamental question of the *why* of happiness. His visual experience with the aged, the sick, the dead and a *sanyasi* completely disrupted his mental equilibrium. What is the cause of difference between the absence and presence of a smile? What is the dividing line between languishing and flourishing? What is key to life and lustre? With deep *sadhana*, Siddhartha becomes Buddha the Enlightened One. His sermons and sayings gave some protection to the suffering humanity. Yet the search for finding the *how* of happiness continues.

The question which was once potent and vibrant in world personalities like Buddha became hunger in peace-starved masses of the world. Obviously social scientists and behavioural scientists joined the parading scientists to locate and learn the formula of happiness.

The publication of Norman Vincent Peale's *The Power of Positive Thinking* book in 1952 created some sensation. Peale remarked: "You can think your way to failure and unhappiness, but you can also think your way to success and happiness. The world in which you live is not primarily determined by outward conditions and circumstances but by thoughts that habitually occupy your mind". This centre of gravity was now shifted to psychological research. More specifically, positive psychology movement surfacing in 1990s was so much attentive and engaging with respect to happiness/well-being research that the movement could otherwise be called as **happiness / well-being movement** (Carr, 2004; Myers, 2002).

It is a healthy sign that researchers with different perspectives, different persuasions joined the search process. As a result, there has been some diversity of opinion. Yet the accumulation of facts and findings has been tremendous. This multiplicity of positions has been represented in this book while discussing issues such as the role of gender, age and marital status. When we approach the most crucial issue of the how of happiness, the respect for multiple viewpoints would be maintained. It is expected that the happiness research agenda would soon experience a period of integration. With its attainment in near future, very specific pinpointed happiness-boosting strategies would be possible to be disseminated. However, it would be wiser and useful to follow the multiple tracks of happiness at this point.

Evolutionary Perspective

Buss (2000) adopts an evolutionary perspective and delineates the barriers to human happiness in modern times. According to Buss, discrepancies between ancestral and modern environments pose major threat to human happiness. In the ancestral environment, people used to live in small groups, consisting of 50 to 200 individuals, with closeness of extended kin, used to live. There was scope for developing deep friendship. In contrast, modern environments contain large populations. Further ancestral humans may have had a dozen or two potential mates to choose them. Modern individuals are surrounded by thousands of attractive potential mates. The media plays an important role in magnifying the attractiveness of possible mates and competition. The extent of hostility and infidelity goes up.

In the past many of negative affects (anger, fear and depression) used to have functional adaptive roles. They used to serve as signals, protect humans and contribute as additional resources. Presently these devices are misdirected and cause subjective distress.

Improving human happiness would require the activity of closing the gap between modern and ancient surroundings. People can take steps to remain in closer proximity. Modern electronic connectivity including E-mail, telephone and video conferencing might be used. With people living longer, communication with grandparents and grand-children is a distinct possibility. Although people these days prefer to live in nuclear families, certain forms of functionally joint family system may inculcate a sense of closeness and togetherness. In many parts of India, married sons/daughters may prefer to visit their elderly parents living elsewhere. Especially they may visit for some days/weeks during festive occasions or family functions. These are also very helpful for reducing child abuse and increasing elder care.

Developing deep friendship is a potent source of

happiness. Although it is always possible to have fake or fair-weather friends, adversity in the past provided an acid test for testing genuine friends. Presently many of the adverse circumstances such as legal problems, natural disasters and physical atrocities have been somewhat controlled. It has rendered friendship test relatively difficult.

Several strategies may help to close the gap between modern and ancestral conditions to deepen friendship and social bonding. People may develop unique attributes and maturate themselves to offer these expertise and contributions where these are valued. They should acquire skills that are irreplaceable.

Reducing distress. A number of steps may be undertaken to reduce stress and distress. One strategy is to select a long-term mate or marriage partner who is similar to you on parameters such as interest, values preferences, and overall "mate value". Much incompatibility may increase the infidelity and eventual breakup.

Child abuse and wife battering may be greater now because modern humans live in isolated nuclear families protected in a shroud of privacy. Having kin in close proximity is likely to reduce certain abuses.

Similarly, education about evolved psychological differences may eliminate a lot of biases. Many sex differences have evolved because of their role as adaptive patterns. For example, men, more than women, infer sexual interest when they observe a smile. This may prompt men to make unwanted sexual advances causing discomfort in women. However, the education that men's and women's mind house different psychological mechanism may help to attenuate sex discrimination.

The most difficult challenge posed by the adaptive demands concerns competition. The stiff competition has generated a number of negative emotions such as rivalry, jealously, hostility and status strivings. One potential method of reducing cut-throat competition is to promote **cooperation**.

Evolutionists have identified a key principle of cooperation – **shared fate**. Genes get selected, in part, for their ability to work cooperatively with other genes. A similar effect occurs with individuals living with shared goals and values.

Axelrod (1984), an evolutionary political scientist, has suggested various strategies to promote shared fate. The first strategy is to enlarge the shadow of the future. If individuals believe that they are going to interact frequently for an extended future, cooperation is likely to increase. A second strategy is to learn reciprocity. Promoting reciprocity not only helps to enhance cooperation, it also works to prevent others' exploitative strategies. People need to understand the benefits of cooperators and the losses of exploiters. The third strategy for the promotion of cooperation is to insist on no more than equity. Greed brings the downfall – this conventional wisdom has to be learned. Finally, the method for promoting cooperation would involve cultivating and building reputation. People know that they are sought after only when they are reputed, they have special skills. The promotion of uniqueness and special skill would foster reciprocity. Thus, the combined effects of these strategies will create a social norm of cooperation. The promotion of cooperation would pave the ways for healthy living attenuating unhealthy climate of competition.

Finally, it is important to recognize that humans have evolved desires whose fulfillment bring deep joy. An evolutionary menu includes desire for health, professional success, helping friends and relatives, achieving intimacy, satisfying the taste for high-quality food, and securing personal safety. The fulfillment of mating desires provides another outlet. A consistent finding in studies of happiness is the link to marriage. Buss and his associates have further found that spouses with higher scores on extraversion, agreeableness, openness, emotional stability and conscientiousness are more satisfied than spouses low on these parameters.

In addition to fulfilling desires, evolution has equipped humans with a host of mechanisms designed to fulfill aesthetic pleasures. Landscape preferences provide a perfect example. Many of the features found satisfying in ancestral environments can be transplanted in modern environments in different forms. It would not be impossible to have situations for appreciating the beauty of a blossom, the loveliness of a lilac, or the grace of a gazelle. A deeper understanding of evolutionary mechanisms provide a heuristic for discovering places where we can intervene and design ingredients in modern environment to fulfill human happiness.

The design of habitat and environment represents a macro-approach to happiness enhancement. It is also possible to contemplate micro-changes. One such method involves mood induction.

Mood Induction

Velten (1968) used the laboratory–method for mood induction. Participants were asked to read silently a list of statements of the kind: "I really do feel good"; "I am elated about things"; "I am cheerful most of the times". They were then asked to read aloud and put themselves in the mood created. Initially there were 60 items and later the list was reduced to 25 items. Westermann, Spies, Stahl, and Hesse

(1996) conducted a meta-analysis involving 46 studies on mood induction and found mood change with an effect size of .38 (this is a proportion of a standard deviation). In another meta-analysis, Gerrards-Hesse, Spies, and Hesse (1994) found that an average 67% of participants reported mood change induced by this method. Although this method worked the elevated mood did not last for more than 10-15 minutes. It has been noted that the Velten method only produces description of emotions that participants think they are expected to be feeling, and any apparent change in mood may be an outcome of "demand characteristics". However, it has been found that the Velten method produces responses on an adjective check list that are different from what participants imagined they would feel. Further, the method produces behavioural responses as well as self-report ones.

A few other methods of mood induction in the lab have been studied. The average effect size found in a meta-analytic study are presented in an Exhibit presented below.

Exhibit
Effect Sizes of Different Methods of Mood Induction

Method	Effect Size
Film / Story*	.73
Film /Story	.53
Gift	.38
Velten	.38
Imagination	.36
Feedback	.33
Music*	.33
Music	.32
Social Interaction	.27
Facial Expression	.19

Adopted from Westermann et al. (1994)

The most effective method is the film /story technique. This consists of showing an emotionally arousing film or asking participants to read an emotionally arousing story. They may also be asked to get involved in the story and the feelings expressed. This is an additional bit of mood manipulation and is shown with * in Exhibit. When this is used the effect is greater (.73 versus .53). It may be indicated that Barbara Fredrickson (2001) asked research participants to watch emotionally charged film clips. The film clips were selected for the purpose of inducing one of four emotions: joy, compassion, anger and fear. A neutral non-emotional clip served as a control condition. After watching the film clip, participants were asked to think of a situation that created feelings similar to those aroused by the clip. Given the feeling created they were asked to list all the things they would life to do right then. They were asked to note whatever comes to their mind. The results showed that participants experiencing positive emotions gave each an elaborate list (e.g., going to hospitals to help patients). In contrast, participants experiencing negative emotion wrote nothing or very limited items. The findings supported **Fredrickson's broaden-and-build theory of positive emotions**. The theory posits that positive emotions such as confidence and engagement broaden the contours of our activities and build our inner resources.

The use of film clips/story is very useful. The experiment has the liberty of manipulating materials and other variables (such as duration of exposure and nature of target groups) to produce desired effect. The findings may offer cause-and-effect inferences. The method has a high success rate, especially with added instructions.

Music was found to be a powerful method in many studies, but overall had an effect size of only .32, though it had an 83% success rate, depending on the music used. Clark (1983) produced large effect; part of the problem is that different kinds of music appeal to different people.

Another successful method for mood induction involves **gift**, especially unexpected gift. The types of gifts such as chocolate, soft drink, dress items can be decided depending upon the target group. Larger gifts may produce larger effects.

Imagination offers a possibility of mood induction. Participants are asked to spend some time, sometimes 20 minutes, remembering a happy event "in as much detail as possible". The effect is greater if concrete images are called up. In an interesting experiment, Kasser and Sheldon (2000) attempted to induce negative mood termed *mortality salience*. Students were assigned to one of two conditions. In the *mortality salience* condition, students were asked to imagine the prospect of their own death in terms of the feelings it aroused and what they believed would happen to their physical bodies after death. In control condition, students listened to music. Next, students in both groups were asked to estimate their financial situations 15 years in the future. It was shown that their behaviours (estimates) were consistent with their induced moods. The estimates were independent of their preexisting values.

Feedback means giving positive feedback about how well subjects have done on some task. In real life outside the lab, success at exams or in getting promotion are major sources of joy. The **social interaction** manipulation has been attempted with help of experimental confederate who is very cheerful and talks in a very pleasant manner. This produces small effect on mood (.27). Schacter and

Singer (1962) in a classic experiment on emotion used a really manic confederate to arouse positive mood. **Facial expression** refers to facial feedback experiments Laird (1984) and others asked participants to arrange their faces corresponding to positive emotions. It produces some effect, though weaker in intensity.

A seminal question relating to the effect intensity concerns its duration of effect. How long the does the induced change last? The mood charge produced by the Velten method is very short-lived, it lasts for 10-15 minutes. Small gifts produce temporary effects, perhaps larger gifts are likely to produce more enduring effects. While the role of exercise as a mood-changer is well-accepted, it is not presented here. Its benefits are described elsewhere.

Although several methods have been contemplated and tried for mood induction and happiness experience, real life scenarios demand relatively more durable and authentic happiness. A great deal of research efforts has been geared towards identifying the sources of sustainable happiness. The network of intentional activities offers an integrative approach in this direction.

Intentional Activities.

The network of intentional activities is not a monolithic concept. The contributions of several contemporary researchers can be brought under this umbrella. However, Lyubomirsky (2007) provides a unifying thread that binds together bits and pieces that deal with happiness-boosting measures.

The core concept: The 40 percent freedom. As shown by the following pie chart, 50 percent of our happiness is genetically predetermined. A great deal of science backs up this conclusion (e.g., Lykken & Tellegen, 1996)

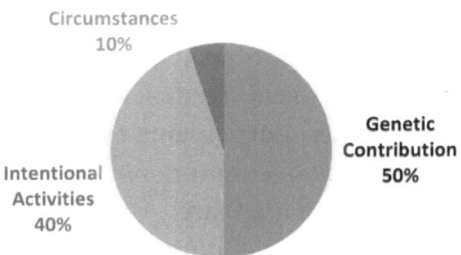

The role of genetic factors has been described in detail in Chapter 4 of this book. Simply stated, the strongest evidence for genetic predisposition comes from a series of fascinating studies involving identical and fraternal twins. Since identical twins share 100 percent and fraternal twins share 50 percent, the comparison of happiness across these two types of twins is a dependable test of genetic role. Research indicates that happiness is largely heritable. Each of us is born with a particular happiness set point that originates from our biological mother or father or both, a baseline or potential for happiness to which we are bound to return, even after big triumph or utter defeat.

The set point for happiness is similar to the set point for weight. Some people have the advantage of a skinny disposition. Even if they are not trying, they maintain their weight. In contrast, others have to work hard to keep to a desired weight. If they are slightly careless, the overweight troubles them. The implication of this finding for happiness is that like genes for weight, the magnitude of our innate set points governs the quantum of our happiness.

A seminal aspect of finding is that *only about 10 percent of the variance in our happiness is explained by differences in life circumstances* (see pie chart). Our richness or poverty, our health or ill-health, our houses or hamlets, race, religion, place of birth and our job gain or job loss can increase or decrease our happiness within the limit of 10 percent.

The discovery that the circumstances of our lives (such as income or marital status) have such little bearing on our happiness sounds pessimistic to most of us. Yet the key to happiness is *not* lost. Even after we take into account our genetically determined personality (implication-wise happiness or unhappiness) to the tune of 50 percent plus 10 percent accruing from life circumstances, we still have the freedom of 40 percent.

Intentional activities: It is important to recognize that differences in our happiness levels are still left unexplained to the extent of 40 percent. What makes up this 40 percent? If genes and situations we confront in lives snatch away 60 percent, we are left with *40 percent freedom of using our cognitive activities and behaviour to achieve happiness*. Thus, the key to happiness does not involve changing genetic make-up or amassing wealth but entails our daily intentional activities. The potentiality of the 40 percent is within our ability to control.

What are the intentional activities with maximal expectation of happiness benefits. Although the list may grow larger, Lyubomirsky (2007) provides a representative list of happiness-boosting activities:
- Devoting a great deal of time to family and friends
- Nurturing and enjoying close relationship
- Experiencing and expressing gratitude to relevant others
- Avoiding overthinking and social comparison
- Offering help to the needy and coworkers
- Practicing optimism
- Savouring life's pleasure, and trying to live in the present moment, Increasing flow
- Regular physical exercise
- Deep commitment to lifelong goals and ambitions

- Facing life's challenges and managing stress
- Avoiding overthinking and social comparison
- Practicing kindness and forgiveness
- Practicing internal religiosity, spirituality and meditation

The hours of activities. According to Lyubomirsky (2007), a list of happiness provides a starting point. With a view to enhancing happiness-boosting potential of such activities, the hours of activities must be taken into consideration.

First, researchers have suggested a wide range of happiness-boosting activities. It may not be possible to undertake each and every activity. But it is possible to identify **person-activity fit.** Individuals must find out activities that fit person's interest, values and needs. With the help of experts, friends and health-advisors, a host of activities may be chosen for the specific individual.

Second, happiness is not wish-fulfillment. It requires **effort, commitment and variety.** Apart from mental planning, the individual needs to have sufficient effort and commitment. The efforts may not be mechanical. One example would illustrate the point. For example, a person enjoys morning walk. The practice of morning walk, in a mechanical fashion (starting everyday at a fixed time of 6 a.m. and covering the same route) may lose its pleasure-giving potential after a large number of repetitions. Hence the person should bring elements of change and variety. Instead of starting at 6 a.m. and finishing at 7 a.m., he or she may start at 6:15 a.m. or 5:45 a.m. some of the days. Similarly he or she may follow a different route for a walk (sometimes going clock-wise and sometimes going anti-clockwise, to include variety).

Third, activities accompanied with positive emotions afford positive benefits. Positive emotions do have self-reinforcing properties. Emotions of joy, love and cheerfulness generated during activities create further motivation for retaining and extending the habit.

Motivation is another key element. It gives sustainability to chosen activities. In the beginning, the person may initiate the activities with efforts and intention. But gradually these positive forms of activities evolve into **habits**. Once habits of happiness boosting activities are formed, they provide the constant source of happiness.

Positive Life Events

In the tradition of stress literature and research, a common measuring instrument is the **Social Readjustment and Rating Scale (SRRS)**. This is also known as Life Event Scale. The scale presents a number of life events (e.g., moving to a new residence; divorce) and participants are asked to indicate the amount of mental energy (on a scale ranging from 0 to 100 units) they need to cope with the situation. They are told that they can have two referents: 50 units for marriage and 100 units for the death of the spouse. The death of the spouse can be replaced by the death of the most loved one. Needless to say, the sum of ratings (score) is indicative of the magnitude of stress experienced. This is an often-used measure.

It is possible to have a similar measure of **Positive Life Events (PLE)**? Michael Argyle (2001) believed that lab-induced positive moods generate short-term happiness, whereas positive life events are likely to produce more enduring happiness. Based on the responses of students of Oxford University Hendersen, Argyle and Furnham (1984) developed PLE scale. The scale presents a number of positive events and participants indicate the frequency with which they experience each event. The list includes sport and exercise, social events, success and recognition, religious activities, and other leisure activities. Some of the events happen naturally without control at our end (e.g., birth of a child in the family), but other events are more often sought and planned. The list given below offers a representative pool of events:

- Falling in love
- Passing the exam
- Gaining qualification
- Getting a new job
- Going on holiday
- Winning a lot of money
- Visiting friends

It is possible to develop similar assessment procedure across cultures. Infact, Magnus, Diener, Fujita and Payot (1993) developed a similar measure for American students. A couple of sample items read: getting into graduate school, getting a car, and joining a club. Some of the events are infrequent (e.g., marriage) while some events are frequent (watching TV). Some events are intense while other events are mild.

Although PLE scale is an interesting one, the issue of computing score in terms of *intensity versus frequency* remains unsolved. Diener, Sandvik and Payot (1991) found that percentage of time that individuals were experiencing positive affect correlated with happiness at about (.50), while the average intensity of positive affect when they were feeling happy correlated at only .25. They concluded that intensity is relatively unimportant; they also report that intense positive experiences occur only on 2.6% of days. However, Argyle (2001) and a few others believe that intensity does play a significant role.

Irrespective of the debate on intensity versus frequency the effects of PLEs are well-accepted. There are also field experiments to demonstrate the positive influence of PLEs. In one field experiment, Reich and Zautra (1981) asked subjects to identify 12 events from a long list of PLEs which they have not experienced for last 2 weeks. Another comparable group of subjects were asked to identify 2 events from the list of PLEs. Then all the participants were provided opportunities to experience their identified events for two weeks. At the end of two weeks, their happiness was measured. Both the groups showed significant improvement in their happiness. It was independent of the condition whether they experienced 12 chosen events or 2 chosen events. In sum, a planned and intended use of PLEs may be exploited for uplifting one's happiness.

Mind Over Matter

Attempts to induce happiness by way of manipulating positive life events and other objective conditions have been successful. Yet spectacular outcomes are not encountered. People turn their attention to certain unusual areas such as fire walk, subliminal awareness and hypnosis where mind power is demonstrated. In the midst of such observations and information, students of psychology ask: '**Is it not possible to reprogramme the mind to experience an unending flow of happiness**?

Of course, the conventional field of soft psychology is not without examples and illustrations. Norman Peale's (1952) book *The Power of Productive Thinking* lighted the candle of hope that thoughts that habitually occupy our mind may change the landscape of our mind. It reaffirmed our belief in body-mind relationship. People have to pull the right kind of psychic lever. Since the dictum that mind influences the brain got accepted, those going for serious pursuit of psychology get closer to Shakespeare's Hamlet: "There are more things in heaven and earth, Horatio, that are dreamt of in your philosophy". While there were several extra-ordinary demonstrations outside the mainstream psychological domains, a few cases would demand our attention.

In certain parts of India and elsewhere some people exhibit **fire walking**. The fire walking phenomenon also surprised Americans during the 1980s after some observations in Sri Lanka and Greece. This is performed as a religious rite. The fire walkers demonstrate a "mind over matter" phenomenon. Just holding the thought in their mind that they are not going to injure their feet alters the chemistry of their body. The physical result of this mind power, walking on red-hot coal without pain or harm is a new found reality. "If I can do this, I can do almost anything including maintaining happiness forever. Although this phenomenon is not without critics, it stands tall as a demonstration.

Another incredible phenomenon relates to **subliminal messages**. The expression 'subliminal' means below "threshold". It is asserted that if imperceptible messages are imparted and people are exposed to such subliminal messages, they would be persuaded by such communication, even if they are not aware of their reception. For example, a theater may manipulate transmitting by way of flashing subliminal message "drink coke" or "eat popcorn". It was found that a large number of people a showed the behaviour as communicated. With publicized success story, many business organizations produced subliminal tapes for their business success.

As with fire walk phenomenon, this was not without critics. There was a legal battle in the United States; parents of a young boy who committed suicide sued a musician alleging that the subliminal message imparted the message 'do it' implying commit suicide. The Court dismissed case saying subliminal message can not be so powerful to force someone to commit suicide. While this is still a fuzzy area, the use of subliminal message for keeping oneself or others happy is a topic of future research.

Finally, **hypnosis** represents another area of mind power. Its benefit at the time of dental operation and surgical intervention has been accepted. Empirically hypnosis has been defined as "**heightened suggestibility**". Although hypnosis in part, has been accepted in scientific discourse and the topic has been included in the text book of medical science, some of the claims have been disputed. For example, past life regression continues to be a controversial area. Further, many critics point out that what hypnosis claims to achieve can be attained by mere procedure of giving suggestion. No elaborate and ritualistic, procedure is needed. Moreover, a person may be hypnotized and the hypnotist may suggest that water would taste salty. In this case, hypnotic suggestion works and water would be salty. In contrast, the hypnotized person would be dehypnotized if the hypnotist suggests that the person takes off his or her dress.

Despite certain limitations of hypnosis, happiness researchers may exploit its positive aspect in the form of self-hypnosis. Person's own auto-suggestion and others' hypnosis like suggestion may be helpful in inducing happiness.

If somewhat controversial areas like subliminal tapes and hypnosis represent possibilities of manipulation, very recent developments in neuroscience offer hard facts regarding possibility of unusual induction.

Rewiring the Brain

Everyone seeks happiness, but a few individuals succeed in experiencing sustainable happiness. In the enactment of life's drama, the trichotomy of brain, mind and behavior complicates the scenarios. Many people and even many scientists believe that the human brain is the finest product of the evolutionary process and the subtle script it carries directs the activities of our mind and diversity of our behavior. Essentially every person is like all other humans, though every person is similar to some other humans to some extent and the person is similar to a few person to a small extent.

The brain provides commonality to human behavior. In fact, human brain is a combination of three brains: a unicellular brain, a mammalian brain and a human brain. Because of the unicellular brain as possessed by unicellular organisms, we are responsive to simple reflexes, such as moving away from a hot object. Our mammalian brain is helpful in guiding us to do a number of voluntary actions. But the most evolved and most recent brain is the neo-cortex or neo-brain that is distinctively human. If we plan to get up at an unusual hour of 4 am just because we have to catch a bus, we rarely fail. Even if our usual habit is to get up at 6 am in the morning, the auto-suggestion of getting up at 4 am works fine with us. The neo-cortex registers the suggestion and we get some sort of signal, such as an unusual dream, to get up. This distinctive property of guiding our behavior is uniquely human.

Although human brain is endowed with unique properties, there are dogmas in the world of brain science. One persistent dogma is that the adult brain is essentially fixed in form and function. The dogma is wrong. Instead, the brain has the property of neuroplasticity, the ability to change the structure and pattern of activity in significant ways not only in childhood, which is not very surprising, but also in adulthood and throughout life. The change can come about as a result of experiences we have as well of purely internal activity – our thoughts.

Experiences may take various forms. The brains of people who have been blind from birth and who learn to read by Braille, the writing system based on tiny raised dots that the finger slide across experience a measurable increase in the size and activity of the motor cortex and somatosensory cortex that control movement and receive tactile sensation from the reading fingers. Even more dramatically, their visual cortex – which is normally hardwired to process signals from the eyes and turn them into visual images – undertakes a career change and takes on the job of processing sensation from the fingers rather than the input from the eyes.

Reading braille is an example of intense, repeated sensory and learning experience of the outside world. But the brain can change in response to messages generated internally (our thoughts and intentions). These changes can increase or decrease the cortical real estate devoted to specific functions. Similarly, thoughts alone can increase or decrease activity in specific brain circuits that underlie psychological illness, as when the therapy quiets the overactivity of the "worry circuit" which causes obsessive–compulsive disorder (OCD). Through mental activity alone, which itself is a produce of the brain, we can intentionally change our brain.

The cortical representation. The idea that there is a one-to-one correspondence between structure and function dates back 1862 when French anatomist Paul Broca announced that he had identified the brain region that produces speech. It is an area towards the back of the frontal lobes. He concluded from autopsy of a man who had lost essentially all the powers of speech. The brain's speech producing area is called the Broca's area.

With this discovery, other brain scientists joined the race of identifying particular brain area for particular function. A German neurologist Korbinian Brodmann, yielded structure function relationship for fifty-two distinct regions. For example, Brodmann number 1 represents the parts of somatosensory cortex that processes tactile sensation from specific spots in the skin. Brodmann area number 52 represents parainsular region where the temporal lobe and insula meet. The visual cortex is known as Brodmann area number 17. Area number 10 is the front-most part of the prefrontal cortex which has increased most in size over the course of evolution and seems to allow us in multi task.

No region of the brain has been as precisely mapped as the somatosensory cortex. This strip of cortex runs roughly over the top of the brain from ear to ear. The left somatosensory cortex receives signal from the right and vice versa. Each part of the body is assigned a particular spot in the somatosensory cortex for processing. As a result, the somatosensory cortex is essentially a map of the body – one that would give Google mappers a heart attack. In experiments in the 1960s, Canadian neurosurgeon Wilder Penfield stimulated systematically different spots of somatosensory cortex and participants reported sensation in different parts of the body in this way. Penfield was able to "map" the somatosensory cortex assigning each spot a corresponding part of the body.

There is an element of humour in cortical representation. Although the hand is below the arm, the somatosensory hand abuts the region that receives signal from the face.

Similarly, the somatosensory representation of the genitals lies directly below the feet. It is observed that with more cortical space, a body part becomes more sensitive. The tip of our tongue, which has a larger representation can feel the ridges of our teeth, whereas the backs of our hands have smaller somatosensory representation.

Because of the past works, the belief was strengthened and carried forward into the idea that particular activity must also be hardwired and if not strictly unchangeable, atleast persistent. According to this view, mental illness such as depression might be caused by underactivity in some area of the prefrontal cortex and overactivity in the amygdala and the underlying biology is as permanent as your finger prints.

Towards the plasticity notion. However, more recently there has been change in the structure-function relationship. Edward Taub and his associates initiated a bold series of experiments, known as the **Silver Spring Experiments,** in the Institute of Behavioural Research Silver Spring (Maryland, USA). The neural centres representing sensory connection to fingers were severed in monkeys. Animals lost all sensation in those limbs. Although the case sparked animal right movement in the USA and Taub had to face criminal investigation, the result of these sensory deprivation studies in 1991 was stunning in the sense it shattered the fixed notion of hardwiring. The region of monkey's somatosensory cortex which originally processed sensation from the fingers, hands and arms had changed jobs. As a result of receiving no signals from body parts, the region now processed signals from the face instead. The amount of brain now receiving sensations from the face had grown to fourteen square millimeters – a "massive cortical reorganization".

Around the same time, other studies of monkeys showed that adult primate brain can change in response to something much less extreme than amputation or nerve-cutting strategy. In the seminal study, scientists at the University of California, San Francisco trained owl monkeys to develop an acute sense of touch in their fingers. They were trained to brush a spinning disk. Day in and day out, monkeys underwent this exercise, until they had done it hundreds of times. The region of their brain – specifically in somatosensory cortex – that received signals from the finger had been trained to feel the grooves in the spinning disks. Structure-function relationships are not hardwired. Instead, the physical lay-out of the brain – how much space it assigns to which tasks and body parts – is shaped by how an organism behaves.

Seeing the thunder, hearing the lightening. The place to look into the application of findings obtained from animal research involves the study of sensory experiences from those who are blind or deaf. The brain is capable of bigger reorganization. Studies of blind and deaf examined much bigger chunks of neural real estate: the visual cortex which occupies nearly one-third of the brain's volume. It is nestled towards the back and the auditory cortex, which stretches across the top of the brain across the ears. We are familiar with a folk wisdom that the blind has especially sharp hearing and the deaf has especially sharp eye sight. But the folk wisdom is not cent percent true. In fact, blind people do not hear softer sounds, and deaf people cannot detect minimal contrasts or see in dimmer light than hearing people can. But compensation works in another way.

In people who are deaf from birth, objects in the peripheral vision are perceived not only in the visual cortex but also in the auditory cortex. **The auditory cortex sees.**

It is as if the auditory cortex, tired of enforced inactivity as a result of receiving no signals from the ears, take upon itself as a regimen of job retraining, so that it now processes visual signals. This has practical consequences. Deaf people are faster and more accurate at detecting the movements of objects in their peripheral vision than are hearing people.

Something comparable happens in people who are blind from birth or an early age. In them, no signals reach the visual cortex. However, the visual cortex does not go waste. In blind people who become proficient in reading, Braille, the visual cortex switches jobs to processing tactile signal from those reading fingers. This discovery was so unexpected that some of neuroscience's most eminent practitioners refused to believe it. As a consequence, the submission turned down by *Science* was published by its arch competitor *Nature* (April 1996).

The brains of the blind change in another way too. When they use their peripheral hearing – to locate the source of a sound, for instance, something they tend to be better at than sighted people – they use their visual cortex. Their brains have gone what we call compensatory reorganization. As a result, **the visual cortex hears**. Once again, William James proved prescient. A century before these discoveries, in his 1892 book *Psychology: The Briefer course*, he wondered whether if neurons get crossed inside the brain, *"we should hear the lightening and see the thunder"* ---- a foreshadowing of the profound alternation in the brain's primary sensory cortices that can result from experience.

In brief, the brain can change assigning a new function to a region that originally did something else. These conclusions were derived from studies conducted on the blind and the deaf. What about normal population?

Pascual-Leone conducted experiments involving

"virtual piano players". It was shown that merely thinking about players' keyboard exercise expanded the region of motor cortex devoted to moving fingers. In another bold experiment, Pascual-Leone recruited healthy volunteers to spend five days in a safe experiment at Beth Israel Deaconess Medical Center in Boston. The participants were blindfolded. To keep from dying of boredom they were provided with sensorially intense activity learning Braille and fine-tuning their hearing. Prior to experimental intervention, they were subjected to fMRI scans. At the end of the five days of such exercise, they were subjected to scans. When they heard something the activity in their visual cortex increased. The visual cortex is supposed to handle sight. Yet, after a mere five days of an unusual sensory activity, scans indicated a radical change in function.

If the visual cortex, which seems like the most hardwired of all the brain's hardwired regions, can so quickly alter its function as a result of sensory input and sensory deprivation, surely it is time to question how much the brain is really fixed and unchangeable. In all likelihood the visual cortex did not grow new connections to the ears and fingers, five days wasn't time enough for that Pascual-Leone suspects that instead "some rudimentary somatosensory and auditory connections to the visual cortex must already be present," left over from the period of brain development when neurons from the eyes and ears and fingers connect to many regions of the cortex rather than just the ones they're supposed to. When input from the retina to the visual cortex ceased because of the blindfold, the other sensory connections were unmasked. Even neural cables that receive no traffic for decades can start carrying signals again.

Therapeutic Application

The realization that sensory experiences can rewire the brain has had important real-world consequences. From the discovery that a region of the brain could be retrained to perform a new function, it is inferred that people in whom a stroke has damaged one region of the brain could train a healthy region of their brain to assume the function of the damaged part. The method of treatment is called **constraint-induced movement therapy.**

The therapy could be explained with the example in whom a stroke has damaged a region of the motor cortex, leaving one arm paralyzed. The therapist would put this patient's good arm in a sling and her good hand in an oven mitt for about 90 percent of waking hours for about two weeks, so she could not use either, leaving her no choice but to try to use her paralyzed arm in activities of daily living and the rehabilitation exercise advised. These exercises, six hours a day for two five-day weeks, involved intensive use of the paralyzed arm, which was actually slightly functional. The patients manipulate cups and eating utensils. After scores of hours of practice, most patients make huge improvements.

Brain plasticity can take several forms. Plasticity is an intrinsic property of the human brain. The potential of the adult brain to reprogram itself might be much greater than has previously been assumed. Neuroplasticity allows the brain to break the bonds of its own genome, which dictates that one region will "see" and another will "hear". The genetical guided blueprint is fine for most people under most conditions, but not all of us all the time – not when we lose our sight or suffer a stroke. **The brain is neither immutable nor static, but continuously remodeled by the lives we lead.** Listed below are the **Take-Aways:**

1. The revolution in neuroplasticity shows that brain can change as a result of the distinct inputs.
2. Brain can change as result of the experiences we have in this world – how we move and behave and what sensory signals arrive in our cortex.
3. The brain changes in response to purely mental activity, ranging from mediation to cognitive (thought) restructuring.

Behavioural Intervention:

Complete mental health is the syndrome that combines high levels of symptoms of emotional well-being, psychological well-being and social well-being as well as the absence of recent illness. The complete state model can schematically be presented:

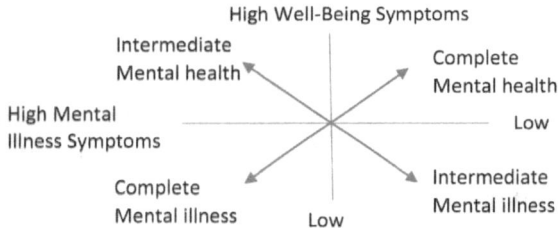

In accordance with complete state model, Fava (1999) articulates happiness therapy as an 8-session intervention programme. It provides a structured, problem-oriented approach with emphasis on self-observation. The therapist's primary responsibility is to help the client cognitively restructure his or her views on concepts central to well-being. These include Ryff's six dimensions of well-being: environmental mastery personal growth, purpose in life, autonomy, self-acceptance and positive relations with others. The intervention is based in Ryff's (1989) eudaimonic model of psychological well-being.

During the session's clients record their thoughts and feeling in a diary. The overall goal is to get clients to see how their thoughts and feelings short-cut the basis of healthy functioning in everyday life. In the first session clients record episodes of healthy functioning and specify the sessions in which these episodes occurred.

Intermediate sessions are used to identify thoughts and feelings that disrupted episodes of well-being. They are asked to identify the causes of disruption. The mutual discussion identifies positive and negative elements. This intervention process has been found to be useful in promoting healthy functioning.

Research on happiness has pointed out several directions. It is important to note that the attainment of happiness is a multi-starter multi-level approach. Depending on personality, situation, and culture, the goal of experiencing happiness has to be approached. The exploration, effort and experimentation with one's own life would often right kind of guidelines.

Chapter 10

Looking Ahead

Happiness is not a cascade of a big joy. It is confluence of several streams of positive experiences. Similarly, a unified body of happiness/well-being is not the contribution of a single thinker. Many philosophers, sociologists, psychologists and neuroscientists have joined in defining and redefining the constructs. Many concerns have been expressed. A number of issues have been tackled; yet new issues have surfaced. The interactions amongst cultures, coherts and disciplines have resulted in a science of happiness.

Compared to the diversity of opinions and accumulation of facts, the present discourse on happiness has a structured form. In view of the centrality of happiness seeking as a human need, both the scientists and lay-persons have been drawn into the thinking circle. Obviously, the present knowledge, though structured, is not a rigid system. Changes and paradigm shifts are inevitable. Yet, it is appropriate at this point to take a pause and to reconsider how some critical challenges have been met and handled. More specifically, there are *three* signals that guide future path-finder: comparability and equivalence, frameworks of integration, and unresolved issues.

Comparability and Equivalence

Research pertaining to happiness/well-being had employed both within culture studies as well as cross-cultural studies. The comparisons across groups and comparison across cultures presuppose certain norms of comparability. To compare two phenomena, they must share some features in common. In other words, two phenomena or cultures must be placed on a dimension of identity (similarity) so that differences on the other dimension can be validly interpreted. For example, when a researcher compares married women with unmarried women, the similarity at the level of gender makes it meaningful to examine some of aspect (say behavioural aspect) of unmarried women vis-à-vis married women. Thus, equivalence (dimensional identity) is a prerequisite for valid comparison and interpretation (Berry, 1980).

Such dimensional identity can be established by demonstrating an underlying *universal* or by searching for *equivalence* (Berry, Poortinga, Segall & Dasen, 1992). Universals can be adopted from biology, sociology, anthropology and linguistics (Sahoo, 1983). For example, researchers can use biological universals such as "all human beings" or "all human groups". Similarly, universals can be adopted from anthropology in terms of common primary needs (reproduction, tools use, language and myth). Since these features or components are common across a wide variety of cultural groups, researchers find it appropriate to place cultures on any one of the dimensional identity and compare them with respect to a particular behavioural facet.

In the context of happiness, universality of the construct may thus be defended. Diener, Seligman and other prominent researchers in the area have argued persuasively that happiness is a pancultural need and it is quite appropriate to undertake cross-cultural comparison in view of this **construct equivalence**. The demonstration of construct equivalence in the form of establishing **universal** offers justification for comparison. However, the how of comparison (use of tests, instruments, and measures) requires another complex process of measurement equivalence.

Measurement Equivalence

Within cross-cultural research tradition, three kinds of *equivalence* could be demonstrated: *functional, conceptual,* and *metric equivalence* (Berry, 1980). First functional equivalence exists when two or more behaviours (in two or more cultural systems) are related to functionally similar problems. In the context of happiness/well-being, this appears to exist. Since all human groups make explicit expression of their happiness needs, this requirement is easily met.

Conceptual equivalence as a precondition is somewhat complex. Conceptual equivalence exists when concepts, test materials, stimuli, tasks, measures and response forms used across cultures are similar. For example, if researchers study how children conserve the notion of volume, they need to use "clay" for children of agricultural communities and "snow" for children of Eskimo community. Similarly, while studying sorting behaviour, grain sorting and card sorting may be treated as equivalent tasks in agricultural and modern acculturated societies.

Traditionally investigators in a cross-cultural research have adopted Osgood's (1965) method of *sematic differential techniques* to examine construct equivalence (a major component of conceptual equivalence) across cultures. In this method, respondents from different cultural groups are asked to rate several dimensions of a construct (e.g., bad-good; passive-active, weak-strong) on a seven-point (or five- or nine-point scale). The statistical analysis reveals whether a construct is similarly conceived across cultures or differently understood. For example, "power" has a positive connotation in western countries whereas it has somewhat negative loading in Japan. This technique of Osgood (1965) has not yet been applied to the construct of happiness. The arguments and writings of scholars in the area of happiness/well-being have assumed its construct equivalence.

The other necessary condition is termed *metric* equivalence or nontechnically *measurement equivalence*. Metric equivalence or measurement equivalence exists when the psychometric properties of two (or more) sets of test/measurement materials from two (or more) cultural groups exhibit essentially the same coherence or structure. This is essentially examined on the basis of data collected.

The issue of measurement equivalence brings to the fore an important aspect of test construction in cross-cultural context.

Etic and Emic Strategy

It is a common observation that a large number of tests

and measures used in non-western countries have originally been developed in western countries. This is also the case with happiness and related measures. Cultural differences are not to be discarded. More specifically, prominent cross-cultural psychologists like Hofstede and Triandis have clearly explicated the distinction between individualistic societies of the West and collectivist societies of the East. In particular, the "self" in the individualistic societies (me society) is relatively *independent* whereas the "self" in collectivist societies (us society) is mainly *inter-dependent*. Obviously, this distinction has a great implication for conceptualization and construction of tests in the two types of cultures.

Researchers have attempted to bridge this gap by adopting etic strategy, or emic strategy or combined etic-emic strategy.

Etic strategy. The terms *etic* and *emic* were coined by the prominent linguist Pike (1954). In linguistics two expressions *phonetics* and *phonemics* are very common. Phonetics refer to sounds common in a number of languages (phono meaning sound). In contrast, *phonemics* refer to sounds peculiar or specific in particular language. Dropping the prefix phono, two expressions are derived: etic and emic. The derivation indicates that etic stands for an approach which is common or "general". In contrast, emic denotes the approach which is "specific". Thus, etic and emic approach refer to transcultural (or pancultural) and culture-specific aspect of a system.

The etic approach has been widely used in the past. Western instruments such as the Minnesota Multiphasic Personality Inventory (MMPI; Hathaway & McKinley, 1967) and the Beck Depression Inventory (BDI; Beck & Steen, 1987) have been translated and used in a large number of nonwestern cultures. The assumption is that concepts and expressions used in the original scales/measures are universal and there is no distortion of meaning in the translated versions. However, Brislin (1970, 1976) has extensively provided specific guidelines for translating test materials from a source language to a target language. The technique of *back-translation* is a valuable feature of the process.

In the context of well-being research, Sahoo and Mohapatra (2009) have used Diener's life satisfaction scale in India. Both the original English version and the translated version have been used by Sahoo and his associates in several studies. Although careful translation in general and back-translation in particular helps in maintaining measurement equivalence, the transportation of an etic construct, mostly Euro-American etic, to a nonwestern situation may not be criticism-free. The problem is termed *imposed etic* (Berry, 1969).

Some researchers in China have used Chinese version of the Scheier and Carver's (1985) measure of optimism: The Life Orientation Test (LOT). They find the items universal and usable in China. This is an instance of etic strategy.

However, it possible to evaluate measurement equivalence in cases where etic strategy has been adopted to use tests in a different culture. **Confirmatory Factors Analysis (CFA)** can be applied for such examination. The first method is to apply the translated test in the new (nonwestern) culture and examine the factor structure. If the CFA yields the structures as derived from the theory, the test is usable in the new culture. If the proposed model is rejected, the adopted test is not usable without modification and refinement.

The single-group CFA informs whether or not the factor

structure is same in source culture and target culture, but it does not reveal whether loadings are same or different. Hence multiple-group of CFA is needed to examine measurement equivalence (or *psychometric invariance*). This reveals whether same constructs are measuring to the same extent. Thus, metric equivalence is a prerequisite for comparing group differences across cultures.

Emic approach. While etic approach has been used in many situations in adapting western tests to nonwestern situations, there are cases where novelty or uniqueness of the construct is of paramount importance. For example, it would be difficult to find an English equivalent of the Buddhist concept of *Karuna* (grossly translated as compassion) or Indian concept of *abhiman* (some sort of loving challenge). These situations would require the development and validation of very culture-specific constructs such as karuna. The development of indigenous test is based on emic approach.

The emic approach posits that behaviours are culture-specific. Researchers need to develop theories and measures sensitive to local contexts in order to increase **ecological validity**.

A good example of indigenous concept and measurement is filial piety in Chinese societies (Ho, 1996). This measure is indicative of relatedness in Chinese context. The locally developed instrument makes prediction of behaviour in their local context. Similarly, Neki's concept of *guru-chela syndrome* in Indian context is a good instance of emic/indigenous measure. Since many countries these days are becoming plural societies, the use of emic approach for various sub-cultures may provide meaningful enterprise. For example, an adequate understanding of Asians in the United States needs culture-specific instruments for evaluation. The disadvantage with this approach involves the difficulty of comparison across cultures whereas within-culture understanding is deepened.

Combined etic-emic approach. Etic and emic approach can be combined to blend the advantages of both the approaches. The idea is that researchers can first identify an etic (pancultural) construct, then its measurement can locally be undertaken. In addition, other indigenous concept can also be combined. The Confirmatory Factor Analysis (CFA) can be used for the data structure to identify the existence of etic (universal) structure as well as emic (indigenous or culture-specific structure).

One recent example from well-being literature involves interpersonal model in Chinese population (Ho & Cheung, 2007). The present concept and measurement of subjective well-being (SWB) mainly includes one's self-appraisal, no special attention is paid to interpersonal dimension of collectivist cultures. In contrast, Chinese are relationally oriented (Ho, 1996). An attempt was made to develop a SWB measure with culture-centric interpersonal focus.

Researchers adopted combined etic-emic approach to construct an indigenous measure "The Satisfaction with Life Scale (SWLS)". Human beings are capable of deriving true happiness from the happiness of significant others and this dimension of happiness is considered very relevant in the measurement of SWB in China. The pre existing measure of SWB is based on self-appraisal of one's well-being and does not explain the total SWB experience of people in collectivist cultures, like the Chinese. Chinese may think about the happiness of significant others and incorporate this appraisal into their own happiness.

With this rationale, Ho and Cheung (2007) used combined etic-emic approach to revise the original SWLS

(Diener et al, 1985) and added to it another five interpersonal items created by them. They selected six items from the initial item pool, based on the exploration factor analysis results. Ho and Cheung refer to this 6-item scale as the Expanded Satisfaction with Life Scale (E-SWLS). These items are for etic components from the original SWLS and measure interpersonal SWB. Another three items are emic components that measure interpersonal SWB. This is a single factor model with both interpersonal and intrapersonal components integrated together. The integrated model is consistent with the assertion that the self-versus other self-appraisal is more appropriate in collectivist cultures.

Similarly, Sahoo (2004) used combined etic-emic approach to modify and develop an instrument of sex role inventory. Bem's Sex Role Inventory (BSRI) is an oft-used test developed and validated by Sandra Bem (1981). It yields an assessment of *androgyny* – the degree of blending of positive masculine and positive feminine traits. The test presents 60 characteristics (20 masculine, 20 feminine and 20 neutral) and people are asked to give their self-endorsement ratings on each of the items on a seven-point scale. The sum of ratings on 20 masculine items is indicative of masculinity and sum of scores on 20 feminine items is indicative of femininity. The small gap between these two sums of scores reveals the degree of androgyny provided the sum of ratings on masculinity and femininity is not too small. A big difference in favour of masculine score describes a person as stereotypically masculine and a big difference in favour of feminine score describes individuals as feminine.

Research has documented that androgyny has health benefits. In other words, androgynous males and females exhibit greater behavioural flexibility, higher self-concept and greater well-being (Sahoo, 2004). Although the construct is a robust one, Sahoo (2004) argued that some of the items used in BSRI were not relevant in India. With view to securing cultural adaptation, he used etic-emic approach. An extensive empirical testing in Indian samples identified the etic items of the original scale. He included a number culturally relevant masculine and feminine items. The etic-emic strategy resulted in a final version of 50-item Sahoo Sex Role Inventory (SSRI; Sahoo, 2004).

Alternative Strategies

It is a common observation that self-report measures of well-being have several limitations. Because health happiness and well-being are valued objectives, the responses are likely to be biased in terms of *social desirability*, *reactivity* (obtrusiveness), and *response set*. Social desirability implies that people tend to respond in a socially desirable ways; this is a big biasing problem in collectivist countries. Reactivity (or obtrusiveness) is the tendency of people to terminate cooperation in responding to items, especially when the items are personal and threatening. Finally, some people have a habitual pattern of responding in a particular way. They do not respond to the contents of test items but repeat their own habits. For example, some people say 'yes' most of the times, whereas others say 'no'. This habitual way of responding pulls up the score or pulls down the score, when all the items are keyed in a positive or a negative direction.

Although psychologists have suggested a number of alternatives to get around the problem, a few important strategies may be indicated.

Projective inventory approach. The classical projective tests such as Word Association Test (WAT), Thematic

Apperception Test (TAT) and Rorschach (Ink-Blot Test) Test are oft-used tests in clinical setting. These are also used for the study and assessment of personality. While the reliabilities are satisfactory, a major problem pertains to the objective interpretation. Because of this difficulty, the test-using agency generally employ multiple experts to determine average score. For example, the Service Selection Board for Indian Army makes use of multiple experts to arrive at a decision.

B.N. Puhan at the Psychology Department of Utkal University (India) has devised an interesting approach (Puhan, 1995) to measure several psychological attributes. This is termed *Projective Inventory Approach*. The approach combines the advantages of both the classical projective tests and self-report personality measures. Like classical projective tests, these are indirect tests such that respondents do not know the real purpose and as such cannot fake. Second, projective inventory materials do have objective scoring format akin to self-report (direct) personality inventories. Thus, the indirect nature of test materials and objective scoring format offer salient features.

In projective inventory method, a small number of stories collected from day-to-day, lives are presented to participating individuals. The stories pertain to the one or two attributes being measured, but this is not disclosed to the participants. Each story is followed by an appreciable number of statements (say, 15 to 25 statements). Participants are asked to read each story and indicate their agreement/disagreement with each statement. The use of a pre-established scoring key assigns scores to an individual on the attribute (say, contentment or calmness). It seems that this procedure attenuates much of social desirability bias (Mishra, Sahoo & Puhan, 1997). More specially, the strategy is useful in collectivist countries like India.

Biological and Other measures. In recent years, several biological measures have been used. Some of these use brain scans such as EEG, MRI, fMRI and PET (Positive emission tomography) to see if individuals show characteristic patterns of good health or ill health. Other measures focus on hormone levels (for example, the level of sex hormone as an indicator of aggressiveness). The level of *adrenalin* as a measure of short-term stress and the level of *cortisol* as an indicator of long-term stress have been accepted in the investigation of health.

In addition, the advent of electronic pager now allows researchers to beep individuals at random (or preestablished) times during the day in order to obtain description of their moods, activities and behaviours at these times. The *experience sampling method* can often reveal much about stable patterns of individual behaviour.

Brunswik's Idiographic strategy: The consideration of alternative strategies of measurement raises a fundamental question: Is it possible to measure an attribute (say, happiness) without the conventional method of psychometric tests? Brunswik's (1952, 1956) conceptual *lens model* and its application provides some possibilities in this direction.

The lens model may be viewed as a representation of any situation in which individuals are making judgments about a criterion. They have several sources of information available none of which predicts the criterion perfectly, although some sources of information may be more useful in predicting the event than others. The task of the individual is to identify the most useful sources of information and learn to employ them skillfully in making accurate judgment. The method requires subjects to make inferences regarding the values of a criterion variable on the basis of cues having uncertain relationships with the criterion. The degree of a subject's success of achievement can be effectively measured by correlating his or her responses with the actual values of the criterion.

Brunswik (1952, 1956) represented this in terms of a convex lends describing the relationship between human judgment, environmental cues, and the object to be judged.

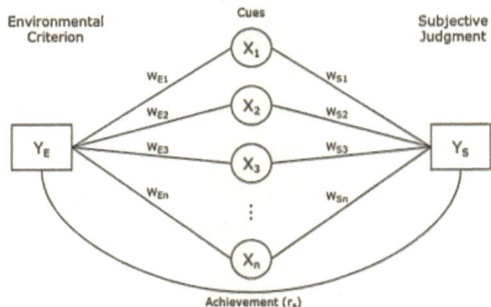

It has been argued that lens model is a unique approach to derive indigenous parameters. Although many studies have been conducted to identify relevant factors in the context of social judgment (decision making behaviour), its use in well-being research has remained under-utilized.

In a novel attempt, Sahoo (2007) employed lens model to identify indigenous parameters of happiness and unhappiness in Indian sociocultural context. The study involved idiographic method where participants were presented cues having variation. A set of six cues was presented as criteria of happiness and a set of six cues of unhappiness was also presented. Each of the participants was presented with 35 profiles (each profile in the form of bar diagrams) and they were asked to indicate their happiness on a 20-point rating scale. Similarly, they were also asked to rate unhappiness on a 20-point rating scales for each of other 35 profiles of unhappiness. It was important to note that the intensity of each of the cues varied from profile to profile.

Participants in the study were asked to see through each profile and indicate their happiness on a 20-point scale. Thirty-five profiles were presented for happiness judgment. Similarly, subjects were asked to judge their unhappiness on a 20-point scale. There were also 35 profiles for unhappiness judgment.

Figure: An Illustrative Profile for Happiness Judgment

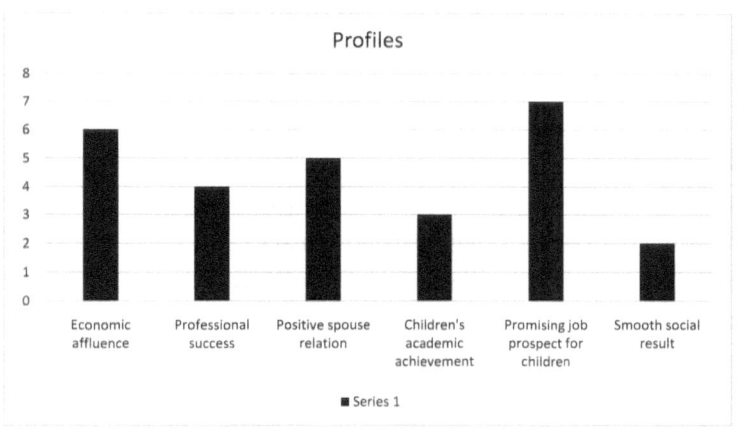

As indicated earlier, study involved an idiographic analysis of predictors of human happiness. Cue values ranged from one to seven units and criterion values from one to twenty units. The weights assigned to cues by participants were determined by computing correlations between values of individual cues and outcome (criterion) ratings across trials (profiles). It is important to note that correlation is computed for each cue (parameter) for each person. Of course, idiographic data (correlation) obtained for each cue (parameter) for each individual can be given nomothetic form to carry out group comparisons.

Sahoo's (2007) study using lens model revealed that all adults perceived children's academic achievement as a significant predictor of happiness. Group-wise, adult males perceived economic affluence and pre-adults judged positive spouse relation as significant factor of happiness. With respect to unhappiness, adult males considered economic hardship as a predictor of unhappiness; all adults viewed economic hardship as a predictor of unhappiness. Elderly females and all females view professional reverses as a predictor of unhappiness. Further, elderly females view as well as all females judge children's academic failure as predictor of unhappiness.

The use of idiographic lens model is a structural method of measurement. It replaces the use of conventional psychometric measure. Researchers may contemplate to think of some innovative methods like lens model to get around he problem of group/cultural bias. This is important especially in plural countries like India. In many plural/multicultural countries, subcultural differences may be greater than intercultural differences.

Apart from measurement bias, there are other issues in the context of happiness research. Though challenges are demanding, attempts are also vigorous to tackle them.

Unresolved Issues

Research on happiness has involved experts of varied persuasions. Considerable amount of consensus has been achieved in many domains; yet some other issues remain unsolved. Two such issues – intensity versus frequency and universality versus specificity – deserve our attention.

Intensity versus Frequency

The issue of intensity versus frequency pertains to

the process nature of happiness/well-being. The leading light in the area of happiness research, Ed Diener, has consistently argued that happiness entails frequent experience of moderate positive affects. In fact, this is one of the key elements in the definition of happiness (Diener, Lucas & Oishi, 2005). Diener further argues that an intense positive event in life such as winning a lottery may generate pleasure for some time, yet the individual gets back to his or her set point (genetically predetermined level) after some time. Accordingly, Diener and his associates consider frequent mild positive emotion as one of the components of authentic happiness while positing a three-component model of happiness (the other two being "life satisfaction" and infrequent negative emotion).

At an empirical level, Diener, Sandvik, and Pavot (1991) showed that the percentage of time that individuals were experiencing positive affect correlated .50, while the average intensity of positive affect when they were being happy correlated at only .25. They concluded that intensity is a relatively unimportant. Further they observed that intense positive events occur only on 2.6% of days.

While a strong case has been made in favour of frequency as a criterion of happiness, some investigators argue in favour of intensity. Argyle (2001) believes that some of the big events may have sustainable effect. The positive experience of sexual union may have long-term effect, so also is the case of visiting a place of spiritual/religious importance. Argyle (2001) further argues that Diener's report that people have intense positive experience only on 2.6% day seems to be a conservative estimate. Many people with religious and spiritual bent of mind go to places of worship/contemplation at least once a week. These activities produce long-term effects.

Reich and Zautra (1981) conducted a field experiment to demonstrate effects of highly pleasant activities. They asked people to choose 12 pleasurable activities (from a long list) which they have not done for last two weeks. A similar group was asked to choose 2 activities. The original list included a large number of activities in the categories of sport, entertainment, cultural pursuits, creative pursuits and other activities. After individuals identified their chosen activities, they were given ample opportunity to have those activities for two weeks. It was found that activities produced happiness and it was relatively stable. This happened for both the groups engaged in 12 activities or 2 activities.

The role of intensity versus frequency may be relative to some psychological parameter yet to be identified in future research.

Universality versus Specificity

Another issue concerns the modality of intervention programmes when intervention for health promotion is planned. Should it be uniform across all subsets of population or should it be tailored specifically for specific groups/cultures?

Like measurement issue here is also the etic-emic dilemma. The etic approach would imply general or universal features of happiness-enhancement programme while emic strategy would denote culture-specific (or group-specific) components.

Although etic-emic strategy appears to be paradoxical, the contradiction can be handled by making a distinction between two levels of analysis. The etic can be placed at the conceptual level whereas emic is positioned on empirical level. For example, *attachment* as a psychological process is an etic construct. People in all cultures exhibit attachment; mothers (caregivers) in all cultures show attachment towards their children. Yet, American mothers' expression mode is primarily verbal. They tell a story or sing a song in the presence of their children. This cements mother child bonding. In contrast, typical Indian or Japanese mothers express their attachment through touch behaviour. They cuddle and embrace their children a lot. Looked through American lens, the lack of verbal story telling may seem somewhat rude. Similarly, absence of touch behaviour on the part of American mothers is likely to be viewed as non-attachment. But a deeper analysis suggests the mothers' behaviour in both cultural contexts are local (emic) expression of universal (etic) tendency of love and affection.

In similar ways, the etic construct of happiness may guide intervention. Yet specific activities and happiness-boosting programmes may be adopted in the form of emic (local) contents.

There is another robust perspective called **saliency approach** (Kanungo, 1982) to solve the universality-specificity incompatibility. Kanungo (1982) explicated saliency model to apply motivational principles both in the cross-cultural and uni-cultural settings. According to Kanungo (1982), each subset of human population has its own priority. Accordingly, certain specific needs may be *salient* (important) to a particular group whereas other needs are found to be salient for the other group. For example, Americans regard challenging and interesting nature of work as the most salient need whereas Indian employees view security as the most salient need. With this rationale, steps need to be taken to satisfy security needs and interesting task-nature in India and America respectively for ensuring work motivation (Sahoo & Bidyadhar, 1995).

In similar ways, Sahoo (2015) has examined the relevance of need saliency model in the health context. More specifically the model in this context posits that well-being is significantly related to salient health needs and unrelated to nonsalient health need satisfaction. Sahoo and his associates have carried out several studies both in the context of work motivation and well-being to examine the model. It has been greatly supported.

Irrespective of the context it is possible to identify salient and nonsalient needs. Typically, a list of needs (factors) may be presented and participants are asked to rank-order these outcome factors. Supposing that the list contains 15 outcome factors, the factors rated first and second (or first, second and third) are considered salient conditions and factors rated fourteenth and fifteenth (or 13th, 14th and 15th) are regarded as nonsalient outcomes. This scheme can easily be applied to any situation including well-being situation.

In sum, the saliency model requires planners and experts to identify salient well-being needs for a given subset of human population and take steps for fulfilling those conditions for promoting happiness. The application of this model would go beyond the etic-emic paradox since etic construct would be implemented in an emic manner.

Towards an Integration

Integration is a continuous process in the evolutionary growth of resilient theories. The conceptual framework of happiness and well-being has also displayed several attempts of integration at growth periods. Although future possibilities do exist with respect to further integration, the past and present attempts also offer many insights.

As described in Chapter 1, happiness/well-being

literature has two distinct perspectives: hedonic and eudaimonic. Hedonic perspective defines happiness in terms of attainment of pleasure whereas eudaimonic definition entails happiness as the realization of one's own potentials. A cursory look at these two perspectives reveals that these are the outcome of four distinct philosophical traditions.

Initially utilitarians such as Jeremy Bentham (1748-1832) and John Stuart Mill (1816-1873) advocated for the greatest happiness for the greatest number. Subsequently it created an echo in positive psychology in terms of working for maximizing happiness within specific groups of people. Similarly, Aristotle's emphasis on virtuous life as good life was respected as another philosophical tradition and positive psychology researchers like Seligman focused character strength as a way to happiness.

Hedonic and eudaimonic thoughts made distinct marks of third and fourth philosophical traditions. A great deal of research along with valid measurement methods placed these two traditions on two distinct theoretical tracks. The distinction between "feeling good" and "doing pleasurable things" is the dividing line. The hedonic denotes the pursuit of pleasure whereas eudaimonia represents a lifestyle whereby individuals strive to be better by using talent and make meaning. In other words, hedonic refers to feeling good and eudaimonia refers to functioning well.

The roots of hedonism can be traced to Indian Carvak school of thought and Greek Cyrrenaic school. Modern psychologists define hedonism as the pursuit of pleasure, gratification and comfort. The focus is on positive emotions. However, positive affect evoked by hedonic activity does not endure beyond the activity itself. Further, individuals engaged in hedonic activity tend to report lower life satisfaction.

Diener and his associates (Diener, Lucas, & Oishi, 2005) often use "subjective well-being (SWB)" interchangeably with happiness. Happiness refers to high levels of positive affect, low levels of negative affect and a high degree of overall life satisfaction. Although life satisfaction is not always a hedonic concept, SWB is used in the literature as an indicator of hedonic well-being.

As a distinct tradition, Aristotle's legacy influenced our contemporary thought on healthy living. Aristotle coined the term *eudaimonia* to refer to a lifestyle based on virtue and realization of potential. It is not a state of feeling, but a way of life.

Drawing on Aristotelian roots, contemporary psychologists considered eudaimonic way of life, wherein an individual strives to be better by developing talents and virtues, and generating meaning. The lifestyle is geared towards growth. Eudaimonic often requires effortful engagement and difficult activity. Such effortful pursuits result in sustainable happiness even if challenging pursuits generate some amount of negative affect. In fact, individuals with an exclusive eudaimoniac focus may experience fatigue; they may seek hedonic activity for making up the physical loss.

The contemporary version of eudaimonic well-being has been termed **psychological well-being** by Ryff (1989). The model psychological well-being (PWB) consists of six dimensions: autonomy, environmental mastery, positive relationship, purpose in life, personal growth, and self-acceptance. Although PWB model has some limitations, this six-factor model has emerged as a valid, effective and integrative framework (Ryff, 2014).

In a parallel development, Ryan and Deci (2000) have articulated another eudaimonic model called **self-**

determination theory (SDT). The model consists of competence, autonomy and relatedness as fundamental human needs and their satisfaction is indicative of well-being. While both PWB and SDT are similar in many respects, there are some differences. In SDT, well-being is fostered by environmental mastery, autonomy and relatedness, while in PWB, these concepts are defining attributes along with other three defining features (personal growth, purpose in life, and self-acceptance). Well-being is attained when individuals meet SDT needs through goal pursuits. There is much empirical support for SDT (Deci & Ryan, 2008).

There is a great deal of correspondence between these two variations of eudaimoniac perspectives. Both forms (PWB and SDT) emphasize activity, goals and relationship. Social well-being as a distinguishing feature of well-being is respected in both the forms.

At a higher level, hedonic and eudaimonic happiness appear to be two distinguishable types of happiness. Hedonic happiness gravitates more towards the "feeling" end and neglects "doing" orientation. Eudaimonic happiness emphasizes functioning aspects ignores feeling dimension. Thus, the incompleteness in each of those two models motivates researchers to look for an integrated framework.

Reconciliation Attempts

Seligman (2002) attempted an integrated framework with his concept of **authentic happiness**. He identified *three* pathways leading to happiness: pleasure, engagement and meaning. The first pathway, the *pleasant life,* is based on positive emotion. This pathway is indicative of hedonic orientation. The second pathway, the engagement, reflects the philosophical approach of eudaimonic and virtue. Engagement is promoted by utilizing virtue and character strength. The third path, meaning, is strongly linked with eudaimonia – the meaningful tendency for helping others and institutions. It also echoes the utilitarian concern – the maximum good for maximum number.

Interestingly Seligman (2002) argues that the centrality of these paths changes across the lifespan. Individuals during adolescence seek for pleasant lives, preadults look for engaged lives, and adulthood and late adulthood prompt them to attain meaningful lives. Thus, the components (pleasure, engagement, and meaning) stay together, but their priorities change as people advance their journey.

In 2011, Seligman revised his authentic happiness model of well-being and proposed a new model – **PERMA**. The PERMA model stands for five pathways instead of three; happiness pathways include *Pleasure* (P), *engagement* (E), *relationship* (R), *meaning* (M) and *accomplishment* (A). The inclusion of positive relationship in the PERMA model emphasizes Peterson's often quoted slogan that other people matter. Seligman (2011) further asserts that happiness depends on these five pillars.

Keyes (2002) furthered the conceptual journey by suggesting the model of **flourishing** as a framework of complete mental health. According to Keyes, flourishing not only includes positive evidence of healthy functioning (feeling good and functioning well), but also entails the absence of psychopathology. Flourishing is contrasted with languishing which denotes the presence of psychopathology and absence of positive mental health. In a way flourishing contains all components of four philosophical traditions discussed earlier.

Hybrid Models

There are a few other attempts where advantages of different models have been combined. One such model is presented by Lyubomirsky, Sheldon, and Schkade (2005). This is termed **sustainable model of well-being**. Three elements are identified as contributing to happiness: genetics, circumstances, and personal choice.

The theoretical models (explanatory framework) have been presented in chapter 8. It may be indicated here that top-down trait theories are used to account for hereditary aspects of well-being. Bottom-up theories of happiness are useful in explaining positive effects resulting from experiences. Finally, cognitive theories are employed to account for cognitive influences (perception and personal choices across situations).

Existential positive psychology model is another hybrid model. Wong (2010) blended existential psychology concepts and positive psychology notions to provide a comprehensive understanding of happiness. Wong posits that only by addressing the totality of life's experiences and existential question can one improve human condition and increase individual happiness. EPP addresses the four existential anxieties – meaning in life, isolation, freedom and death.

Wong expanded the category of happiness by specifically denoting spiritual happiness as a distinct type of happiness. Spirituality can be conceptualized as a fourth key psychological need in addition to the three SDT needs (Ryan & Deci, 2000) of competence, autonomy and relatedness. The EPP hybrid model is an amalgamation of four philosophical traditions of the utilaterian, virtue, hedonic and eudaimonic elements.

Future Directions

Fertilization and cross-fertilization is a principle that continues indefinitely. In the context of well-being research, paradigm crises and paradigm shifts are taking place constantly. A major concern expressed through this bulk of research involves the thought of going beyond the individual happiness. Is it possible for an individual to be happy *when others are unhappy*? This brings to the fore the fundamental concept of **collective happiness.** In fact, a large number of studies during past decades have delineated the social component (positive relation with others). Yet, this component requires further operationalization and nomological network. This would be future challenge.

In addition, researchers in future are likely to study new areas relevant for happiness domain, use-more of qualitative data. The concept of "true self" and "other-oriented hope" may feature in future research. The happiness and well-being in children and adolescents is also a candidate for future research. Finally, it is important to recognize that many developments in neuroscience would provide many pointers for upcoming research. The combined growth of positive psychology and neuroscience of happiness carries immense possibilities for future research.

❏❏

References

Chapter – 1

Baumgardener, S.R., & Crothers, M.K. (2009). *Positive psychology*. New Delhi: Pearson Education.

Biswas-Diener, R., &Diener, E. (2001). Making less of a bad situation: Satisfaction in the slums of Calcutta. *Social Indicators Research*, 55, 329-352.

Dalai Lama & Cutler, H.C. (1998). *The art of happiness*. London: Hodder & Stoughton.

Diener, E. (1984). Subjective well-being. Psychological Bulletin, 95, 542-575.

Diener, E., & Biswas-Diener, R. (2002). Will money increase subjective well-being? A literature review and guide to needed research. *Social Indicators Research*, 57, 119-169.

Diener, E., & Oishi, S. (2000). Money and happiness and subjective well-being across nations. In E. Diener & E.M. Suh (Eds) *Culture and subjective well-being* (pp. 185-218). Cambridge, MA: MIT Press.

Diener, E., & Seligman, M.E.P. (2004). Beyond money: Toward an economy of well-being. *Psychology in the Public Interest*, 5(1), 1-31.

Diener, E., Sapyta, H., & Suh, E. (1998). Subjective well-being is essential to well-being. *Psychological Inquiry*, 9, 33-37.

Easterbrook, G. (2003). *The progress paradox: How life goes better while people feel worse*. New York: Random House.

Goyal, M. (2016). Why India is one of the unhappiest nations in the world? *The Economic Times* (Nov 4).

Helliwel, J.F. (2003). How is life? Combining individual and national variables to explain subjective well-being. *Economic Modelling*, 20, 331-360.

Kahneman, D., Diener, E., Schwarz, N. (Eds) (1999). *The foundations of hedonic psychology*. New York: Russell Sage Foundation.

Kasser, T., & Kanner, A.D. (Eds) (2004). *Psychology and consumer culture: The struggle for a good life in a materialistic world*. Washington D.C.: American Psychological Association.

Little, T.D. (1997). Mean and covariance structures (MACS) analysis of cross-cultural data: Practical and theoretical issues. *Multivariate Behaviour Research*, 32, 53-76.

Myers, D.G. (2000a). The funds, friends and faith of happy people. *American Psychologist*, 55, 56-67.

Myers, D.G. (2000b). *The American Paradox: Spiritual hunger in a age of plenty*. New Haven: Yale University Press.

Ryan, M., & Deci, E.L. (2001). On happiness and human potential: A review of research on hedonic and eudiamonic well-being. *Annual Review of Psychology*, 52, 141-166.

Ryan, R.M., & Deci, E.L. (2000). Self-determination theory and the facilitation of intrinsic motivation, social development, and well-being. *American Psychologist*, 55, 68-78.

Ryff, C.D., & Keyes, C.L.M. (1995). The structure of psychological well-being revisited. *Journal of Personality and Social Psychology*, 57, 1069-1081.

Ryff, C.D., & Singer, B. (1998). The contours of positive human health. *Psychological Inquiry*, 9, 1-28.

Ryff, C.D., & Singer, B. (2000). Interpersonal flourishing: A positive health agenda for the new millennium. *Personality and Social Psychological Review*, 4, 30-44.

Sahoo, F.M. (2007). Promoting human happiness. In M.B. Sharan & D. Suar (Eds) *Psychology matters* (pp. 26-44). New Delhi: Allied Publishers.

Seligman, M., & Csikszentmihalyi, M. (2000). Positive psychology: An introduction. *American Psychologist*, 55, 5-14.

The Economic Times (Sept 27, 2020). Mental health in India.

Thoits, P., & Hanna, M. (1979). Income and psychological distress: The impact of an income - - maintenance experiment. *Journal of Health and Social Behaviour*, 20, 130-138.

Waterman, A.S. (1993). Two conceptions of happiness: Contrasts of personal expressiveness (eudaimonia) and hedonic enjoyment. *Journal of Personality and Social Psychology*, 64, 671-691.

Chapter – 2

Alfonso, V., Allinson, D., Rader, D. & Gorman, B. (1996). The Extended Satisfaction with Life Scale: Development and Psychometric Properties. Social Indicators Research, 38, 275-301.

Argyle, M. (2001). *The psychology of happiness*. London: Routledge.

Brickman, F. & Campbell, D.J. (1971). Hedonic relativism and planning the good society. In M.H. Appley (Ed.), *Adaptation level theory* (pp 287-305). New York: Academic Press.

Cacioppo, J.T., Gardner, W. L. & Berntson, G.G. (1999). The affect system has parallel and interpretive processing components. *Journal of Personality and Social Psychology*, 76, 839-855.

Cohn, M. & Fredrickson, B.L. (1009). Positive emotions. In S.J. Lopez & C.R. Snyder (Eds) *Oxford handbook of positive psychology* (pp. 13-24). New York: Oxford University Press.

FACIT (Functional Assessment of Chronic Illness Therapy) (1993). Journal of Clinical Oncology, 11(3), 570-579.

Fordyce, M. (1988). A review of research on the happiness measure: A sixty second index of happiness and mental health. *Social Indicators Research*, 20, 355-381.

Kahneman, D., Diener, E., & Schwarz, N. (1999). *Well-being: The foundation of hedonic psychology*. New York: Russell Sage Foundation.

Keyes, C.L.M. (1998). Social well-being. *Social Psychology Quarterly*, 61, 121-140.

Lyubomirsky, S. & Lepper, H.S. (1999). A measure of subjective happiness: Preliminary reliability and construct validation. *Social Indicators Research*, 46, 137-155.

Myers, D. & Diener, E. (1996). The pursuit of happiness, Scientific American, 274 (May), 54-60.

Ryff, C.D. & Singer, B. (1998). The contours of positive mental health. *Psychological Inquiry*, 1998, 9, 1-28.

Ryff, C.D. (1989). Happiness is everything, or is it? Exploration on the meaning of psychological well-being. *Journal of Personality and Social Psychology*, 57, 1069-1081.

Sahoo, F.M. (2009). *Life Orientation Scale (LOS)*. Unpublished Report, Psychology Department, Utkal University, Bhubaneswar, Odisha, India.

Sandvik, E., Diener, E., & Seidlitz, L. (1993). Subjective well-being: The convergence and stability of self-report and non-self-report measures. *Journal of Personality*, 61, 317-342.

Stone, A., Schiffman, S. & DeVries, M. (1999). Rethinking self-report methodologies; An argument for collecting ecologically valid, momentary measurements and selected results of EMA studies. In D. Kahneman, E. Diener & N. Schwartz (Eds.), *Well-being: The foundation of hedonic psychology* (pp 26-39). New York: Russell Sage Foundation.

Watson, D., Clark, L.A.& Tellegen, A. (1988). Development and validation of brief measures of positive and negative affects: The PANAS scales. *Journal of Personality and Social Psychology*, 54, 1065-1070.

WHOQOL Group (1998). The World Health Organization Quality of Life scale (WHOQOL): Development and general psychometric properties. Social Science and Medicine, 46, 1569-1585.

Chapter – 3

Argyle, M. (2001). *The psychology of happiness*. New York: Routledge.

Bandura, A. (1977). Self-efficacy: Towered a unifying theory of behavior change. Psychological Review, 84, 191-215.

Bandura, A. (1991). Self-efficacy mechanism in physiological activation and health-promoting behavior. In J. Madden, IV (Ed) *Neurobiology of learning, emotion and affect*) (pp. 229-270). New York: Raven.

Bandura, A. (1997). Self-efficacy: The exercise of control. New York: Freeman.

Bar-On, R. (1997). *Bar-On Emotional Quotient Inventory (EQ-1): Technical Manual* Toronto: Multi-Health System.

Beck, A.T. (1967). Depression: *Clinical, experimental, and theoretical aspects*. New York: Hoeber.

Beck, A.T. (1991). Cognitive therapy: A 30-year retrospective. *American Psychologist*, 46, 368-375.

Bonanno, G.A. (2007). Psychological resilience. *Psychological Science*, 17, 181-186.

Carver, C.S. & Scheier, M.F. (2005). Optimism. In C.R. Snyder & S.J. Lopez (Eds.), *Handbook of positive psychology* (pp. 231-243). New York: Oxford University Press.

Davidson, R. & Begley, S. (2012). *The emotional life of your brain*. London: Hodder.

Finchman, F.D. & Bradbury, T.N. (1992). Assessing attributions in marriage: The Relationship Attribution Measure. *Journal of Personality and Social Psychology*, 62(3), 457-68.

Frankl, V. (2004). *Man's search for meaning*. London: Rider.

Gardner, H. (1993). *Frames of mind: Theory of multiple intelligence*. New York: Basic Book.

Garmezy, N. (1971). Vulnerability research and the issue of primary prevention *American Journal of Orthopsychiatry*, 41, 101-116.

Goleman, D. (1995). *Emotional intelligence*. New York: Bantam

Greenwald, A.G. (1980). The totalitarian ego: Fabrication and revision of personal history. *American Psychologist*, 35, 603-618.

Jerusalem, M. & Mittag, W. (1995). Self-efficacy in stressful life transition. In A. Bandura (Ed), *Self-efficacy in changing societies* (pp 177-201). New York: Cambridge University Press.

Keyes, C.L.M., & Lopez, S. (2005). Toward a science of mental health: Positive directions in diagnosis and intervention. In C.R. Snyder and S.J. Lopez (Eds), *Handbook of positive psychology* (pp. 45-59). New York: Oxford University Press.

Lazarus, R.S. (1983). The costs and benefits of denial. In S. Benitz (Ed), *Denial of stress* (pp. 1-30). New York: International Universities Press.

Maddux, J.E. (2005). Self-efficacy: The power of believing you can. In C.R. Snyder & S.J. Lopez (Eds.) *Handbook of positive psychology* (pp. 277-287). New York: Oxford University Press.

Marlatt, G.A., Baer, J.S., & Quigley, L.A. (1995). Self-efficacy and addictive behavior. In A. Bandura (Ed0, *Self-efficacy in changing societies* (pp. 289-315). New York: Cambridge University Press.

Masten, A.S. (2001). Ordinary magic: Resilience process in development. *American Psychologist*, 56, 227-238.

Moskovitz, S. (1985). Longitudinal follow-up of the child survivors of the Holocaust. *Journal of the American Academy of Child Psychiatry* 24(4), 402.

Mowrer, O.H. (1960). Learning theory and behavior. New York: Wiley.

Myers, D.G. (1990). *The pursuit of happiness* New York: Harper.

Pargament, K. (1997). *The psychology of religion and coping*. New York: Guilford Press.

Peterson, C. & Chang, E.C. (2003). Optimism and flourishing. In C.L.M. Keyes (Ed) *Flourishing: Positive psychology and life well-lived* (pp. 55-79). Washington D.C.: APA.

Peterson, C. (2000). The future of optimism. *American Psychologist*, 55, 44-55.

Philippot, P. & Blairy, S. (2002). Respiratory feedback in the generation of emotion. *Cognition and Emotion*, 16(5), 605-627.

Sahoo, F.M. & KhandayatRay, L. (2008). The lotus-in-the-mud phenomenon: A study of resilient children's need expression and gratification. *Indian Journal of Psychological Issues*, 16, 1-13.

Salovey, P. & Mayer, J.D. (1990). Emotional intelligence. *Innovation, Cognition, and Personality*, 9, 185-211.

Scheier, M.F., & Carver, C.S. (1985). Optimism coping ad health: Assessment and implications of generalized expectancy on health. *Health Psychology*, 4, 219-247.

Scheier, M.F., Matthews, K.A., Owens, J.F., Magovern, G.J., Lefebvre, R.C., Abott, R.A., & Carver, C.S. (1989). Dispositional optimism and recovery from coronary artery bypass surgery: The beneficial effects on physical and psychological well-being. *Journal of Personality and Social Psychology*, 57, 1024-1040.

Schneider, S.L. (2001). In search of realistic optimism. *American Psychologist*, 56, 250-263.

Schwarzer, R. & Fuchs, R. (1995). Changing risk behaviors and adopting health behaviors: The role of self-efficacy beliefs. In A. Bandura (Ed), *Self-efficacy in changing societies* (pp. 259-288). New York: Cambridge University Press.

Seligman, M.E.P. (1998). *Learned optimism. How to change your mind and your life* (2nd Edn.). New York. Pocket Books.

Seppala, E. (2016). *The happiness track*. New York: Harper Collins.

Snyder, C.B. (2000). *Handbook of hope: Theory measures, and application*. San Diego, CA: Academic Press.

Snyder, C.B. (2002). Hope theory: Rainbows of the mind. *Psychological Inquiry*, 13, 249-275.

Snyder, C.R., Lopez, S.L., & Pedrotti, T. (2011). *Positive psychology: The scientific and practical explorations of human strengths*. (2nd Edition). Sage: New Delhi.

Snyder, C.R., Rand, K.L., & Sigman, D.R. (2005). Hope theory: A member of the positive psychology family. In C.R. Snyder and S.J. Lopez (Eds.) *Handbook of positive psychology* (pp. 257-276). New York: Oxford University Press.

Taylor, S.E. & Brown, J.D. (1988). Illusion and well-being: A social psychological perspective on mental health. *Psychological Bulletin*, 103, 193-210.

Taylor, S.E. (1989). *Positive illusion*. New York: Basic Books.

Tiger, L. (1979). *Optimism: The biology of hope* New York: Simon & Schuster.

Werner, P.E. & Smith, R.S. (2001). *Journeys from childhood & midlife.* Syrancuse, N Y: Cornel University Press.

Wilde, G. (2001). *Target risk 2: A new psychology for health and safety.* Toronto: PDE

Chapter – 4

Argyle, M. & Lu, L. (1990). The happiness of extraverts. *Personality and Individual Differences,* 11, 1011-1017.

Argyle, M. (2001). *The psychology and happiness.* New York: Routledge.

Baruch, G.K., & Bernett, R. (1986). "Role quality", multiple role involvement and psychological well-being in midlife women. *Journal of Personality and Social Psychology,* 51, 578-585.

Battista, J., & Almond, R. (1973). The development of meaning in life. Psychiatry, 36, 409-427.

Biswas-Diener, R. & Diener, E. (2001). Making less of a bad situation: Satisfaction in the slums of Calcutta. *Social Indicators Research,* 55, 329-352.

Bradburn, K.M. (1969). *The structure of psychological well-being.* Chicago: Aldine.

Brickman, P., & Campbell, D. (1971). Hedonic relativism and planning the good society. In M.H. Appley (Ed.), *Adaptation-level theory: A symposium* (pp 287-302). New York: Academic Press.

Campbell, A., Converse, P.E., & Rogers, W.L. (1976). *The quality of American life.* New York: Sage.

Canter, N. & Sanderson, C.A. (1999). Life task participation and well-being. In D. Kahneman, E. Diener, & N. Schwartz (Eds.), *Well-being: The foundations of hedonic psychology* (pp 230-243). New York: Russell Sage.

Carr, A. (2004). *Positive psychology*. New York: Routledge.

Carstensen, L.E., Isaacowitz, D.M., & Charles, S.T. (1999). Taking time seriously: A theory of socio-emotional selectivity. *American Psychologist*, 54, 165-181.

Caspi, A., Sugden, K., Moffitt, T.E., Taylor, A., Crang, I.W., Harrington, H.I., McClay, J., Mill, J., Martin, J., Braithwaite, A., & Poulton, R. (2003). Influence of life stress on depression: Moderation by a polymorphism in the 5-HTT gene *Science*, 301, 386-389.

Costa, P.T., McRae, R.R., & Norris, A.H. (1981). Personal adjustment in aging: Longitudinal prediction from neuroticism and extraversion. *Journal of Gerontology*, 36, 78-85.

Csikszentmihalyi, M. (1999). If we are so rich, why aren't we happy? *American Psychologist*, 54, 821-827.

Danner, D., Snowdon, D., & Friesen, W. (2001). Positive emotions in early life and longevity: Findings from the nun study. *Journal of Personality and Social Psychology*, 80, 804-813.

DeNeve, K.M., & Cooper, H. (1998). The happy personality: A meta-analysis of 137 personality traits and subjective well-being. *Psychological Bulletin*, 124, 197-229.

Diener, E. & Oishi, S. (2000). Money and happiness: Income and subjective well-being across nations. In E. Diener and E.M. Suh (Eds.), *Culture and subjective well-being* (pp. 185-218). Cambridge, MA: MIT Press.

Diener, E. (2000). Subjective well-being: The science of happiness and a proposal for national index. *American Psychologist*, 55, 34-43.

Diener, E., & Biswas-Diener, R. (2000). *Income and subjective well-being: Will money make us happy?* University of Illinois, Unpublished report.

Diener, E., & Diener, M. (1995). Cross-cultural correlates of life satisfaction and self-esteem. *Journal of Personality and Social Psychology*, 68, 563-663.

Diener, E., & Larsen, R.J. (1984). Temporal stability and cross-situational consistency of affective, behavioral and cognitive responses. *Journal of Personality and Social Psychology*, 47, 580-592.

Diener, E., & Lucas, R. (1999). Personality and subjective well-being. In E. Kahneman, E. Diener & N. Schwartz (Eds.), *Well-being: The foundations of hedonic psychology* (pp. 213-29). New York: Russell Sage Foundation.

Diener, E., & Seligman, M. (2004). Beyond money: Toward an economy of well-being. *Psychology in the Public Interest*, 5, 1-31.

Diener, E., Suh, E.M., Lucas, R.E., & Smith, H.L. (1999). Subjective well=being: Three decades of progress. *Psychological Bulletin*, 125, 275-302.

Frankl, V.E. (1959). *Man's search for meaning*. London: Hodder Stoughton.

Fredrickson, B.L. (2001). The role of positive emotions in positive psychology: The broaden-and-build theory of positive emotions. *American Psychologist*, 56, 218-226.

Fujita, F., & Diener, E. (2005). Life satisfaction and set point: Stability and change. *Journal of Personality and Social Psychology*, 88, 158-164.

Fujita, F., Diener, E., Sandvik (1991). Gender differences in negative affect and well-being. *Journal of Personality and Social Psychology*, 61, 427-434.

Furnham, A., & Cheng, H. (2997). Personality and happiness. *Psychological Reports*, 80, 761-762.

Gottman, J., & Silver, N. (1999). *The seven principles for making marriages work*. New York: Growth.

Gray, J.A. (1972). The psychophysiological nature of introversion extraversion: A modification of Eysenck's theory. In V.D. Neblitsyn & J.A. Gray (Eds.) *Biological basis of individual behaviour* (pp. 182-205). New York: Academic Press.

Haring, M.J., Okun, M.A., & Stock, W.A. (1984). A quantitative synthesis of literature on work, status and subjective well-being. *Journal of Vocational Behavior*, 25, 316-324.

Harker, L., & Keltner, D. (2001). Expressions of positive emotion in women's college yearbook pictures and their relationship to personality and life outcomes across adulthood. *Journal of Personality and Social Psychology, 80,* 112-124.

Heady, B., & Wearing, A. (1989). Personality, life events and subjective well-being. *Journal of Personality and Social Psychology, 57,* 731-739.

Helson, H. (1964). *Adaptation-level theory.* New York: Harper & Row.

Hills, P. & Argyle, M. (2001). Happiness, introversion-extraversion and happy introverts. *Personality and Individual Difference, 30,* 595-608.

Inglehart, R. (1990). *Cultural shift in advanced industrial society.* Princeton: Princeton University Press.

Isaacowitz, D.M. (2007). Understanding individual and age differences in well-being. In A.D. Ong, &M.H.M. Van Dulmen (Eds.), *Oxford handbook of methods in positive psychology* (pp 220-232). New York: Oxford University Press.

Johnson, D.R., & Wit, J. (2002). An empirical test of crisis, social selection, and role explanation of the relationship between marital disruption and psychological distress. *Journal of Marriage and the Family, 64,* 211-224.

Kagan, J., & Snidman, N. (2004). *The long shadow of temperament.* Cambridge, MA, USA: Belknap Press.

King, L.A., & Nappa, C.R. (1998). What makes a life good? *Journal of Personality and Social Psychology, 75,* 156-165.

Kunzmann, U., Stange, A., & Jordan, J. (2005). Positive affectivity and lifestyle in adulthood: Do you do what you feel? *Personality and Social Psychology Bulletin, 31,* 574-588.

Langer, E.J. (1983). *The psychology of control.* Beverly Hills, California: Sage.

Lu, L., Shih, J.B., Lin, Y., & Ju, L.S. (1997). Personal and environmental correlates of happiness. *Personality and Individual Differences, 23,* 453-462.

Lucas, R. E., Clark, A. E., Georgellis, Y., & Diener, E. (2003).

Reexamining adaptation and the set point model of happiness. *Journal of Personality and Social Psychology*, 84, 527-539.

Lykken, D. & Tellegen, A. (1996). Happiness is a stochastic phenomenon. *Psychological Science*, 7, 186-189.

Lyubomirsky, S. (2007). *The how of happiness.* New York: Penguin Books.

Mastekaasa, A. (1992). Marriage and psychological well-being. *Journal of Marriage and Family*, 54, 901-911.

Mastekaasa, A. (1993). Marital status and psychological well-being: A changing relationship? *Social Indicators Research*, 29, 249-276.

McCrae, R.R., & Costa, P.T. (1991). Adding liebe and arbeit. The full Five Factor model and well-being. *Personality and Social Psychology Bulletin*, 17, 227-232.

McCrae, R.R., Costa, P.T., & Martin, T.A. (2005). The NEO-PI-3: A more readable revised NEO personality inventory. *Journal of Personality Assessment*, 84, 261-270.

McGregor, I., & Little, B.R. (1998). Personal projects, happiness, and meaning. *Journal of Personality and Social Psychology*, 74, 494-512.

Meehl, P.E. (1975). Hedonic capacity: Some conjectures. *Bulletin of the Menninger Clinic*, 39, 295-307.

Michalos, A.C. (1991). *Life satisfaction and happiness: Global report on subjective well-being* Vol. 1, New York: Springer - Verlag.

Myers, D. (1992). *The pursuit of happiness.* New York: Harper.

Myers, D. G. (2000). The funds, friends and faith of happy people. *American Psychologist*, 55, 56-67.

Nolen-Hoeksema, S. & Rusting, C.L. (1999). Gender differences in well-being. In D. Kahneman, E. Diener and N. Schwartz (Eds.), *Well-being: The foundations of hedonic psychology* (pp. 330-350). New York: Russell Sage Foundation.

Nolen-Hoeksema, S. (1991). Responses on depression and their effects on the duration of depressive episodes. *Journal of Abnormal Psychology*, 100, 569-585.

Nolen-Hoeksema, S. (1995). Epidemiology and theories of sex difference in depression. In M. Seeman (Ed), *Gender and psychopathology* (pp. 63-87). Washington D.C.: American Psychiatric Association.

Rodin, J. (1986). *Aging and health: Effects of the sense of control. Science*, 233, 1271-1276.

Rosenberg, M. (1965). *Society and the adolescent self-image.* Princeton, USA: Princeton University Press.

Rotter, J.B. (1966). Generalized expectancies for internal versus external control of reinforcement. *Psychological Monograph*, 80, 1-28.

Ryff, C.D., & Singer, B. (2000). Interpersonal flourishing: A positive health agenda for the new millennium. *Personality and Social Psychology Review*, 4, 30-44.

Schmutte, P.S., &Ryff, C.D. (1997). Personality and well-being. Reexamining methods and meanings. *Journal of Personality and Social Psychology*, 73, 549-559.

Schwartz, B. (2004). *The paradox of choice: Why more is less.* New York: Ecco Press.

Seligman, M.E.P. (2002). *Authentic happiness.* New York: Free Press.

Sheldon, K.M., & Elliot, A.J. (1999). Goal striving, need satisfaction, and longitudinal well=-being: The self-concordance model. *Journal of Personality and Social Psychology*, 76, 482-497.

Suh, E.M., Diener, E. & Fujita, F. (1996). Events and subjective well-being. *Journal of Personality and Social Psychology*, 70, 1091-1102.

Veenhoven, R. (1994). *Correlates of happiness* (3 Vols.). The Center for Socio-Cultural Transformation. The Netherlands.

Watson, D. (2005). Positive affectivity. In C.R. Snyder and S.J. Lopez (Eds.), *Handbook of positive psychology* (pp 106-119). New York: Oxford University Press.

Wood, W., Rhodes, N., & Whelan, M. (1989). Sex difference in positive well-being. *Psychological Bulletin*, 106, 249-264.

Chapter – 5

Allport, G.W., & Ross, J.M. (1967). Personal religious orientation and prejudice. *Journal of Personality and Social Psychology*, 5, 432-443.

Amabile, T.M. (1983). *The social psychology of creativity*. New York: Springer Veriay.

Argyle, M. (2001). *The psychology of happiness*. New York: Routledge.

Battista, J. & Almond, R. (1973). The development of meaning in life. *Psychiatry*, 36, 409-427.

Baumeister, R.F. (1991). *Meanings of life*. New York: Guilford Press.

Benson, H., & Proctor, W. (1984). *Beyond the relaxation response*. New York: Times Books.

Brown, K.W., & Ryan, R.M. (2003). The benefit of being present: Mindfulness and its role in psychological well-being. *Journal of Personality and Social Psychology*, 84, 822-848.

Bryant, F.B., & Verhoff, J. (2007). *Savouring: A new model of positive experience*. Mahwah, N.J.: Lawrence Erlbaum.

Csikszentmihalyi, M. (1990). *Flow: The psychology of optimal experience*. New York: HarperCollins.

Csikszentmihalyi, M. (1997). *Finding flow*. New York: Basic Books.

Ellison, C.G., Gay, D.A., & Glass, T.A. (1989). Does religious commitment contribute to individual life satisfaction? *Social Forces*, 68, 100-123.

Emmons, R.A. (1999). *The psychology of ultimate concerns: Motivation and spirituality in personality*. New York: Guilford Press.

Goleman, D. (1995). *Emotional intelligence*. New York: Bantam Books.

Goleman, D. (2003). *Destructive emotion*. London Bloomsbury.

Guilford, J.P. (1950). Creativity. *American Psychologist*, 5, 444-454.

Hill, P.C., & Pargament, K.L. (2003). Advances in the conceptualization and measurement of religion and spirituality. *American Psychologist*, 58, 64-74.

Inglehart, R. (1990). *Culture shifts in advanced industrial society*. Princeton: Princeton University Press.

James, W. (1985). *The varieties of religious experiences*. Cambridge, USA: Harvard University Press.

Kabat-Zinn, J. (1990). *Full catastrophe living*. New York: Delacourt.

Kirkpatrick, L.A. (1992). An attachment-theory approach to the psychology of religion. *International Journal for the Psychology of Religion*, 2, 3-28.

Kuhn, T. (1966). *The structure in scientific revolution*. Chicago: Chicago University Press.

Langer, E.J. (2005). Well-being: Mindfulness versus positive psychology. In C.R. Snyder & S.J. Lopez (Eds), *Handbook of positive psychology* (pp. 214-230). New York: Oxford University Press.

Moberg, D.O., & Taves, M.J. (1965). Church participation and adjustment in old age. In A.M. Rose and W.A. Peterson (Eds), *Older people and their social world* (pp. 113-124). Philadelphia: F.A. Davis.

Myers, D. (1992). *The pursuit of happiness*. New York: Avon Books.

Myers, D. (2000). The funds, friends, and faith of happy people. *American Psychologist*, 55, 56-67.

Okun, M.A., & Stock, W.A. (1987). Correlates and components of subjective well-being among the elderly. *Journal of Applied Gerentology*, 6, 95-112.

Osbern, A.F. (1963). *Applied imagination: Principle and procedures of creative problem-solving* (3rd ed.). New York: Scribner.

Pargament, K., Tarakeshwar, N., Ellison, C.G., & Wulff, K.W. (2001). Religious coping among the religious: The relationship between religious coping and well-being in a national sample of Presbyterian clergy, elders, and members. *Journal for the Scientific Study of Religion* 40, 496-513.

Pargament, K.I. (1997). *The psychology of religion and coping: The theory, research and practice*. New York: Guilford Press.

Poloma, M.M., & Pendleton, B.E. (1991). *Explaining neglected dimensions of religion in quality of life research*. New York:

Edwin Mellon Press.

Sahoo, F.M. (2013). *Wonders of mind*. Bhubaneswar: ASHRA.

Simonton, D.K. (2000). Creativity: Cognitive, personal, developmental and social aspects. *American Psychologist*, 55, 151-158.

Snyder, C.R. & Lopez, S.J. (2005) (Eds). *Handbook of positive psychology*. New York, Oxford University Press.

Sternberg, R.J., & Lubart, T.I. (1996). Investing in creativity. *American Psychologist*, 51, 677-688.

Veenhoven, R. (1994). *Correlates of happiness* (3 Vols). Rotterdam, The Netherlands: RISBO, Center for Socio-Cultural Transmission.

Walsh, R., & Shapiro, S.L. (2006). The meeting of meditative disciplines and Western psychology. *America Psychologist*, 61, 227-239.

Walsh, R.N. (1983). Meditation research and practice. *Journal of Humanistic Psychology*, 23, 18-50.

Witter, R.A., Stock, W.A., Okun, M.A., & Haring, M.J. (1985). Religious and subjective well-being in adulthood: A quantitative synthesis. *Review of Religious Research*, 26, 332-342.

Zinnbauer, B.J., Pargament, K.I., Cole, B., Rye, M., Butter, E.M., & Belavich, T.G. et al (1997). Religion and spirituality: Unfuzzying the fuzzy. *Journal for the Scientific Study of Religion*, 36, 549-564.

Chapter – 6

Argyle, M, (2001). *The psychology of happiness*. New York: Routledge.

Argyle, M., & Furnham, A. (1982). The ecology of relationships. Choice of situations as a function of relationship. *British Journal of Social Psychology*, 21, 259-262.

Baumeister, R., & Leary, M.R. (1995). The need to belong: Desire for interpersonal attachment as a fundamental human motivation. *Psychological Bulletin*, 117, 497-529.

Baumgarden, S.R., & Crothers, M.K. (2009). *Positive psychology*. New Delhi: Pearson Education.

Brief, A.P., Bucher A. H., George, J.M., & Link, K.E. (1993). Integrating bottom-up and top-down theories of subjective well-being: The case of health. *Journal of Personality and Social Psychology*, 64, 646-653.

Buss, D.M. (2000). The evolution of happiness. *American Psychologist*, 55, 15-23.

Carr, A. (2004). *Positive psychology*. New York: Routledge.

Corin, E. (1995). The cultural frame: Context and meaning in the construction of health. In B.C. Amick, S. Levined, & D. Chapman Walsh (Eds), *Society and health* (pp.272-304). New York: Oxford University of Press.

Deci, E.L., & Ryan, R.M. (1985). *Intrinsic motivation and self-determination in human behavior*. New York: Plenum Press.

Diener, E. & Suh, E.M. (Eds) (2000). *Culture and subjective well-being*. Cambridge: MIT Press.

Diener, E. (1995). A value-based index for measuring national quality of life. *Social Indicators Research*, 36, 107-127.

Diener, E. (2000). Subjective well-being: The science of happiness and a proposal for a national index. *American Psychologist*, 55, 34-43.

Diener, E., & Diener, M. (1995). Cross-cultural correlates of life satisfaction and well-being. *Journal of Personality and Social Psychology*, 68, 653-663.

Diener, E., & Seligman, M. (2004). Beyond money: Toward an economy of well-being. *Psychology in the Public Interest*, 5, 1-31.

Diener, E., Diener, M., & Diener, C. (1995). Factors predicting the subjective well-being of nations. *Journal of Personality and Social Psychology*, 69, 851-864.

Diener, E., Oishi, S., & Lucas, R.E. (2003). Personality, culture, and subjective well-being: Emotional and cognitive evaluations of life. *Annual Review of Psychology*, 54, 403-425.

Fredrickson, B.L., & Losada, M.F. (2005). Positive affect and the complex dynamic of human flourishing. *American Psychologist*, 60, 678-686.

Frey, B.S., & Stutzer, A. (2000). *Happiness, economy and institutions*. Paper presented at the Nuffield College Conference on Well-being.

Gable, S.L. (2000). *Appetitive and aversive social interaction*. Unpublished doctoral dissertation, University of Rochester.

Gottman, J. & Silver, N. (1999). *Seven principles for making marriages work*. New York: Crown.

Hills, P., & Argyle, M. (1998). Positive moods derived from leisure and their relationship to happiness and personality. *Personality and Individual Differences*, 25, 523-535.

Hofstede, G. (1980). *Cultures' consequences*. New Delhi: Sage.

Kitayama, S. & Markus, H.R. (2000). The pursuit of happiness and the realization of sympathy: Cultural pattern of self, social relations and well-being. In E. Diener & E.M. Suh (Eds), *Culture and subjective well-being* (pp 113-162). Cambridge: MIT Press.

Klein, M.H., & Greist, J.H., & Guttman, A.S. (1985). A comparative outcome study of group psychotherapy vs exercise treatments for depression. *International Journal of Mental Health*, 13, 148-177.

Larson, R.W. (1990). The solitary side of life: An examination of the time people spend alone from childhood to old age. *Developmental Review*, 10, 155-183.

Lee, Y.T., & Seligman, M.E.P. (1997). Are Americans more optimistic than the Chinese? *Personality and Social Psychology Bulletin*, 21, 32-40.

Lynn, R. (1981). Cross-cultural differences in neuroticism, extraversion and psychotism. In R. Lynn (Ed), *Dimensions of personality* (pp. 263-286). Oxford, UK: Pergamon.

Lyubomirsky, S. (2007). *The how of happiness*. New York: Penguin.

Marks, D.F., Murray, M. & Estacio, E.V. (2018). *Health psychology* (5th Edition). New Delhi: Sage.

Meyers, D.G. (2000). The funds, friends, and faith of happy people. *American Psychologist*, 55, 56-67.
Myers, D.G. (1992). *The pursuit of happiness*. New York: Harper.
Okun, M.A., Stock, W.A., Haring, M.J., & Witter, R.A. (1984). The social activity/subjective relationship: A quantitative synthesis. *Research on aging*, 6, 45-65.
Reis, H.T. (1990). The role of intimacy in interpersonal relation. *Journal of Clinical Psychology*, 9, 15-30.
Reis, H.T., & Gable, S.L. (2003). Toward a positive psychology of relationship. In C.L.M. Keyes &J. Haidt (Eds), *Flourishing: Positive psychology and the life well-lived* (pp. 129-159). Washington D.C.: American Psychological Association.
Reis, H.T., Collins, W.A., & Berscheid, E. (2000). The relationship context of human behaviour and development. *Psychological Bulletin*, 126, 844-872.
Sahoo, F.M. (1983). Recent development in cross-cultural psychology. *Psychological Studies*, 28, 56-61.
Sahoo, F.M., Sia, N., & Panda, E. (1987). Individualism – collectivism and coping styles. *Journal of Psychological Researches*, 3(2), 72-81.
Steptoe (1998). *Effects of exercise on mind*. Seminar at Oxford.
Sternberg, R.J. (1986). A triangular theory of love. *Psychological Review*, 93, 119-135.
Suh, E. (2000). Self, the hyphen between culture and subjective well-being. In E. Diener and E.M. Suh (Eds), *Culture and subjective well-being* (pp. 63-86). Cambridge: MIT Press.
Tajfel, H. (1982). Social psychology of intergroup relations. *Annual Review of Psychology*, 33, 1-39.
Thayer, R.E. (1989). *The biopsychology of mind and arousal*. New York: Oxford University Press.
Triandis, H.C. (2000). Cultural syndrome and subjective well-being. In E. Diener and E.M. Suh (Eds), *Culture and subjective well-being* (pp.13-36). Cambridge: MIT Press.
Veenhoven, R. (2000). *Freedom and happiness*. Paper presented at the Nuffield College Conference on Well-being.

Worcester, R.M. (1998). More than money. In I. Christie and I. Nash (Eds). *The good life* (pp. 19-25). London: Demos.
World Value Survey Study Group (1994). *World Values Survey, 1981-1984 and 1990 – 1993*. Ann Arbor, Michigan, US: Institute for Social Research, University of Michigan.

Chapter – 7

Argyle, M. (2001). *The psychology of happiness*. New York: Routledge.
Arvy, R.D., McCall, B.P., Bouchard, T.J., Taubman, P., & Cavanaugh, M.A. (1994). Gender influences on job satisfaction and work values. *Personality and Individual Differences*, 17, 21-33.
Baumgardener, S.R. & Crothers, M.K. (2009). *Positive psychology*. New Delhi: Pearson Education.
Betz, N.E., & Luzzo, D.A. (1996). Career assessment and the Career Decision Making Self-Efficacy scale. *Journal of Career Assessment*, 4, 413-428.
Boehm, J.K. & Lyubormisky, S. (2008). Does happiness promote career success? *Journal of Career Assessment*, 16, 101-116.
Bronfrenbrenner, U. (1989). Ecological systems theory. In R. Vista (Ed.), *Anals of child development (Vol. 6). Six theories of child development: Revised foundations and current issues* (pp. 187-249). Greenwich, CT: JAI Press.
Buss, D.M. (1994). *The evolution of desire: Strategies of human mating*. New York: Basic Books.
Buss, D.M. (1995). Psychological sex difference: Origin through social selection. *American Psychologist*, 50, 164-168.
Buss, D.M. (2000). The evolution of happiness. *American Psychologist*, 55, 15-23.
Carr, A. (2004). *Positive psychology*. New York: Routledge.
Clark, A.E. (1998). Job satisfaction and gender: Why are women so happy at work? *DEELSA*, France.

Csikszentmihalyi, M., & Csikszentmihalyi, I. (Eds) (1988). *Optimal experience: psychological studies of flow in consciousness*. Cambridge: Cambridge University Press.

Dana, K., & Griffin, R.W. (1999). Health and well-being in the workplace: A review and synthesis of literature. *Journal of Management*. 25(1), 357-384.

Davidson, R.J., & Begley, S. (2013). *The emotional life of your brain*. London: Hodder.

Diener, E. & Seligman, M. (2004). Beyond money: Toward an economy of well-being. *Psychology in the Public Interest*, 5, 1-31.

Diener, E.& Lucas, R. (1999). Personality and subjective well-being. In D. Kahnemann, E. Diener, and N. Schwartz (Eds.), *Well-being: The foundations of hedonic psychology* (PP. 213-229). New York: Russell Sage Foundation.

Goldberg, D. (1978). *Manual of the General Health Questionnaire*. Windsor, U.K.: NFER.

Gottman, J., & Silver, N. (1999). *The seven principles for making marriage work*. New York: Crown.

Hackman, J.R., & Oldham, G.R. (1976). Motivation through the design of work: Test of a theory. *Organizational Behavior and Human Performance*, 16, 250-279.

Harter, I.K., & Schmidt, F.L. (2002). Employee engagement and business-unit performance. *Psychologist Manager Journal*, 4, 215-224.

Harter, I.K., Schmidt, F.L., & Hayes, T.L. (2002). Business-unit-level relationship between employee satisfaction, employee engagement and business outcomes: A meta-analysis. *Journal of Applied Psychology*, 87, 268-279.

Herrbach, O. (2006). A matter of feeling? The affective tone of organizational commitment and identification. *Journal of Organizational Behavior*, 27, 629-643.

Hoppock, R. (1935). *Job satisfaction*. New York: Harper.

Kanungo, R.N. (1982). *Work alienation*. New York: Praeger.

Karasek, R.A. (1979). Job demands, job decision latitude, and mental strain: Implications for job redesign. *Administrative Science Quarterly*, 24, 285-308.

Kenrick, D.T., Neuberg, S.L., Zierk, K.L., & Krones, J.M. (1994). Evolution and social cognition: Contrast effect as a function of sex, dominance and physical attractiveness. *Personality and Social Psychology Bulletin*, 20, 210-217.

Locke, E.A. (1976). The nature and causes of job satisfaction. In M.D. Dunnette (Ed.), *Handbook of industrial and organizational psychology* (PP. 1297-1347). Chicago: Rand McNally.

Luthans, F., Youssef-Morgan, C.M., & Avolio, B. J. (2015). *Psychological capital and beyond*. New Delhi: Oxford.

Murphy, G.C., & Athanasru, J.A. (1999). The effect of unemployment on mental health. *Journal of occupational and Organizational Psychology*, 72, 83-99.

Myers, D. (2000). The funds, friends and faith of happy people. *American Psychologist*, 55, 56-67.

Myers, D.G. (2002). *The pursuit of happiness*. New York: Harper.

Rath, T., & Harter, J. (2010). *Well-being: The five essential elements*. New York: Gallup Press.

Rathunde, K. (1988). Optimal experience and the family context. In M. Csikszentmihalyi and I. Csikszentmihalyi (Eds.), *Optimal experience: Psychological studies of flow in consciousness* (PP. 342-363). Cambridge: Cambridge University Press.

Ross, C.E. & Mirowsky, J. (1995). Does employment affect health? *Journal of Health and Social Behavior*, 36, 230-243.

Sahoo, F.M., Mitra, A., & Mohanty, A. (2014). Need saliency and job involvement: Test of a cross-cultural model. *Journal of the Indian Academy of Applied Psychology*, 40(2), 279-288.

Seligman, M.E.P. (2002). *Authentic happiness*. New York: Gallup Press.

Snyder, C.R., Lopez, S.J., & Pedrotti, J.T. (2011). *Positive psychology*. New Delhi: Sage.

Tait, M., Padgelt, M.Y., & Baldwin, T.T. (1989). Job satisfaction and life satisfaction: A reexamination of the strength of the relationship and gender effect as a function of the date of the study. *Journal of Applied Psychology*, 74, 502-507.

Turner, N., Barling, J., & Zacharatos, A. (2005). Positive psychology at work. In C.R. Snyder and S.J. Lopez (Eds.), *Handbook of positive psychology* (PP. 715-728). New York: Oxford University Press.

Wanous, J.P., Reichers, A.E., & Hudy, M.J. (1997). Overall job satisfaction: How good are single-item measures? *Journal of Applied Psychology*, 82, 247-252.

Warr, P.B. (1994). A conceptual framework for the study of work and mental health. *Work and Stress*, 8, 84-97.

Warr, P.B. (1999). Well-being and the workplace. In D. Kahnemann, E. Diener and N. Schwartz (Eds.), *Well-being: The foundations of hedonic psychology* (PP. 393-412).New York: Russell Sage Foundation.

Chapter – 8

Andrews, F.M. (1974). Several indicators of perceived life quality. *Social Indicators Research*, 1(3), 279-299.

Davidson, R.J. & Begley S. (2012). *The emotional life of your brain*. London: Hodder.

DeNeve, K.M., & Cooper, H. (1998). The happy personality: A meta-analysis of 137 personality traits and subjective well-being. *Psychological Bulletin*, 124, 197-219.

Diener, E., & Ryan, K. (2009). Subjective well-being: A general overview. *South African Journal of Psychology*, 39, 391-406.

Diener, E., Kesebir, P., & Lucas, R. (2008). Benefits of accounts of well-being- to success and for psychological science. *Applied Psychology*, 57, 37-53.

Ebersole, P. (1998). Types and depth of written life meanings. In P.T.P. Wong & P.S. Fry (Eds). *The human quest for meaning: A handbook of psychological research and clinical application* (pp. 179-191). Mahway, New Jersey: Erlbaum.

Emmons, R.A. (1991). Personal strivings daily life events, and psychological and physical well-being. *Journal of Personality*, 59, 453-472.

Emmons, R.A. (1999). *The psychology of ultimate concern: Motivation and spirituality in personality*. New York: Guildford Press.

Emmons, R.A. (2007). Personal goals, life meaning and virtue: Wellsprings of a positive life. In C.L.M. Keyes (Ed), *Flourishing: Positive psychology and the life well-lived* (pp. 105-129). Washington D.C.: American Psychological Association.

Emmons, R.A., & Kaiser, H. (1996). Goal orientation and emotional well-being: Linking goals and affect through the self. In A. Tesser & L. Martin (Eds), *Striving and feeling: Interactions among goal, affects, and self-regulation* (pp. 79-98). New York: Plenum Press.

Fordyce, M. (1977). Development of a program to increase personal happiness. *Journal of Consulting Psychology*, 24, 511-520.

Forgas, I.P., Bower, G.H., & Moylan, S.I. (1990). Praise or blame? Affective influence on attribution of achievement. *Journal of Personality and Social Psychology*, 59, 809-819.

Goleman, D. (2003). *Destructive emotion*. London: Mind and Life Institute.

Gregory, R.L. (2015). *Eye and brain: The psychology of seeing*. Princeton: Princeton University Press.

Heckhausan, J., Wrosch, C., & Schulz, R. (2010). A motivational theory of lifespan development. *Psychological Review*, 117, 32-60.

Kahneman, D. (1999). Assessment of individual well-being. In D. Kahneman, E. Diener & S. Schwatz (Eds), *Well-being: The foundation of hedonic psychology*. New York: Russel Sage Foundation.

Kasser, T., & Ryan, A.M. (1996). Further examining the American dream: Differential correlates of intrinsic and extrinsic goals. *Personality and Social Psychology Bulletin*, 22, 280-287.

King, L.A. (2010). *The science of psychology: An appreciative view*. New York: MacMoran.

Locke, E.A. (2005). Setting goals for life and happiness. In C.R. Snyder & S.J. Lopez (Eds), *Handbook of positive psychology* (pp. 299-312). New York: Oxford University Press.

Lyubomirsky, S. (2007). *The how of happiness*. New York: Penguin Bases.

Lyubomirsky, S., & Diekerhoof, R. (2010). A construal approach in increasing happiness. In I. Tangency, & J. Maddux (Eds), *Social psychological foundation of clinical psychology*, (pp. 229-244). New York: Guilford Press.

Parducci, A. (1968). The relativism of absolute judgments. *Scientific American*, 219, 84-90.

Ryan, R.M., & Deci, E.L. (2000). Self-determination theory and the facilitation of intrinsic, motivation, social development, and well-being. *American Psychologist*, 55, 68-78.

Siegel, D.J. (2007). *The mindful brain: Reflection and attunement in the cultivation of well-being*. New York: W.W. Norton.

Stewart, T.L., Chipperfield, J.G., Ruthing, J.C., & Heckhaussen, J. (2013). Downward social comparison and subjective well-being in late life: The moderating role of perceived control. *Aging and Mental Health*, 17(3), 375-385.

Wills, T.A. (1981). Downward social comparison principle in social psychology. *Psychological Bulletin*, 90, 245-271.

Wong, P.T.P. (1998). Spirituality meaning, and successful aging. In P.T.P. Wong & P.S. Fry (Eds), *The human quest for meaning* (pp. 359-394). Mahwah, New Jersey: Erlbaum.

Wood, J.V. (1989). Theory and research concerning social comparisons of personal attributes. *Psychological Bulletin*, 106, 231-248.

Zajonc, R.B. (1998). Emotion. In D.T. Gilbert, S.T. Fiske, & G. Lindzey (Eds) The handbook of social psychology (4th Ed., Vol. 1, pp. 591-632). New York: McGraw Hill.

Chapter – 9

Argyle, M. (2001). *The psychology of happiness*. New York: Routledge.

Axelrod, R. (1984). *The evolution of cooperation.* New York: Basic Books.

Buss, D.M. (2000). The evolution of happiness. *American Psychologist,* 55, 15-23.

Carr, A. (2004). *Positive psychology.* New York: Routledge.

Clark, D.M. (1983). On the induction of depressed mood in the laboratory: Evaluation and comparison of the Velten and musical procedure. *Advances in Behaviour Research and Therapy,* 5, 24-49.

Diener, E., Sandvik, E., & Payot, W. (1991). Happiness is the frequency not the intensity of positive versus negative affect. In E. Strack, M. Argyle, & N. Schwarz (Eds.), *Subjective well-being* (119-139). Oxford, U.K.: Pergamon.

Fava, G.A. (1999). Well-being therapy: Concept and technical issues. *Psychotherapy and Psychosomatics,* 68, 171-179.

Fredrickson, B. (2001). The role of positive emotions in positive psychology: The broaden-and-build theory of positive emotions. *American Psychologist,* 56, 218-226.

Gerrards-Hesse, A., Spies, K., Hesse, F.W. (1994). Experimental inductions of emotional states and their effectiveness. *British Journal of Psychology,* 85, 55-78.

Henderson, M., Argyle, M., & Furnham, A. (1984). *The assessment of positive life events.* Oxford, UK: University of Oxford.

Kasser, R., & Sheldon, K.M. (2000). Of wealth and death: Materialism, mortality salience and consumption behavior. *Psychological Science,* 11, 352-355.

Laird, J.D. (1984). Facial response and emotions. *Journal of Personality and Social Psychology,* 47, 909-937.

Lykken, D., & Tellegen, A. (1996). Happiness as a stochastic phenomenon. *Psychological Science,* 7, 186-189.

Lyubomirsky, S. (2007). *The how of happiness.* New York: Penguin.

Magnus, K., Diener, E., Fujita, F., & Payot, W. (1993). Extraversion and neuroticism as predictors of objective life events: A longitudinal analysis. *Journal of Personality and Social Psychology,* 65, 1046-1053.

Myers, D. (2002). *The pursuit of happiness*. New York: Harper.
Reich, J.W., & Zautra, A. (1981). Life events and personal causation. *Journal of Personality and Social Psychology*, 41, 1002-1012.
Ryff, C.D. (1989). Happiness is everything, or is it? Explorations on the mearing of psychological well-being. *Journal of Personality and social Psychology* 57, 1069-1081.
Schachter, S., & Singer, J. (1962). Cognitive, social, and physiological determinants of emotional state. *Psychological Review*, 69, 379-399.
Velten, E. (1968). A laboratory task for induction of mood states. *Behaviour Research and Therapy*, 6, 473-482.
Westermann, R., Spies, K., Stahl, G., & Hesse, F.W. (1996). Relative effectiveness and validity of mood induction procedure: A meta-analysis. *European Journal of Social Psychology*, 26, 557-580.

Chapter – 10
Argyle, M. (2001). *The psychology of happiness*. New York: Routledge.
Beck, A., & Steen, R.A. (1987). *Beck Depression Inventory Manual*. San Antonio, Texas: Psychological Corporation.
Bem, S.L. (1981). *Bem Sex Role Inventory (BSRI)*. Palo Alto, California: Consulting Psychologists Press.
Berry, J.W. (1969). On cross-cultural comparability. *International Journal of Psychology*, 4, 119-128.
Berry, J.W. (1980). Introduction to methodology. In H.C. Triandis & J.W. Berry (Eds) *Handbook of cross-cultural psychology* (Vol.2) (pp. 1-28). London: Allyn & Bacon.
Berry, J.W., Poortinga, Y.H., Segall, M.H., & Dasen, P.R. (1992). *Cross-cultural psychology: Research and application*. New York: Cambridge University Press.
Brislin, R. (1970). Back translation for cross-cultural work. *Journal of Cross-Cultural Psychology*, 1, 185-216.

Brislin, R. (Ed) (1976). *Translation: Application and research*. New York: Wiley – Halsted.

Brunswik, E. (1952). *The conceptual framework of psychology*. Chicago: Chicago University Press.

Brunswik, E. (1956). *Perception and the representative design of psychological experiments*, Berkley, California: University of California Press.

Deci, E., & Ryan, R. (2008). Hedonic, eudaimonia, and well-being: An introduction. *Journal of Happiness Studies, 9*, 1-11.

Diener, E., Emmons, R.A., Larson, R.J., & Griffin, R. (1985). The Satisfaction with Life Scale. *Journal of Personality and Social Psychology, 49*, 71-75.

Diener, E., Lucas, R.E., & Oishi, S. (2005). Subjective well-being: The science of happiness and well-being. In C.R. Snyder & S.J. Lopez (Eds), *Handbook of positive psychology* (pp. 63-730. New York: Oxford University Press.

Diener, E., Sandvik, E., & Pavot, W. (1991). Happiness is the frequency not the intensity of positive versus negative affect. In E. Strack, M. Argyle & N. Schwarz (Eds), *Subjective well-being* (pp. 119-139). Oxford, UK: Pergamon.

Hathaway, S.R., & McKinley, I.C. (1967). Minnesota *Multiphasic Personality Inventory Manual Revisited*. New York: Psychological Corporation.

Ho, D.Y.E. (1996). Filial piety and its psychological consequences. In M.H. Bond (Ed), *The handbook of Chinese psychology*, (pp. 155-165). Hong Kong: Oxford University Press.

Ho, S.M.Y., & Cheng, W.L. (2007). Using the combined etic-emic approach to develop a measurement of interpersonal subjective well-being. In A.D. Ong & M.H.M. Van Dulmen (Eds), *Oxford handbook of method in positive psychology* (pp. 139-152). New York: Oxford University Press.

Kanungo, R.N. (1982). *Work alienation*. New York: Praeger.

Keyes, C.L.M. (2002). The mental health continuum: From languishing to flourishing in life. *Journal of Health and Social Behavior. 43*, 207-222.

Lyubomirsky, S., Sheldon, K., Schkade, D. (2005). Pursuing happiness: The architecture of sustainable change. *Review of General Psychology*, 2, 111-131.

Mishra, G., Sahoo, F.M., & Puhan, B.N. (1997). Cultural bias in testing: India. *European Review* of Applied Psychology, 47(4), 309-316.

Osgood, C. (1965). Cross-cultural comparability in attitude measurement via multilingual semantic differentials. In I. Steiner & M. Fishbein (Eds), *Current studies in social psychology*. Chicago: Holt, Rinehart, and Winston.

Pike, K.L. (1954). *Language in relation to a unified theory of the structure of human behavior*. Glendale, Connecticut: Summer Institute of Linguistics, and the Hague: Mouton.

Puhan, B.N. (1995). Projective-inventory: An indigenous approach to personality assessment. *Psychology and Developing Societies*, 7, 115-137.

Reich, J.W., & Zautra, A. (1981). Life events and personal causation. *Journal of Personality and social Psychology*, 41, 1002-1012.

Ryan, R., & Deci, E. (2000). Self-determination theory and the facilitation of intrinsic motivation, social development and well-being. *American Psychologist*, 55, 68-78.

Ryff, C.D. (1989). Happiness is everything, or is it? Explanations on to meaning of psychological well-being. *Journal of Personality and Social Psychology*, 57, 1069-1081.

Ryff, C.D. (2014). Psychological well-being revisited: Advances in the science and practice of eudaimonia. *Psychotherapy and Psychosomatics*, 83, 10-28.

Sahoo, F.M. & Bidyadhar, S. (1995). A cultural validation of need saliency model: An empirical investigation in a non-western context. *Psychological Studies*, 40(1), 120-125.

Sahoo, F.M. (1983). Recent development in cross-cultural psychology. *Psychological Studies*, 28, 56-61.

Sahoo, F.M. (2004). *The sex roles in transition*. New Delhi: Kalpazam.

Sahoo, F.M. (2007). Promoting human happiness. In M.B. Sharan & D. Suar (Eds), *Psychology matters* (pp. 26-44). New Delhi: Applied Publishers.

Sahoo, F.M. (2015). Need saliency and subjective well-being in the aged. International *Journal of Development and Social Research*, 1-10.

Sahoo, F.M., & Mohapatra, L. (2009). Psychological well-being in profession groups. *Journal of the Indian Academy of Applied Psychology*, 35(2), 211-217.

Scheier, M., & Carver, C.S. (1985). Optimism, coping and health: Assessment and implications of generalized outcome expectancies. *Health Psychology*, 4, 219-247.

Seligman, M.E.P. (2002). *Authentic happiness: using the new positive psychology to realize your potential for lasting fulfillment*. New York: Free Press.

Seligman, M.E.P. (2011). *Flourish: A visionary new understanding of happiness and well-being*. New York: Free Press.

Wong, P.T. (2010). What is existential positive psychology. *International Journal of Existential Psychology and Psychotherapy*, 3, 1-10.

About the Authors

Dr Fakir Mohan Sahoo Ph.D. (Queen's, Canada) is now a Visiting Professor in XIM University, Bhubaneswar, India. He a former Professor and Head of the Centre of Advanced Study in Psychology, Utkal University, Bhubaneswar, India. He was Research Professor, Xavier University. He also enjoys the status of Visiting Professor at IIM, Ranchi, IIT, Bhubaneswar, Central University, Hyderabad and Ravenshaw University, Cuttack. He received Canadian Commonwealth Scholarship and obtained doctoral degree from Queen's University at Kingston, Canada. His other achievements include University Grants Commission's Emeritus Fellowship, Career Award in Humanities and Social Sciences, Indo-Shastri Fellowship offered by Indo-Canadian Institute and Professional Associateship accorded by the East-West Center, Honolulu, the U.S.A.

He has completed a large number of national and international research projects. Apart from directing several national and international seminars, he has participated in more than 25 international seminars. He has authored more than 50 books including 16 books in English. As a well-known writer in the State of Odisha, he has received several literacy awards.

The second author **Dr. Satyabrata Tripathy** is a management professional. He has been working with a large public sector company for last 29 years. He graduated in science and received his MBA degree from Utkal University. He completed his Ph.D. from the same University in 2017. Apart from being a corporate manager, he loves to read, write and engages himself in multitasking responsibilities. His research papers have been published in many national and international management journals. He has also received the 'Best M M Executive' award from his company. You can connect Dr. Tripathy through e-mail: sbtripathy.2010@gmail.com.

The third author Dr.**Kalpana Sahoo** is an Assistant Professor in Organizational Behaviour at School of Human Resource Management, XIM University, Bhubaneswar, India. She has more than 15 years of teaching experience. She has completed her Ph.D. from Utkal University, Psychology Department on the topic Critical Predictors of Human Happiness. She has published several papers in the areas of Learned Optimism, Positive Psychology, Competency Mapping, Employee Engagement, Emotional Intelligence and Personality in national and international journals. Her teaching interests are in the areas of quality of work life, EQ & SQ, Psychological wellbeing, personality, and leadership. You can connect Dr. Sahoo through e-mail: klpnsahoo@gmail.com.

Black Eagle Books

www.blackeaglebooks.org
info@blackeaglebooks.org

Black Eagle Books, an independent publisher, was founded as a nonprofit organization in April, 2019. It is our mission to connect and engage the Indian diaspora and the world at large with the best of works of world literature published on a collaborative platform, with special emphasis on foregrounding Contemporary Classics and New Writing.

www.ingramcontent.com/pod-product-compliance
Lightning Source LLC
Chambersburg PA
CBHW020514080526
44583CB00013B/592